New Churches: A Theology

New Churches:
A Theology

Edited by

Joshua Cockayne and Will Foulger

scm press

© Editors and Contributors 2024
Published in 2024 by SCM Press
Editorial office
3rd Floor, Invicta House,
110 Golden Lane,
London EC1Y 0TG, UK
www.scmpress.co.uk

SCM Press is an imprint of Hymns Ancient & Modern Ltd
(a registered charity)

Hymns Ancient & Modern® is a registered trademark of
Hymns Ancient & Modern Ltd
13A Hellesdon Park Road, Norwich,
Norfolk NR6 5DR, UK

All rights reserved. No part of this publication may be reproduced,
stored in a retrieval system, or transmitted,
in any form or by any means, electronic, mechanical,
photocopying or otherwise, without the prior permission of
the publisher, SCM Press.

The editors and contributors have asserted their right under the Copyright,
Designs and Patents Act 1988 to be identified as the Authors of this Work.

British Library Cataloguing in Publication data
A catalogue record for this book is available
from the British Library

Unless otherwise indicated, Scripture quotations are from The New Revised Standard Version of the Bible, Anglicized Edition, copyright © 1989, 1995 by the Division of Christian Education of the National Council of the Churches of Christ in the United states of America, and are used by permission. All rights reserved.
Scripture quotations marked NIV are taken from The Holy Bible, New International Version (Anglicised edition) copyright © 1979, 1984, 2011 by Biblica (formerly International Bible Society). Used by permission of Hodder & Stoughton Publishers, an Hachette UK company. All rights reserved.
Bible extracts marked KJV are from the Authorized Version of the Bible (The King James Bible), the rights in which are vested in the Crown, and are reproduced by permission of the Crown's Patentee, Cambridge University Press.

ISBN: 978-0-334-06615-6

Typeset by Regent Typesetting

Contents

Contributors ix

Introduction: Why on Earth a Theology about Starting New Churches? 1

Part One: Missiology: New Churches and the *missio Dei*

1 Do Church Planters Believe in the *missio Dei*? 21
  Mark Collinson

2 (Why) We Need to Talk About Method 34
  Mark Powley

3 Telling Stories for Transformation: Theodrama and Discipleship Formation in Church Planting Contexts 47
  Helen Miller

4 Church Planting, Community and the Triune God of Grace 62
  Joshua Cockayne

5 Who is Doing the Planting? Understanding Human Agency while Keeping the Focus on the Work of the Spirit 73
  James Butler

6 'Don't offer help ... ask for it': Towards an Ethics of Church Planting in Conversation with Aquinas 86
  Beth Honey

Reflections on Part One 96

Part Two: Praxis: Theological Method for New Churches

7 Leveraging Indigenous Theologies for Church Growth
   in Light of the Emergence of World Christianity   101
   Paul Ayokunle

8 From the Margins to the Mainstream? Four Questions
   for the Theology of Church Planting   116
   Andy Wier

9 Is Church Planting a Craft? Training Lessons from
   Medieval Guilds   128
   Christian Selvaratnam

10 Venturing Upstream: Community Organizing as a
   Resource for Church Planting in a Post-Christian Culture   144
   Ayo Audu and Catherine Butt

Reflections on Part Two   153

Part Three: Context: Learning from New Churches

11 Small, Simple, Slow: Missional Community as Faithful
   Ecclesial Expression in the Context of Late Modernity   159
   Paul Bradbury

12 Co-creating Churches Playfully   172
   Tina Hodgett

13 A Tale of Two Churches   185
   Stephen Squirrell

14 Anglo-Catholic Church Planting: It Does Happen!   196
   John Wallace

Reflections on Part Three   203

Part Four: Ecclesiology: A Theology of New Churches

15 Growth in the Gaps and Cracks: A Reflection on Polity, Tradition and Praxis in Planting and Pioneering   209
   Ali Williams

16 'We're going to plant a church on Friday': Reflections and Learnings on Church Planting   220
   Cathy Ross

17 Just What is it That You Want to Plant? A Dissenting Missional Ecclesiology   233
   Simon Hall and Roy Searle

18 Giving the Church Away: Fresh Theology for Church Planting?   244
   Michael Moynagh

19 Movement, Diversity and Leadership in the Early Roman Churches: Explorations of Church Planting Hints in Romans 16   256
   John Valentine

Reflections on Part Four   264

Index of Names and Subjects   269

Contributors

Ayo Audu grew up in the Middle Belt region of Nigeria. He trained for ordination at St Mellitus College, London and since 2021 has been serving his curacy at St Frideswide's Water Eaton, Bletchley, Milton Keynes. He is currently reflecting on the interplay of culture and soteriology and the implications this presents for our calling as pilgrims.

Paul Ayokunle is a theologian and a mission-minded scholar. His Doctor of Philosophy research degree from Liverpool Hope University explored church growth dynamics among African diaspora congregations in Liverpool. Paul's other research interests include African perspectives on leadership and mission. In addition, he enjoys working with second-generation diaspora Africans on issues of their religious lives. As a Baptist-trained and ordained minister, he currently serves as the pastor of Victory Baptist Church, Liverpool.

Paul Bradbury is an ordained pioneer minister in the Church of England, based in Poole, Dorset. He is the founder and leader of Poole Missional Communities, which plays host to a number of fresh expressions of church and pioneer mission initiatives. He is an associate tutor with Sarum College, CMS and Ripon College, Cuddesdon. He is currently studying for a DTh with the University of Roehampton exploring the connections between emergence and the ecclesiology of pioneers. He has published two books reflecting on his experience as a pioneer, *Home By Another Route* (BRF, 2019) and *In The Fullness of Time* (Canterbury Press, 2024).

James Butler is pioneer MA lecturer and assistant coordinator at the Church Mission Society. He also works as a postdoctoral researcher at the University of Roehampton, researching themes of learning, discipleship and social action. He teaches in the areas of mission, ecclesiology and practical theology. His PhD explored how Small Missional Communities sustain their social action.

Catherine Butt is incumbent at St Frideswide's Water Eaton, Bletchley, Milton Keynes and Project Lead for the Diocese of Oxford's Resourcing Hub for Community Organising and Church Growth. She grew up in the north-east and has lived in Milton Keynes for 20 years since her ordination (after training at Cranmer Hall) in 2003. Exploring, experimenting, teaching and learning are what keep her going. She likes asking questions just as much as finding solutions and is keen to keep real people and their experiences at the heart of any effort to facilitate worship and spiritual growth.

Joshua Cockayne is the Director of the Centre for Church Planting Theology and Research at Cranmer Hall, where he also teaches mission and evangelism. He has taught theology and philosophy at the University of St Andrews, the University of York, St Hild College, and Westminster Theological Centre. He was previously the leader of Holy Trinity Boar Lane, a church plant started to engage with the those who work in the city centre of Leeds. He has published books on areas related to ecclesiology and spirituality and is currently the editor of the Durham Studies in Church Planting and Theology at SCM Press.

Mark Collinson is Rector of Six Fen Churches in the Diocese of Ely, where he is learning about missional ecclesiology in a small church rural context. He tutors students at the Oxford Centre for Mission Studies and Ridley Hall, Cambridge. He studied theology at Cambridge University and the Vrije Universiteit in Amsterdam, where he also completed his doctorate on missional ecclesiology. After a curacy in suburban Manchester he spent 14 years in Amsterdam planting two multicultural congregations. From 2015 to 2024 he was Canon Principal of the Winchester School of Mission, residentiary canon of Winchester Cathedral and later served as Director of Ministry.

Will Foulger is the vicar of St Nic's Church in Durham and the founder of the Centre for Church Planting Theology Research. He teaches ecclesiology and missiology at Cranmer Hall. Prior to his doctoral research, Will studied Theology at St Andrews University and at Princeton Seminary. He is clear that his most challenging theological work up to now has been to teach Religious Studies in secondary schools in south-east London, where he grew up. He is author of *Present in Every Place: The Church of England's New Churches and the Future of the Parish* (SCM Press).

Simon Hall is a Baptist Minister and Church Planter based in Leeds. After training in philosophy and theology and then youth ministry, he and his wife Anna were involved in planting Joy, one of the UK's first youth congregations, in Oxford. Simon also worked for Oasis Trust, where he was founding Principal of Oasis College. He writes and teaches mainly in the area of practical theology as it applies to youth ministry, worship and Christian formation; his current focus is exploring what neuroscience can teach us about discipleship. Simon is a member of The Northumbrian Collective (northumbrian.org), which seeks to apply the principles of contemplative practice to contemporary issues through blogs, podcasts and retreats.

Tina Hodgett loves to dwell in possibility. This thread runs through her life in secondary education, lay and ordained ministry, pioneering and study, and as an ordained pioneer she planted two fresh expressions of church. Tina co-designed and led the Pioneer Project in the Diocese of Bath and Wells and currently has a dual role at the Church Mission Society leading an initiative aimed at enabling parishes to become more pioneering and facilitating experiential learning among emerging pioneers in the CMS Southwest Region Hub. Tina is co-author of the Pioneer Spectrum and writes and speaks anywhere she's invited. She serves a parish in Yeovil and a white cat called Willow.

Beth Honey has been an ordained pioneer planter in the Church of England since 2009 in often marginal urban contexts and now finds herself exploring pioneer enabling and practice in rural, town and city life in Cumbria, living between Carlisle and Penrith. She is married to Ben, a lay pioneer and youth worker, and they have three children who ask them the truly courageous questions day to day.

Helen Miller is Head of Research and Professional Development at Moorlands College. She oversees the College's MA Applied Theology programme and also teaches on the College's undergraduate programmes. Her areas of teaching include ecclesiology and missiology, alongside helping students to engage with contemporary cultural shifts and trends. She is the author, as Helen D. Morris, of *Flexible Church: Being the Church in the Contemporary World* (SCM Press, 2019), and co-edited *Evangelicals Engaging in Practical Theology: Theology that Impacts Church and World* (Routledge, 2022) with Helen Cameron. Helen and her husband Tim are actively involved in their local church, in particular in teaching and preaching.

Michael Moynagh is an Anglican minister who has spent the past 20 years researching, advocating and providing support for new forms of Christian community. Among his publications are *Church for Every*

Context (SCM Press, 2012) and *Church in Life* (SCM Press, 2017). He is currently a consultant to the Church of England Greenhouse Initiative and the Diocese of Oxford's New Congregations Programme.

Mark Powley is the Archbishop's Mission Enabler for the North of England, a role focused on revitalizing parishes and planting new churches across the Northern Province of the Church of England. He was previously the Principal of St Hild College, a theological training institution in Yorkshire. His PhD research was on the presence of God in worship, drawing on Hans Urs von Balthasar, and addressed the question of divine and human synergy.

Cathy Ross is Lecturer in Mission at Regent's College, Oxford and MA Coordinator for Pioneer Leadership Training at CMS (Church Mission Society) in Oxford. She has written widely in areas of mission and contextual church, and her work includes *Women with a Mission* (Penguin, 2006); *Mission in the 21st Century* (DLT, 2008, edited with Andrew Walls); *Imagining Mission with John V. Taylor* (SCM Press, 2020, with Jonny Baker).

Roy Searle, having pioneered in urban Teesside and rural Northumberland, was the Senior Pastor of a large evangelical charismatic church in Wearside prior to becoming one of the founding leaders of the Northumbria Community. A former President of the Baptist Union of Great Britain, he is a leadership mentor and spiritual director and one of the denominations Pioneer Ambassadors. He recently founded the Northumbrian Collective, an initiative that seeks to encourage people to listen well, think deeply and live authentically. Roy is a Free Church tutor at Cranmer Hall, and helped in the formation of the college's Free Church Missional Leadership Track and training for Baptist ministry in the north-east. He lives with his wife, Shirley, in Alnwick, Northumberland.

Christian Selvaratnam is the Dean of Church Planting at St Hild College where he leads the Centre for Church Planting, the Church Planting Track and the Seedbed programme. Christian is the author of several books on church planting, including *Why Plant Churches? Theological and Practical Reasons* (Grove, 2023) and *The Craft of Church Planting: Exploring the Lost Wisdom of Apprenticeship* (SCM Press, 2022), which is the result of his doctoral studies.

Stephen Squirrell is a Year Tutor on the Local Ministry Programme (Diocese of Guildford), where he teaches ordinands and local lay ministers in training. He is undertaking a PhD in systematic and eucharistic theology at the University of Exeter. Before returning to study and teaching he was a pastor and church planter. He lives in north London.

John Valentine is the Dean of the Local Ministry Programme in the Anglican Diocese of Guildford, where he teaches and trains ordinands, local lay ministers and other lay leaders for local mission and ministry. He is also a Gregory Associate with the Gregory Centre for Church Multiplication. He planted a church from Holy Trinity Brompton into central London, which went on to plant two other churches in London. He hosted the Gregory Centre's Plant course for five years. He has a Doctor of Ministry in church planting from Asbury Theological Seminary. He is the author of *Jesus, the Church and the Mission of God: A Biblical Theology of Church Planting* (Apollos, 2023).

John Wallace has a degree in Classics from St John's College, Cambridge, an MSc in Human Resource Management from Luton (now the University of Bedfordshire), an MA in Theology, Politics and Faith-Based Organisations from King's College, London and most recently a Doctorate in Theology and Ministry from the University of Durham with a thesis on Anglo-Catholic Church Planting. He has been at his current liberal Catholic parish since 1983 and been churchwarden (twice). He is a member of the ministry team so preaches on occasion as well as undertaking other liturgical roles. He was Lay Chair of Deanery Synod for over 20 years and served as Lay Vice President of St Albans Diocesan Synod for 15 years as well as serving on the Diocesan Mission and Pastoral Committee.

Andy Wier is the Research Team Leader at Church Army. Andy is a researcher, consultant and practical theologian. He has worked for Church Army since 2014 and led the research team since 2019. During this period, he has written numerous research and consultancy reports on contemporary mission and evangelism. These have included research on mission with young adults, sustaining fresh expressions of church, growing leaders on urban estates, and the changing landscape of pioneering.

Ali Williams has been working in pioneer and planting ministries for 20 years as a lay person and since ordination, in gloriously varied contexts – cathedrals, to former mining villages, city centre to rural arts festivals. She is a mentor and coach supporting lay and ordained pioneers with a little and capital 'P', working with dioceses and networks to enable pioneer ministries and new gatherings within our parish polity. She is currently serving in Peterborough Diocese.

Introduction:
Why on Earth a Theology about Starting New Churches?

There are at least two groups of people who might ask this question.

The first are the doers: the planters, the pioneers, the go-to-it-quick types. For these folk, a 'theology' of planting is the last thing we should be spending our time on. The task is clear, the need is even clearer, and the opportunities abundant. Planting is an activity; it is something we do. There is a healthy suspicion here of our talking, which so often seems to distract us from the doing. We can talk and think all we want but at the end of the day that talking doesn't start or pioneer or re-enliven churches. And anyway, hasn't the church already got a theology and an ecclesiology and got these in abundance? The issue, it seems, hasn't been with our theorizing; it has been with our (in)ability to put all that into practice.

The second group ask the question from a very different place. These are the thinkers; the reflectors, those who might consider themselves worthy of the title 'theologian'. For them, the problem isn't with our practice, it's with the desire to try and relate theology to any and every facet of the church's life and ministry. A 'theology of starting new churches' sounds a bit like a 'theology of church furniture', or a 'theology of small-group ministry' or whatever it is that some group seems especially interested in at that moment. The problem isn't that theology is seen to have nothing to say to these things. Far from it: the claim would be made by this group that theology is about *everything* ('God, and all things in relation to God' as Aquinas so pithily put it). The problem is more that by attaching a qualifier to theology ('a theology of *x*') we somehow make it too specific, too limited and too controlled by whatever the qualifier happens to be. In this sense, we can't have a theology of new churches, because whatever such a theology has to say can only ever be one very small part of the Christian vision of the world. Furthermore, there is a hint of arrogance here. Rather than starting with theology and seeing where it takes us, we now have determined in advance the object of investigation and then use theology to make sense of that thing. But what if 'theology' *questions* rather than offers a rationale for starting new churches? What if we were to really dig into Scripture, the Christian tradition and experience, and find that – in fact – starting new churches is the very last thing we should be doing? Theology cannot be co-opted to support one's ecclesiological preferences. Well, it can, but it shouldn't.

I (Foulger) have much empathy for both perspectives. Elsewhere I have written of the importance of recognizing our theological instincts (Foulger, 2023, pp. 12–16). Each group here is working with a set of instincts that leads to their different responses, and both sets of instincts have truth within them. On the one hand is the instinct to act, to get done. I receive this instinct as a good one. Like me, you may be humbled whenever you spend time with those whose hearts hurt (often literally) for the communities and the people they know and love, who believe deeply that church might be a gift to such people and places, and who desire people to come and know of the love of God and of the community he has established. There is an appropriate, gospel-shaped urgency here: they see no reason why all this can't be happening now, and their frustration is thus often (not always) a holy dissatisfaction with the inflexibility of our structures and systems of which our tendency to theologize-rather-than-act is just one symptom. On the other hand, I recognize the instinct to be wary of 'using' theology as a means of justifying whatever seems to us worthwhile in the moment; that is, to jettison the task of real, slow, deep theological reflection for the quick win of something to offer. It is not hard to point to examples where theology has been done like this. At best it leaves our praxis wafer-thin, disconnected from the depth of the tradition, and thus vulnerable to being blown away by the wind that is whatever the next vision or strategy or focus of attention happens to be. And at worst (we don't need to dig too hard for examples) our theologizing becomes a way of legitimizing something bad, foolish and even directly counter to the work and ways of God.

Both instincts lead therefore to a healthy suspicion of 'a theology of new churches'. For the former the problem lies with the 'theology' bit, for the latter it is the 'of new churches' that causes the problems.

So why then attempt it? In other words, why this book?

Well, to answer that in the first instance, it's probably best to pick up the good instincts of these fictional groups and run with those. For the doers, we need a theology *to* new churches. And for the thinkers, we need a theology *from* the new churches.

INTRODUCTION

For the doers: a theology *to* new churches

We need a theology *to* new churches because we need serious theological reflection if we are to start new churches well. And by 'well' we mean of course 'faithfully' which is, after all, our only real appropriate measure as theological practitioners. We need deep theological reflection to support, correct, challenge and guide us in this complex work of starting new things. In this, the instinct of the thinkers is surely right: if this is to be *faithful* practice, rather than simply, say, 'effective', then it needs to make sense within the riches of the Christian tradition. It must be resonant with the gospel the church has received. A few months ago, I was completing a Strategic Development Fund bid for some financial support to get off the ground what became the Centre for Church Planting Theology and Research. And in the paperwork there was a question that asked, 'What is your theory of change?' It's a good question. But I reflected on it for a while, and then, after some time, I typed one word: 'God'. Now, I'm not someone who tends towards facetiousness, so this move didn't come naturally. Indeed, in the end my pragmatic side got the better of me, and I engaged with the question in a manner more attuned to what I think its inventors had intended. However, for the day or two that 'God' sat in that textbox I felt more than a little smug, and certainly justified. It's been a good talking point since. For surely that is indeed the only answer we can give, theologically that is. For those of us who claim to follow a Christ who was dead and then raised to life again, our theory of change must indeed be God. It is God's church in the world; his is the idea, his is the implementation, his is the fruit. This is therefore why theology cannot be a luxury to us as a church and in our churches. Theology is simply the task of asking how this thing – whatever it is – is of God. If we claim that this is the Christian church faithful to the God revealed in Jesus Christ, then we must be intentionally doing theology all the time.

The theologian John Webster speaks of the church as having a *proximate* and a *principal res*. That word *res* is a Latin word meaning a 'thing'. In other words, the church is two 'things'. The proximate (or closest/obvious/immediate) thing of the church is what you see, for example, on a Sunday: it's the human community, gathered. This is directly accessible to all and everyone. If you ask a passer-by what the church is, she would be able to say 'It's a building' or 'It's a group of people' or whatever. But for Webster, this is one aspect of the church. For the principal *res* of the church is her identity as the body of Christ; the community of Christ in the world, called and established by God. And this, he argues, is harder to know; and certainly more difficult to observe. Indeed, it's not really a reality that you can 'get to' from the ground up, as it were. One may walk into church on a Sunday, or during a midweek activity, and make a whole host of observations from what one notices about the church. Some of these may even be quite grand ('This is how all humanity should be', 'This is what I always dreamed of', 'This is true love in communal form') or may not be. But what one wouldn't be able to do is to simply observe the community and conclude, 'This is the called of Christ, given as gift to and for the world, broken and yet redeemed.' For such a claim is a claim not so much about the community as seen, but about God as the one who calls. And that – of course – is theology: God, and the things of God. It is why we must be constantly doing theology. Not because we enjoy theology as a discipline (though we might), but simply because of the nature of the church itself. If it is to be a *church* that we start, launch, graft or re-imagine, and not simply a human movement or institution, then we cannot *but* do theology.

Sadly, of course, 'doing theology' conjures up a host of unhelpful connotations. 'Academic' theology can sometimes seem distant, disconnected from actual goings on, and dispassionate. (The discipline of 'theology' too frequently doesn't help itself in this regard.) I will return below to the question of how theology might be seen as different from this, but for now it is to say that the type of theology we want to do in this book will, it is hoped, not feel like that. Whether we have succeeded remains to be seen, but we do hope that this is a rich theology that serves the church and churches rather than simply making observations from a distance. We hope therefore that this theology is integrated into actual goings on, even as it rightly remains critical and rigorous. Not because the goal is to score theological points, but because they are passionate about how the reality of God might be more fully realized in actual goings on. This I what I hope a theology to starting new things might be able to gift us doers.

A theology *from* new churches

As well as a theology *to* new churches however, we need a theology that is *from* new churches. And this, I think, is where the instinct to act needs to find its place alongside the instinct to reflect. Put simply, there is much that can be learnt about the church (ecclesiology) and mission (missiology) from the activity of starting new things. In his book *Church Planting in the Secular West,* the missiologist Stefan Paas explores some of the many rationales that have been found for starting new churches in our Western context. And at the end of the book, he asks us to think why we might start new churches in a context (the post-Christendom West) where we already have a lot of existing churches. Clearly, Paas argues, starting new churches has been an important part of the church's mission at different times and different places (e.g. the book of Acts!), but this doesn't necessarily justify why we should be doing it now, and in this context where we have a plethora of existing local churches. And this is his conclusion:

> Church planting is not a biblical mandate for all times and places. The New Testament was written in a pioneer situation. Whoever decides to plant a church in Europe or in other nations with a long history of Christianization must find additional, contextual reasons that justify this action. ... The strongest theological defence of church planting in Europe can be found in the relationship between mission and church ... A Christianity that denies itself the experience of church planting may have only an abstract notion of what it means to be called to mission ... As an intersection of ecclesiology and missiology, church planting provides the Western church with a rich potential for missionary experience and reformation. (Paas, 2016, p. 265).

It is this 'rich potential' that we want to embrace in this book: the unique intersection of church and mission, and the fruits that result. There are two points Paas is making here, one conceived negatively and one positively, and we will address them in turn.

First then, in terms of the negative construal, Paas' claim is that without a practice of starting new things, the church risks having only an 'abstract' notion of mission. That is, if we stay within our inherited churches, and never seek to do church in a new way, we risk losing something vital. When I was part of a team that started a new church in Nottingham, we would speak of church planting as simply 'doing church intentionally'. That is, the task of starting from scratch as it were, with a blank canvas and asking, 'What is this church going to look like and behave like and do?' is of a different order from the task of taking on an existing church and working within what already exists. This, Paas argues, is a good process for us as a church to go through since it challenges our assumptions and all the ways we have imbibed a way of being church without ever thinking too hard about it. When we start from scratch we must ask: 'What does it mean to be "missional" here and now? What must church look like and be like? Why do we do things this way; is there another way?'

Now, it should be pointed out that the word 'mission' here might be seen as immediately problematic. Paas is working with the assumption, argued to the point of consensus by many theologians through the twentieth century and into our own, that the church is missional by her very nature. That is, that the church exists only because of mission, and that mission is her purpose. Yet we do have to be careful here. The problem comes when we define 'mission' too narrowly, with the result that, for example, we end up saying that the church exists for evangelism, or for social justice or whatever.

Once again, we are in danger of conflating the purpose of the church with whatever happens to be our particular theological or even political commitment. Many have been rightly wary of this claim, pointing out, for example, how little of the New Testament seems to be about intentional mission and is instead more about the quality of the community, its formation and its ethics. Others might claim therefore that 'faithfulness' and indeed 'worship' should be finally what defines the church rather than 'mission'. But the claim that 'the church is missional by her nature' can become less problematic if we simply allow – at least for a moment – the term 'missional' to be as broad as possible, and thus incorporating both faithfulness and worship within it. In John 20, after his resurrection, Jesus commissions the church by sending them (that word 'sending' is the word that would eventually become 'mission', i.e. 'to be sent') 'as the Father has sent me'. That is mission. Before this call, there is no church, only a ragtag group of scared followers of a failed messianic sect. (John makes clear that the doors are locked, and that fear rather than love is the prevalent atmosphere.) It is at this point of commissioning that they become the church: called, given a purpose. And this purpose is in the sending.

This is why we must say, theologically, that mission defines the church. Not in the sense that there is a task ('mission') that the church must fulfil to validate her existence; a sort of reductionistic ecclesiology. But in the sense that the church exists – to be faithful and to worship – only through the commissioning of God. She is what she is only by being *sent* by God: it is this sending that defines her reality. The moment she forgets this, thinking that she has some other basis for existence, or that she can simply 'be' the church without recourse to the purposes of the living God who is actively at work to reconcile all things, she gives up on being the church and becomes something else. Thus this mission – this sending – is deliberately broad. It is a sending in the pattern of Jesus ('As the Father has sent me …'), and as we know all too well, it is impossible to limit the breadth of Christ's mission. All of our designators – such as 'to bring the kingdom', 'to proclaim the kingdom', 'to preach good news to the poor' – can only ever shine a light on one aspect of the fullness of God's salvific purposes, which is to bring reconciliation to all things. In this sense, wherever we are in terms of our tradition and understandings of the task of mission, we can afford a very open reading of Paas' claim at this juncture.

INTRODUCTION

Starting new churches – as particular points within the broad ecology of God's mission – helps us to grasp what the 'sent-ness' of the church really does mean and look like. To remain only within the inherited churches, avoiding doing anything new, risks conditioning us to think of this mission of the church only in 'abstract': a neat theological idea, but devoid of any present reality. As though, for example, the church is being 'missional' by showing up week by week and worshipping. Again, there is a deep theological instinct at play here; the church is sent not to do something, but to *be* something, and thus in her faithfulness and worship she is in a deep way being the church as the sent people of God. However, this truth can quickly become meaningless if it is divorced from any empirical ground at all (e.g. the church that gathers to worship every week, and which loves one another well, but is essentially closed to outsiders, inhospitable and unwelcoming).[1] If there is one thing we can say with confidence about the sending of the Son, it is that he takes on flesh, dwelling among us in the earth and dust that is reality. And thus starting new churches can help us know something of that reality. It allows us to witness our ecclesiology and our missiology taking on flesh. Not mission as an idea or theological principle, but as a happening, an event; an actual encounter.

Which leads to Paas' second, positive, construal. As an 'intersection' of mission and ecclesiology, starting new churches provides new learnings for the church about both church and mission, and thus ultimately about God. In this sense, starting new churches can be theologically generative. There is a more general point here, about how our theology must in some sense always be lived; that the gospel is not a closed book, as it were, but is always being discovered afresh in and through the process of attempting to be faithful in the contemporary situation. New questions are asked, and new perspectives emerge. Theologians debate endlessly about the place that we should afford to what is often labelled 'experience' – and much of this is vital work – but essentially most theologians agree that we can say that while the gospel is objectively true, we are continually being opened to new perspectives *on* this truth, and to depths that we hadn't before reached. This is what Ben Quash speaks of when he describes the relationship between the 'given' and the 'found', between, that is, our theological commitments on the one hand (the given) and the new realities we encounter in the world (the found). Starting a new church is thus just one of many ways in which this process happens and is not unique in that sense. In the long history of the Christian church, no one has ever pioneered a new community in the suburbs of Birmingham in 2023. But so likewise, no one before has attempted to minister within a 400-year-old parish in 2023, or lead a medieval cathedral in this time either. So starting a new church is not unique when it comes to the task of trying to make sense of what the gospel looks like here in this time. And yet it is one of the commitments of this book that there is something at least more intense about the way that new churches approach this task. That is, new churches have a particular contribution to make to this conversation, given that for them the question of contextualization is an especially urgent one. A new church, or pioneer project, has no other ground on which it can stand; it exists and is sustainable only to the extent it can engage with people who are not yet involved with it. In this way, new churches – because they are asking the 'why' question all the time ('Why are we here, what is our purpose?') without the immediacy of an answer that comes from being well established and settled – thus afford the church a moment of learning: of learning about the contemporary context, about how people receive the church and its News, and thus ultimately about what God might be doing ahead of us in the world. In this way, rather than seeing the praxis of starting new things as somehow incongruent with 'real' theology (whatever this might be), we need to see that our theology can be shaped and honed and developed in the process of starting and sustaining new things. Simply put, our claim in this book is that if we pay proper attention there is an awful lot to be learnt about God, the world and about human creatures by observing the process of starting a new church. Much to learn, that is, from this process carried out well, and most certainly from where it has been carried out less well.

We know this to have been the case within the denomination of which we are part, the Church of England. Since the Church of England started taking pioneering and planting seriously, there has a been a wealth of discussion and reflection. Clearly not all of this – on any 'side' – has been very good (anxious, knee-jerk, cynical) and not much of it has really been, in any true sense, theological. But some has been both. And we have found that when people have been genuinely open to learning from what is going on – whether one arrives as basically suspicious or positive in the first instance – and willing to think properly, a good deal of rich theological work has emerged. Even in negative reactions to new churches, some people have sharpened their ecclesiology for the better.

In summary then, this book exists as a piece of theology *to* new churches: helping to sharpen our praxis so that it might be faithful, more fully participative in the movements of God revealed in Christ. And it exists as a theology *from* new churches: helping to draw out the theological (missiological, ecclesiological) learning from this process of starting new things.

Given all that has been said thus far, it is worth setting out explicitly what we believe to be the *character* of the book before you.

INTRODUCTION

A critical friend

This book seeks to be a critical friend to the movement of planting and pioneering new churches. *Friend*, because each of the contributors is sympathetic to the concept of starting new things. That is, each contributor has not ruled out the possibility that starting a new church might be a good, wise and faithful thing to do. Some contributors have been involved in starting new churches or have supported those who have been; others have observed from a distance. Some of us would say that we are fully bought in, seeing the starting of new things as *the* thing we should be focused on. Others see starting new things as just one (albeit potentially important) aspect of what God is calling us to do in this time. We thus want this book to be a gift: to planters and pioneers, to gatekeepers and decision makers, to planting or pioneering networks, and to teachers and coaches. We recognize the challenge of actually *being* the church faithfully in our time – doing mission that has integrity, which is integrated and vital – and of the hard decisions and choices that are faced at the coalface and in supporting those who are there.

A *critical* friend, however, because each of us recognizes that irrespective of where one stands in regards planting/pioneering, there is an onus on us all to ensure that we start new things well. As argued above, if this is to be the church, and if these are churches (or expressions of), then it matters how and why we do what we do, and in this regard not all options are open to us. The measures of 'success' we think we are working to must be evaluated, as much as the processes and forms that we think will get us there. Good, wise friends are those who take us out of the immediate concerns of the moment and remind us of the long game, the deeper work and the sometimes imperceptible and easily missed work of God. It should be noted therefore that we are doing theology in the sense of seeking a critical engagement with the broad issues around starting and sustaining new things. In this respect this book is different from other 'theologies of planting', which are working backwards as it were, seeking some basis or justification for what is already happening. These are important works of course, and it is important we seek to locate our mission within Scripture, tradition and reason/experience. What we want to do here, however, is pull out from the immediate paths we might have set ourselves on, not seeking a theological justification or validation for planting/pioneering, but thinking critically about these issues. As Paas says in the quotation above, simply because Paul planted churches in his world and in his way does not mean that we must do the same today. The call is to faithfulness in our time: to respond to what God is calling us to be and do now, in the time and places he has set us within, and with the gifts he has placed in our hands.

Non-partisan

We recognize that much of the conversation around new churches has been marked by the same sorts of polarized and binary thinking that so shapes our contemporary political and cultural life. We want to try and overcome some of these polarities here, or – better – explore what fruit might be borne through the conversation and the wrestle between different perspectives. That is, the goal is not synthesis (though there may be some of this that happens as we go) but rather conversation. There are three such polarities worth naming here: between practitioners and theologians; between inherited and new; between planting and pioneering.

The first of these has been the basis of this Introduction; we are seeking a theology rooted in praxis since ultimately this is what the church is. As a body called into the world to speak of God, it is thus theological all the way down. The task of theology, then, is one that very much concerns the forming and sustaining of churches.

Second, we want to refuse the basic distinction between old (inherited) and new. Such a distinction is a difficult one to uphold given that – as has been said now many times – every church was new once. In this sense, there is no fundamental distinction between old and inherited churches; the only difference is time. What this means, of course, is that technically there is no universal 'character' to new churches, in contrast to inherited ones. Sometimes, for example, it can be assumed that new churches are all necessarily 'modern' in whatever way this is imagined. In such a formulation, one can easily therefore make the pivot to argue that it is inherited churches that must necessarily be the bastions of true, historical faith, in contrast to the new things. But there is no reason why this must be the case. If the only difference between new and inherited (at least in principle) is when they started, then old/new cannot in any way be a measure of fidelity. It might be that a new church better models faithful, historic credal Christianity, for example, than does a church that has been around for 500 years (each of us will of course have our own measures as to what constitutes 'fidelity'). This is not the same as saying there is no value whatsoever in 'age'. We only have the perspective of our very short lifetime and we should be extremely wary of the sort of arrogance that leads us to give nothing more than a mere passing glance at the accumulated wisdom of the saints who have come before us and which is bound up in our ecclesial forms. Rather it is to say that we would need different measures of how and why what we receive really is such a gift. We do not decide what we are bequeathed, and many times an inheritance turns out to be more of a hindrance than a value. Overall, then, each of us who has contributed to this book would want to respect in some sense the concept that has become known as the mixed ecology; that we are called to start new things as much as we are called to sustain inherited models. The point is that the measures of how and why and when are not weighted in favour of the old or the new; there is no *absolute* value to either.

Third, and finally, in this book we want to address the assumed polarity between pioneering and planting. As far as we know, no one has named this difference explicitly in text; however, we are aware that it is a common distinction among practitioners and decision makers. The closest someone has come for arguing for such a difference would be Michael Moynagh, who has argued for two different approaches to starting churches: 'worship first' and 'serving first'.[2] Though Moynagh does make clear that these are 'models' rather than literal description, it is clear that he does see here a crucial difference, and one which I think plays out in the ways we have tended to approach starting new churches. The former – serve first – is about listening and responding to what one finds. Church here *emerges*: from the context one finds oneself within, and the people encountered. One might well expect such a process to take time and there may be multiple steps (the introducing of the reality of Christ carefully and appropriately) before what emerges can be defined as 'a church' by any accepted measure. This is the 'pioneering' approach – it is church that seeks to be for and in the 'edges'. It is necessarily contextual because, so the claim is made, established (inherited) church culture is necessarily an obstacle for many. Thus, rather than seeking to bring people in from the outside as it were, it seeks to form church where people are, and in a form that is relevant, appropriate and accessible. In contrast, Moynagh's 'worship first' approach, which most resembles what we would call classic church 'planting', is about forming church intentionally as a first rather than second step. In the pioneering model, worship may not emerge for some time whereas, in the planting model, worship happens immediately, and people are invited into this.

There is a great deal that needs to be said about this distinction. First, Moynagh is clearly right to say that 'Nothing in real life is quite like a model.' Thus, although we think this basic difference – pioneering and planting – remains, in reality most practitioners we speak to tend to merge these categories in their practice all the time. For example, the pioneer who starts with (albeit accessible, relevant) worship gatherings as a first step, or the planter who first spends a year simply being with a community before starting a small group with those who have shown some interest. We think this blurring-distinctions-in-reality is why the pioneering/planting distinction is largely unrecognized outside of the UK, where the term 'planting' tends to be used as a catch-all for any activity of starting new Christian communities. In the UK though, the distinction has been a significant one in the mainline established churches because of the particularities of the 2004 *Mission-shaped Church* report in the Church of England, and the resulting Fresh Expressions movement. Such fresh expressions of church were understood to be very much in the pioneering mould; that is, contextual expressions of church that might look potentially very different from inherited forms. In the past 15 years or so, however, there has been a shift within the Church of England, and planting has become far more prominent, not least because of the activity of Holy Trinity Brompton and the Church Revitalisation Trust, which has established several 'resource churches' in major cities in the UK. This approach – establishing a church by sending leaders and a team into a new place (potentially not a new building) – has proved popular for many, not least because it offers immediate 'impact' (both numerical and in terms of social capital). The result is that within the UK missional conversation we see these two 'streams' at play – planting and pioneering – and very often one is set against the other.

The assumption of this book is that within the 'mixed ecology' of church we will need all sorts of approaches to starting new things, and there can be no one-size-fits-all approach to ecclesiology. In this sense, we want to embrace planting/pioneering as something more akin to a spectrum, within which there are specific charisms that are important to hold on to. Others have worked hard in this regard: something like the 'pioneer spectrum' (CMS) or 'church trellis' (Northern Mission Centre, 2022) shows how we might make sense of a variety of church forms and missional approaches within the same place or ecclesial structure. We want to acknowledge the charisms, however, because we believe that the conversation benefits from distinctive instincts, rather than seeking a lazy 'mush' in which we don't recognize the gifts that different parts of the church are bringing to our ecclesiology. Pioneering reminds the church of the edge, and of those who will not ever or cannot ever 'come' to our churches. It reminds us that mission is not about conquest or coverage, but is about the slow, patient and emerging work of God in real people's lives. It reminds us of a vital theological truth that the church does not 'have' God but that God is found outside of the church, well before we show up. These are distinctive and sharp claims that we simply cannot forget as a church. But likewise, 'planting' (as we take it in distinction to 'pioneering') also has its own gifts to offer. Worship (and sacrament) is a primary rather than secondary aspect of church, of the witness of a diversity gathered together as one, of the sharing of the charisms of the people of God together in mission. What matters is not whether a church emerges following a 'serve first' journey or whether it is planted overnight; what matters is how this process happens and the extent to which it is a faithful witness to the beauty of Christ. One can 'plant' a church that is deeply contextual, seeking to respond to the needs of its place, just as one can plant a church that is parasitic on its place, driven by a colonial mentality.

Above all then, this book is an attempt to shine a light on the unique theological instincts that are at play in our starting of new churches, while refusing the slide into polarization and dichotomies that might result. We believe that we have the same aim – to see the church of Christ sent as he is sent – and that our distinctive contributions (and even challenges to one another) are not a threat but a gift so long as we are willing to listen and speak well.

Key themes

The 19 chapters of the book are divided into four parts, grouped around four themes: missiology, praxis, context and ecclesiology. In many respects these divisions are artificial. For all 19 chapters address all four of these themes to some degree; how could any reflection on church planting worth engaging with *not* address these issues? Yet the four parts allow us to pause for some more general reflections arising from each theme, before moving on to the next. As such, we hope the chapters – representing different contexts and approaches to starting new churches – offer a coherent and connected reflection on these issues of the theology and practice of missional ecclesiology in context.

The chapters in Part One all seek to ask questions related to divine and human agency in starting new churches. In a nutshell, they ask: What is God's to do and what is ours? In missiology more generally, the past 50 years have seen an important emphasis placed on the *missio Dei*, in recognition that the starting point for thinking about the task of mission is the work and mission and God, and not the activities and programmes of the church. Perhaps most influential in this shift is the work of David Bosch, in his seminal publication, *Transforming Mission*. As Bosch puts it, 'Mission is not primarily an activity of the church but an attribute of God' (Bosch, 1991, pp. 389–90). In seeking to reflect on the theology of new churches, a key question thus arises: What does it mean to think of God as the primary agent of mission for the task of planting new churches?

In Chapter 1, Mark Collinson asks provocatively whether church planters *really* believe in the *missio Dei*. If they really did, Collinson argues, they would take more seriously the need to challenge and shape the polity of the church to ensure missiology is at the heart of our church structures and traditions. Building on this theme of God's agency in the work of the church, Mark Powley seeks to challenge the false dichotomy often found in discussions of the *missio Dei*, which thinks of human agency as opposed to, or distinct from, divine agency, leading to a downplaying of strategy, planning and human effort. Instead, Powley offers an account of 'passionate co-agency', according to which the work of the Holy Spirit is expressed in and through human agents. Similarly, in Chapter 3, Helen Miller explores the tensions that arise from seeking to engage in church planting which is both faithful to Christ and responsive to context. Like Powley, Miller thinks that we must find a way of making sense of both human and divine agency in ministry – utilizing recent theological work on 'theodrama', Miller offers an account in which purposeful human action is empowered and situated within the work of God in the church.

In contrast to the accounts of Miller and Powley, seeking to situate human action as a kind of cooperative agency with God, emphasizing the importance of divinely infused strategy and planning, the chapters by Joshua Cockayne and James Butler seek instead to emphasize the need for a more robust spirituality in the context of church planting. Cockayne's argument presents a theology of divine–human participation as central to our ecclesiology, suggesting that planting must be rooted in the inaction of silence and discernment before it can be said to join in the ministry of God in church planting. Butler too emphasizes the need for prayer and discernment in planting but arrives at this conclusion via a different route. For Butler, our theology of new churches must take seriously the messiness of the lived reality of planting, and not merely offer a 'blueprint ecclesiology' from a distance. Thus, in reflecting on the ministry of participants in missional communities, Butler offers an account of divine–human agency in church planting that is dynamic, provisional and Spirit-led.

Last, in the final chapter of Part One, Beth Honey seeks to draw from the work of Thomas Aquinas to explore the relationship between divine and human agency in the work of starting new churches. As Honey argues, the key to understanding the relationship between our contribution and God's is the language of 'posture', seeking to hold our own narratives and understandings of planting with humility, and being willing to lay these down to allow for fresh and diverse voices to be heard.

In Part Two, the conversation takes a more practical turn, seeking to explore how our theology of church planting can influence our praxis.

Developing Honey's plea to see more diverse voices in church planting contexts, Paul Ayokunle seeks to look to the blossoming ministry of church planters in the global church. Ayokunle makes clear that the conversation cannot only focus on Western theological voices and their sometimes myopic focus on institutional decline. Ayokunle argues that in drawing non-Western, indigenous voices into the conversation, the church is better able to communicate and translate its message; it is better able to express the twin blessings of unity and diversity.

There follow two chapters exploring the leadership, training and deployment of practitioners. Andy Wier explores the concept of the 'paid pioneer', a kind of leadership role that has become increasingly common in the Church of England. The relationship between pioneers and the wider church is not always straightforward. Wier argues for the need for a more robust theology of pioneering as a distinct role within the church, to allow us to think creatively about the practical training and deployment of pioneers. Following this, Christian Selvaratnam explores this theme of training in more detail. Taking his lead from the medieval craft guilds as well as more modern apprenticeship models, Selvaratnam makes the case that church planting is a 'craft', and our training methods ought to reflect this, ensuring training is embodied, practical and embedded within a community of fellow craft practitioners.

Last, Ayo Audu and Catherine Butt seek to draw from the tools and methodology of Community Organizing to reflect on the ministry of church planting. Like Selvaratnam, they emphasize the need for leadership development and community, focusing especially on how these can help create communities deeply engaged with issues of injustice. Told through a powerful recounting of their own narratives and stories, Audu and Butt offer a framework for thinking about leadership that engages with the social and cultural issues of context, rather than focusing only on the *worshipping* life of communities.

After considering these important theological issues on a wider scale, Part Three takes a more fine-grained approach to the theology of new churches, seeking to learn from specific contexts and communities. The first two chapters offer reflections on what might typically be thought of as 'pioneering' contexts. First, Paul Bradbury seeks to draw lessons from the contexts of small missional communities, a sometimes overlooked context in the funding processes of the Church of England, which has often focused on larger, so-called 'resource churches'. As such, the voices of smaller contexts are sometimes missing from the conversation on church planting. Bradbury provides a summary of his interviews with seven leaders, seeking to offer a distinctive account of the missional ecclesiology found within missional communities, which he argues can provide an important way shaping of future ministry in starting new churches. Second, Tina Hodgett in Chapter 12 reflects on the ministry of seven full-time paid pioneers in the Diocese of Bath and Wells. Hodgett's focus is on the theme of 'play', seeking to explore the creativity of pioneering and the application of research in education, psychology and neuroscience on this theme. Hodgett's reflections promise to provide a different perspective from the sometimes scientific or mechanistic focus on planting, to see the need for artistic and affective approaches to starting new church communities.

The next two chapters consider two reflections on contexts that would more typically be called 'church plants' than 'pioneering contexts'. In Chapter 13, Stephen Squirrell explores two church revitalization projects in both the Charismatic-Anglican and Anglo-Catholic traditions. Squirrell unpacks the themes of 'parish' and 'sacrament' in these two very different contexts, seeking to reflect on the specific ministry of revitalization, and to emphasize the importance of a diversity of tradition in our theology and practice of church planting. Building on this importance of highlighting diverse traditions, John Wallace explores two Anglo-Catholic contexts of church planting, which are still very much in the minority of the church planting movement. Wallace's research offers concrete examples of Anglo-Catholic planting and also reflects on the distinctive challenges of starting new churches within a tradition that is sometimes peripheral to the central strategies and networks of church planters.

Finally, Part Four concludes the book with five chapters devoted to the topic of ecclesiology, asking questions about the shape and nature of the church and how this affects our theology of starting new churches. It begins with three chapters exploring the intersection between missiology and ecclesiology. In Chapter 15, Ali Williams argues that mission ought to be foundational for our ecclesiology. Seeking to avoid the risk of mission being merely 'epistemological' (i.e. something we believe), Williams argues for the need to see mission as an outworking of God's nature, and therefore integral to an ontology of the church. Thus, Williams argues, in shifting our ontology of mission, we see the importance of the church's relationship with its context and community. In a similar vein, in Chapter 16 Cathy Ross draws on her extensive expertise in missiology to pose important questions for those in the ministry of starting new churches. As Ross argues, it is important to see the role of the ministry and work of God through the Holy Spirit in reflecting on our ecclesiology of planting. In doing so, she offers a vision of the church that is deeply engaged in its context: listening in the neighbourhood, discerning how God is already at work there, committing to living in the context to establish relationships, living and working on the edges, allowing the locals to engage in their own transformation and leadership.

Then, in Chapter 17, Simon Hall and Roy Searle reflect on ecclesiology 'from the edge'. They begin by considering the reception of the concept of 'church planting', outside of the academy and the church. They contend that for many people, 'church' is synonymous with a building or a minister in a dog collar. In contrast to this centralized, institutionalized ecclesiology, Hall and Searle seek to offer a vision of the church that emphasizes community over institution and disperses leadership widely and creatively to all involved. They maintain that a decentralized model of church whose primary focus is on discipleship and mission is culturally pertinent, and needed if we are to re-engage with the ministry of church planting today.

The final two chapters outline two perspectives on different models of the church, which offer to shape our theology of new churches. First, in Chapter 18, Michael Moynagh explores the theme of 'gift', offering a model of the church that can expand our ecclesiological vision. For Moynagh, it is a part of the church's nature to be self-donating; to give itself away. This emphasis on gift, Moynagh argues, can provide an ecclesiology that can promote a healthy and generous approach to starting new churches, avoiding the risks of insularity and fear. Finally, John Valentine in Chapter 19 looks to the pages of Paul's Epistle to the Romans to ask ecclesiological questions about the uniformity and diversity of church planting structures. Valentine argues that what emerges from exegesis is an emphasis on three key themes: diversity, freedom and unity. These themes can provide a lens through which to see the contemporary ministry of church planting, stressing the importance of ministry that draws from a range of voices and contexts, and in which there is space for innovation and creativity to flourish within the one church of Christ.

Notes

1 We should also question the language of 'faithfulness' here. Faithful to what? If God is at work to redeem his creation, then we cannot possibly be faithful without participating in this work intentionally. Faithfulness is not opposed to intentional mission (be it social justice or evangelism) rather faithfulness to *this* God; that is, the God revealed in Jesus Christ (the Father who sends and the Son who is sent in the power of the Spirit) must look like mission. We might want to retreat from the world, imagining ourselves as moving towards God, but we risk missing him as he comes the other way: always moving towards the world. One could make a similar – though distinctive – claim about worship. We worship a God who is 'a fountain of sending love' as David Bosch famously put it (Bosch, 1991, p. 392). And thus to worship him – to give him worth – must entail following him in his reconciling love towards the world. This is why the Old Testament prophets are so consistently

angry at worship practices that are disconnected from 'mission' (justice, service and holy living).

2 See Moynagh, 2012; 2017, chapter 2. He summarizes: 'Like any model, they do not mirror reality, but are generalizations and simplifications of it. ... They offer partial, not complete knowledge. So while the models are to be taken seriously, they are not to be taken literally. Nothing in real life is quite like a model' (2012, p. 206).

References

Bosch, D. J., 1991, *Transforming Mission: Paradigm Shifts in Theology of Mission*, New York: Orbis Books.
CMS, 'Pioneer Spectrum', https://pioneer.churchmissionsociety.org/pioneer-spectrum/ (accessed 09.06.23).
Foulger, Will, 2023, *Present in Every Place? The Church of England's New Churches, and the Future of the Parish*, London: SCM Press.
Paas, Stefan, 2016, *Church Planting in the Secular West: Learning from the European Experience*, Grand Rapids, MI: Eerdmans.
Moynagh, Michael, 2012, *Church for Every Context: An introduction to Theology and Practice*, London: SCM Press.
———, 2017, *Church in Life: Innovation, Mission and Ecclesiology*, London: SCM Press.
Northern Mission Centre, 2022, 'Imaginative Mission in and Around Cumbria', https://godforall.org.uk/wp-content/uploads/2022/11/FX-Booklet-2022-FINAL-RFS.pdf (accessed 09.06.23).
Vatican II, *Ad Gentes*, https://www.vatican.va/archive/hist_councils/ii_vatican_council/documents/vat-ii_decree_19651207_ad-gentes_en.html? (accessed 22.03.24).

PART ONE

Missiology: New Churches and the *missio Dei*

I

Do Church Planters Believe in the *missio Dei*?

MARK COLLINSON

Introduction

Partly what drew me to minister in Amsterdam after initial ministerial training was the potential to plant new church congregations. I found the experience of focusing ministry within the boundaries of a parish in suburban Manchester somewhat stifling. One step too far, cross the road, and you're outside the parish. Drive over the River Mersey and you're in a different diocese. The concept of jurisdiction that restricted my role assisting the incumbent in the cure of souls defined clear and understandable limits, but the lives of our parishioners ebbed and flowed across invisible ecclesiastical frontiers. The divisions we encountered in society were more concerned with whether you support Man City or Man United. People shop in either the town-centre bargain stores, Tesco or Sainsbury's. Few parishioners work within the boundaries of the parish in which they live. There is an inevitable tension between the significance of ecclesiastical place and the spaces people occupy as they live from day to day.

Why was this important for an eager minister a little wet behind the ears? I remember one ecumenical evangelistic campaign in the town centre that gave out free food to passers-by. How does one follow up with those who want to find out more when even they don't know which parish they live in? What *is* so significant about ecclesial jurisdiction that the rights of the incumbent to have no other Anglican incumbent ministering in her parish must be defended by law? How do you avoid treading on sensitive ecclesiastical toes that are defending their territory from invasion? This is an essential component of the parish system in England.

The grass looked rather greener in the Diocese in Europe, where the ecclesial form of the Church of England is rather different. There are no parishes, just chaplaincies, where the clergy serve as chaplains in their communities, serving, in principle, just a segment of the population who speak English. What attracted me about the Anglican chaplaincy in Amsterdam was that it was a major European city with a burgeoning English-speaking population, but it had not seen the same kind of growth of Anglican congregations as other northern European cities. Paris had two Anglican churches in the heart of the city, and a chain of ancillary chaplaincies around its ring roads. Brussels too had a large congregation on the outskirts of the city as well as its older congregation in the city centre, and yet further congregations not far off in Waterloo and Leuven. The English-speaking population in Amsterdam was considerable, and one of the aspects that drew me to apply for the post of Chaplain was the possibility of planting congregations on the outskirts of the city, without infringing ecclesiastical boundaries.

Or so I thought. Within weeks of arriving in Amsterdam, I was invited to lunch by the priest of the Old Catholic Church, who enthusiastically told me about the Bonn Agreement of 1931, which, lamentably, had been omitted from my Initial Ministerial Education. Then, at diocesan synod, we met the Bishop of the Convocation of Europe, The Episcopal Church of the USA, who is one of a number of bishops in the wider Anglican family of churches who claim overlapping jurisdiction with the Church of England's Bishop of the Diocese in Europe. While the Church of England in England was able to literally hold the line of where parochial boundaries are drawn, the Diocese in Europe operated in a contested world of overlapping Anglican jurisdictions and had done so for many decades. It is a fact of ecclesial existence.

Frequently, missionary couples financed by churches in the USA arrived in Amsterdam because they perceived it to be a city in need of the gospel and overrun by drug gangs and prostitutes. Such well-meaning evangelists obviously thought the indigenous Dutch churches were putting on a poor show. Meanwhile, there were also Dutch pastors from all different stripes of the Reformed traditions who were also picking up on the mission-shaped church agenda of the Church of England and the church planting ministry of Redeemer Presbyterian Church in New York. They also wanted to plant churches. I was immersed in the ecumenical deep end and had to learn quickly how ecumenical and worldwide Anglican relationships had an impact on the mission to which I believed I was called.

Eventually, out of desperation, to learn more about the nature of the church and mission I enrolled in a research masters at the local university in Amsterdam, which developed into doctoral study (Collinson, 2021). It was a rich multicultural environment of students from a whole host of confessional entities. One of the tensions I discovered that has been evident since the European Reformation, evolving throughout the twentieth century and manifest in the opening decades of the twenty-first, is the tussle between the disciplines of missiology and ecclesiology. In the last century, missiology as an academic discipline within systematic theology established itself, but with some rather threatening claims.

If we believe in the *missio Dei,* then the only logical consequence is that it challenges the primacy of ecclesiology. My observation is that in practice, the ecclesial polity of the Church of England is so strong that it relegates missiology to an also ran. That makes me wonder whether we, and church planters in particular, really do believe in the *missio Dei*. If we did, would we be more confident about challenging the ecclesial polity that shapes the life of the church? I suggest this theological hypocrisy can be exposed by briefly tracing the interrelationships between missiology and ecclesiology and examining the ecclesial polity we find operating as we reflect on 20 years since the publication of the influential *Mission-shaped Church* report (Archbishops' Council, 2004).

What's so important about mission?

While 'mission' has been part of the church since before the day of Pentecost, missiology is a relatively new kid on the block of systematic theology. I believe the word 'mission', and its Greek (*apostellō* and *pempō*) and Latin (*missio*) antecedents are more important than we have assumed even in the last century. When *apostellō* appears in the New Testament (and it appears together with its cognates in 225 verses) it provides us with a perspective on the action of God bringing salvation to the world. Most of the time, it's translated by 'send'. The Gospel writers also use the word *pempō* less frequently but in a similar way, and to some extent the two words are interchangeable. Both words are used to describe the sending of people and, most significantly for Christology, they describe the relationship between the Father and the Son.

The Father 'apostled' the Son and the Son sent (*pempō*) the Holy Spirit[1] – or to use the English derivation from the Latin, the Father missioned the Son, and the Son missioned the Holy Spirit. This places mission at the heart of our Christology. This mission embraces the vibrance of *kenosis,* the self-emptying of the divine Son of God expressed in the hymn of Philippians 2. The human form of Jesus of Nazareth is perpetuated in the Father and the Son sending the Holy Spirit into the world to be the presence of Christ in the hearts of those who believe in his resurrection.

In the Gospels, Jesus defines not just the persons of the Father, Son and Holy Spirit in terms of 'being sent', but he also defines the disciples in the same terms. He sends the disciples into the world so that the world may believe that the Father sent the Son. The disciples therefore become 'the sent ones', the apostles, the ones who are missioned by Christ to go into the world and make disciples of all nations.

Here we encounter the dynamic of mission that is illustrated in the first Pentecost of the church. This sending of the disciples crosses cultural boundaries. The Son crossed the boundary from heaven to earth, and the apostles cross the boundaries of language and culture as they speak in other tongues proclaiming the glory of God to those who are gathered for the Jewish festival in Jerusalem. As the church is born, so the apostles discover that they are sharing the good news of Christ not just in Jerusalem, but in Judea, Samaria and to the ends of the earth. The book of the Acts of the Apostles starts in Jerusalem and ends in a completely different culture, in Rome.

The significance of this cultural transition from Aramaic- and Hebrew-speaking apostles sharing the gospel with Jews, to its reaching the heart of the Latin- and Greek-speaking Roman Empire is witnessed by the New Testament writings. The impact of the New Testament being written in Greek for Greeks, not Aramaic or Hebrew for Jews, is all too easily forgotten. The story of the sending of the Son to the people of Israel has embedded within it the demonstration of how the gospel crosses the cultural boundaries between Jews and Greeks. Some parts of this story explicitly address the tensions of this cultural transition. These tensions are expressed throughout the New Testament. Do Christians eat the blood of animals sacrificed in Greek temples because Jews never would? Do we participate in Greek festivals, or do we observe the sabbath? How do we translate the significance of the cleanliness rules that Jews would observe in daily life and especially when worshipping in the Temple? Do we even need a Temple? Christians discovered they didn't need the Temple even before the Jews had to adjust to its destruction in 70 CE.

I think the significance of this cultural shift that is inherently part of the New Testament is largely lost on contemporary Christians. Perhaps this is because both Greek and Hebrew cultures are foreign to us, and we're trying to understand a context that existed two millennia ago. We merge the two cultures together in the process of trying to translate it to ours. Perhaps, because we study the New Testament in Greek, we don't even notice that an enormous cultural shift happened when the Gospel writers expressed in their first drafts the words of Jesus in a language other than the one Jesus spoke. Just a few untranslated Aramaic words remain in the text to indicate the hard work that has gone on translating all the rest. The work of translation that the authors of the New Testament did in writing their Gospels and letters in Greek is largely hidden from us. That work, I suggest, is essential in the dynamic of the mission of God. That hidden work is the secret ingredient of conveying the gospel to a culture that does not know about Jesus. It's as if the canon of the New Testament is formed, as a ready-made package to be followed by future generations, already demonstrating that the message of Jesus crosses cultural frontiers.

It is the apostles who did this work. So when we consider the traditional understanding of what it means for the church to be apostolic, ecclesiology gives us two possible answers. First, the church sits under the oversight of bishops who can trace their consecrations in a direct line of transmission back to the Apostle Peter, the first Bishop of Rome. Second, we assess whether we stand in the teaching of the first apostles as a measure of our authenticity to their gospel.

But how much do we consider that being apostolic means sharing the gospel in a different culture? Sharing the gospel in different cultures was very much the motivation of the modern missionary movements. Lesslie Newbigin, on his return in 1974 from being an ecumenical missionary bishop after 40 years in India, helped the Western church recognize that there is just as much of a mission field in Western society as in India. In contemporary Western society we may not need to speak a different language in order to share the gospel, but we certainly need to recognize the culture of church. This culture of church holds and propagates the gospel, and has to engage within sub-cultures of society in order to be able to communicate the story of Jesus. As the Anglican Preface to the Declaration of Assent reminds us whenever a priest is licensed to a benefice, we are 'to proclaim afresh in each generation' the faith of the church.

Each generation produces its own new subcultures, which become increasingly mystifying to the parents and grandparents of older generations. But subcultures are not just defined by generations. The significance of place is that every place has its own culture. Culture is composed of history and stories, of people who lived lives and sang songs, who interacted, argued and forgave one another, and who gave birth to the next generation. Every town, suburb and village as well as every generation has a specific culture, and part of what we understand by incarnating the gospel means making Jesus Christ understood, alive and relevant in every context. This, I suggest, is the relevance of being apostolic in contemporary Western society.

Who believes in the *missio Dei*?

It was in the middle of the twentieth century that the term *missio Dei* evolved. Back in 1932 at a missionary conference in Brandenburg, Karl Barth related the significance of the word *missio* to the Trinity. Barth asked,

> Must not even the most faithful missionary, the most convinced friend of missions, have reason to reflect that the term *missio* was in the ancient Church an expression of the doctrine of the Trinity – namely the expression of the divine sending forth of the self, the sending of the Son and the Holy Spirit to the world? Can we indeed claim that we can do it any other way? (Thomas, 1995, 2003, pp. 105–6)

Here Barth reminds missionaries that they are not what mission is about. Mission is not what missionaries do, it is something God does, because *missio* is part of who God is. He picks up on the term *missio* because of its significance to the identity of the Trinity. The significance of this is that missiology is located primarily in the doctrine of the Trinity, rather than ecclesiology or soteriology. Ecclesiology and soteriology locate missiology as theological praxis, the practice of the church's mission. But this cannot be the case if missiology is derived principally from the doctrine of the Trinity. It is taking nearly a century of theological reflection for this to be recognized.

According to John Flett, the pastor and missionary Karl Hartenstein (after tours in India, China and Africa) is the first to be credited with coining the term *missio Dei* in an essay written in 1934 (Flett, 2010, p. 131). It was not until after the 1952 Missionary Conference in Willingen that two concepts of the *missio Dei* emerged that describe a tension between ecclesiology and missiology that continues today.

The first recognizes the primary significance of the church as the agent by which God works in the world. Echoing the action of the birth of the church, when 120 faithful followers of Christ devoted themselves to prayer, so today the church gathered around Word and sacrament is the instrument of God's salvation in the world. The church proclaims the gospel to the world; the church serves humanity as a sign of God's love; as people hear and respond to the gospel, they join the church. This view places the church at the centre of God's mission as the vehicle for personal redemption. In this sense the church has a specialized role in the *missio Dei* (Van Gelder and Zscheile, 2011, p. 30). This view resonates deeply with contemporary understandings of the church.

The second view defines a more generalized role of the church, and recognizes that God's agency cannot be restricted by the church's action. God embraces not just people whose lives are saved, but the whole of creation is caught up in the mission of God to bring the kingdom of heaven to earth. God is active outside the church revealing 'Godself' to humanity and working through the structures of human institutions both ecclesial and secular. This view acknowledges that mission is not primarily an activity of the church, but the action of God in the world. God's mission embraces the witness of the church in the world, but is certainly not restricted to it: God's mission does not even need the church, and frequently extends beyond it.

While both views recognize the nature of the church as missionary,[2] this second view of the *missio Dei* challenged the centuries-old understanding that God related to the World through the church: the popular formula of God – Church – World was turned around to God – World – Church. Not surprisingly, this ruffles some ecclesiastical feathers. This displaces the primacy of the church and its mediating role. It is tempting to try to collapse the dichotomy and say that both ways are true: God relates to the world both through the church and through God's agency directly outside the church. But this is essentially the second view.

Furthermore, the corollary of the church being missionary by its very nature (Vatican Council II, 1965) is that ecclesiology is really derived from missiology. Prior to the emergence of the *missio Dei*, the nature of the church was derived directly from Christology, as the body of Christ. But now our understanding of Christology has changed so that we recognize mission is at the heart of the dynamic and salvific work the Trinity. Mission has slipped into a theological space which means the nature of the church must always be responding to the missionary nature of God.

What's this got to do with church planting?

These two understandings of the *missio Dei* continue to influence and, I would argue, frustrate the mission of the church today. Since the publication of the *Mission-shaped Church* report in 2004, the Church of England has been increasingly polarized in its attitude to church growth. The two perspectives of the *missio Dei* outlined above make uncomfortable bedfellows. The first view of the specialized role of the church, with an ecclesio-centric view of the church, appeals to both the contemporary inheritors of the evangelical tradition and Anglo-Catholics.

Defenders of the parish system celebrate the prayer-soaked walls of centuries of witnesses in our ancient medieval churches and cathedrals. The church building is the location of forgiveness proclaimed, where the gospel of freedom is announced, where the Word of God is preached. As John Milbank so romantically evokes the image of the parish church where 'only pure geography encompasses all without exception ... only the located place, situated round the buried bones of the martyrs ... extends this embrace back into the mists of historical time and forward into a trusted future' (Milbank, 2008, p. 125). The church building is where God is met in worship, where the word is preached and where baptism seals the membership of the redeemed people of God into the Body of Christ.

While these images are reminiscent of a glorious past, this church-centric view of the mission of God has its problems. First, we must remember that the rise of the missionary movement through mission societies happened because missionaries believed the churches were *not* taking their responsibilities seriously enough to proclaim the gospel to people of other nations and faiths around the world. The church had ignored the call to mission, so missionary societies of the protestant churches acted and were governed outside of and independently of the structures of the established churches. They were often resourced by women whose gifts, callings and sacrificial ministries were unappreciated within the established churches. It's as if the mission of God could not be contained within the suppressive confines of the existing church structures.

Second, the ecclesial structures of the Church of England are so strong and influential that they actually influence our ecclesiology. Indeed, as some critics of the *Mission-shaped Church* report highlight, there is a union between the form and content of the church (Davison and Milbank, 2010, pp. 1–27). Drawing on the philosophy of Wittgenstein, what Andrew Davison and Alison Milbank mean by this is that the meaning is conveyed in the message, that words and language express content through shared common practice. The problem with this union between form and content is that it also fuses the ecclesial polity of the Church of England with its ecclesiology. Davison and Milbank may say that this isn't a problem at all, but that's not the experience of Anglicanism.

The Reformation of the sixteenth century was a laboratory of experiments demonstrating how different ecclesial forms were derived from ecclesiology. Anglicans, Lutherans, Calvinists and Anabaptists all evolved different forms of church governance and authority. For Anglicans, the most significant changes were between the Pope and the King, but the threefold order of bishops, priests and deacons remained, as did parishes. In subsequent centuries the ecclesial structures of the church evolved into the synodical structures we have today. These structures do change, and they evolve over time, and sometimes quite quickly as they did in the sixteenth century. Ecclesial polity shifts and changes. Furthermore, these structures are derived from ecclesiology, not the other way around. The ecclesial structures that each confession evolved and adopted served their understanding of the nature of the church. The historic creeds that state what we believe about God and the church have not changed. Only the ecclesial structures changed. To suggest therefore that form and content are one means that the ecclesial structures of the Church of England are in fact influencing its ecclesiology.

When we think about the church (typified in Hampshire where I live), we think about beautiful medieval buildings, set in pretty churchyards, serving their village communities. Each village often has its own parish. These ecclesial forms of the church describe the nature of the church. It is very difficult to imagine church in these communities in other ways. So much so that, when someone proposes a new form of church that meets in the village cricket club, the pub or in the primary school, it is very hard to imagine how it compares with inherited church.

When form and content are fused, we forget that it is the role of ecclesiology to define the nature of the church and not our ecclesial polity. The nature of the church concerns whether it is one holy catholic and apostolic. A church in the Church of England must have ministry conducted according to the canons, by ministers who are duly ordained, who believe in the faith of the historic creeds. Worship is defined by the ministry of Word and sacrament. When we unite form and content we tend to forget that it is the creeds, our orders, the Scriptures and the sacraments that define the nature of the church, rather than the Church Representation Rules. Far be it from us to use the prerogative of ecclesial structures to change the nature of what we believe the church to be.

Do church planters believe in the *missio Dei*?

This is an interesting question. In the introduction to the *Mission-shaped Church* report, the chair of the working group suggested that 'a mixed economy of parish churches and network churches will be necessary, in an active partnership across a wider area, perhaps a deanery' (Archbishops' Council, 2004, p. xi). In his detailed research conducted by Church Army, George Lings analysed fresh expressions of church and church plants in the twenty-year period between 1992 and 2012 (Lings, 2016). From a sample of 21 dioceses he found that the numbers of people attending fresh expressions of church equated to an average-sized diocese, and was equal to the decline in average worshipping attendance. Only 25% of those attending these new forms of church are already Christians; the remainder being people who are dechurched (35%) or non-churched

(40%). Only 17% of the fresh expressions of church in these dioceses crossed parish boundaries, and always with consent of those affected. This, Lings suggests, has been a very consistent statistic. Over four-fifths, therefore, of fresh expressions of church are within parish boundaries, and should be accountable to the incumbent of the benefice. The non-parochial legal status initiated by the *Mission-shaped Church* report, the Bishop's Mission Order, is the primary legal instrument that challenges the parochial structures, providing deanery and diocesan synodical representation. However, only 2% of fresh expressions of church/church plants opted for this route up to 2012. Tim Sumpter in his analysis of the impact of fresh expressions of church in historic church buildings suggests that they are 're-traditioning' parish churches (Sumpter, 2015, pp. 24–6). The impact of the Church Revitalisation Trust working in partnership with the national church and dioceses has led to most dioceses in the Church of England establishing resource churches. With the exception of some early experiments, most of these are being established within existing parochial structures, without the use of Bishop's Mission Orders. They are also beginning to revitalize urban areas as teams of people leave the resource church to breathe new life into neighbouring parishes.[3]

All this suggests that the parish structure is, by and large, absorbing and sustaining the new growth coming from fresh expressions of church and church plants. The mixed economy envisaged 20 years ago, and still enshrined in the current Church of England vision framed as mixed ecology, is still a future aspiration. The ecclesial structures of parish have not been threatened or disrupted by church planting and fresh expressions of church, because the parish system is such a robust ecclesial structure. The critics of the *Mission-shaped Church* report and the current advocates of Save the Parish have nothing to fear.

In *The Once and Future Parish*, Alison Milbank laments in a litany of woes why the parish needs to be saved. According to Milbank the parish needs saving from a 'contentless' sense of mission, managerialism, the centralization of power in dioceses and the national church, a crisis in ordination training, and the inappropriate resourcing of diocesan functions in preference to parochial clergy (Milbank, 2023, p. 53). While she does acknowledge some of the demands of compliance in administration in dioceses, such as safeguarding and health and safety (Milbank, 2023, pp. 132–4), she is somewhat dismissive of safeguarding training, and does not seem to recognize the significance of the change in cultural awareness that is so vital to the church's integrity in safeguarding. Furthermore, compliance also involves charities law and governance requirements, GDPR and employment law. She fundamentally believes that after decades of numerical decline, there is 'no financial necessity' to reduce the number of stipendiary clergy (Milbank, 2023, p. 66). Milbank clearly believes that the church must grow, and she provides encouraging examples of parish churches from different traditions that have grown, together with mission initiatives that any resource church leader would applaud (Milbank, 2023, pp. 1, 28, 135–45).

Milbank's objections to resource churches and pioneering appear to be more related to the culture she feels they reject than any discernible ecclesiological marks of the church. After all, the priests who lead resource churches supported by the Church Revitalisation Trust have been ordained by the historic episcopate, believe in the historic creeds, the Scriptures containing all things necessary for salvation, the sacraments, and that the church is one holy catholic and apostolic. They couldn't be more Anglican according to recognized ecclesiological terms. The difference is that most couldn't be less culturally bonded to the supporters of Save the Parish. These cultural differences are represented, for example, in the way liturgy is viewed. For the traditional Hampshire parish church, liturgy will be exemplified by the Book of Common Prayer, *Common Worship* Holy Communion and Evensong. For the urban resource church it will be exemplified by a style of worship that is nonetheless still authorized as a Service of the Word by *Common Worship*. The days are long gone when we define what is Anglican by liturgy alone.

If our ecclesial structures are as robust as they appear to be, then if we follow Milbank, it does seem that they are driving our understanding of the nature of the church. Ecclesial polity is in fact influencing ecclesiology. And this is something that should concern us if we believe in the *missio Dei*. As I have argued above, if we believe in the *missio Dei*, then we understand that the nature of the church should be derived from the God of mission. We are then able to reform and revitalize our ecclesial polity in response to the leading of the Holy Spirit. Traditionally this has been done through orders in the church that typically exhibit the prophetic gifts and make the traditional church uncomfortable: the Desert Fathers, the Benedictines, Dominicans, Jesuits and Franciscans, to name but a few. Over the past 20 years, we had an opportunity for fresh expressions of church and church plants to challenge the parish system. But we choose to subsume them within our existing polity. The emerging church hasn't yet emerged.

This is further evidence that, as Andrew Root warns us, we continue to believe that the church is the star of its own story (Root, 2022, pp. 83–91). If we believe in the *missio Dei*, then we will not persist in joining in with God's mission in a way that puts church at the centre of who we are and what we do.[4] As Root suggests, the church is not the primary subject in the story, but God is. Church isn't even the object of the story. The world is the focus of God's revelation, and when the world starts seeking who God is, then the church will be revived, revitalized and renewed. Missional church really is about birthing the church in a particular context as cultural boundaries are crossed. We have only begun to rediscover the power of the gospel for those who believe as we see fresh expressions of church, resource church and revitalizations bringing new life to parishes. There is a greater journey of discovery ahead of us if we believe in the *missio Dei* and trust God to nurture new ecclesial forms of church to create a mixed ecology.

Notes

1 Take, for example, the Gospel of John, which uses *pempō* interchangeably with *apostellō* when he refers to the sending of himself by the Father and the sending of the Holy Spirit. *Pempō* is used in John chapters 1, 4—9, 12—16 and 20 to refer to the Father sending the Son/Jesus and the Holy Spirit (including the filioque clause of 15.26). *Apostellō* is used in John chapters 1, 3, 5—8, 11 and 17 to refer to the Father sending the Son/Jesus. Virtually every chapter in John's Gospel apart from the crucifixion scenes reminds the reader of this key theme.

2 Significantly, Vatican II recognized: 'The pilgrim church is missionary by her very nature, since it is from the mission of the Son and the mission of the Holy Spirit that she draws her origin, in accordance with the decree of God the Father' (*Ad Gentes*, §2). This demonstrates how much Karl Rahner and Hans Küng were able to introduce Barth's understanding of the *missio Dei* to the Council.

3 I speak here with knowledge primarily of the Diocese of Winchester, which has invested significantly, with the assistance of training and support provided by Church Revitalisation Trust and national church grants, in five resource churches that are now having a significant impact on revitalizing and reviving parishes across all the major urban areas of the diocese.

4 Tim Keller makes the same mistake in his overview of church revitalization in his book *Centre Church* (2012).

References

Archbishops' Council, 2004, *Mission-shaped Church: Church Planting and Fresh Expressions of Church in a Changing Context*, London: Church House Publishing.

Collinson, Mark P. C., 2021, *Witnessing God's Mission: Towards a Missional Ecclesiology of the Church of England*, PhD thesis, Vrije Universiteit Amsterdam.

Davison, Andrew and Alison Milbank, 2010, *For the Parish: A Critique of Fresh Expressions*, London: SCM Press.

Flett, John G., 2010, *The Witness of God: The Trinity, Missio Dei, Karl Barth, and the Nature of Christian Community*, Cambridge: Eerdmans.

Keller, Timothy J., 2012, *Centre Church: Doing Balanced, Gospel-Centered Ministry in your City*, Grand Rapids, MI: Zondervan.
Lings, George, 2016, *The Day of Small Things: An Analysis of Fresh Expressions of Church in 21 Dioceses of the Church of England*, Sheffield: Church Army's Research Unit.
Milbank, Alison, 2023, *The Once and Future Parish*, London: SCM Press.
Milbank, John, 2008, 'Stale Expressions: The Management-Shaped Church', *Studies in Christian Ethics* 21(1), pp. 117–28.
Root, Andrew, 2022, *Churches and the Crisis of Decline: A Hopeful, Practical Ecclesiology for a Secular Age*, Grand Rapids, MI: Baker Academic.
Sumpter, Tim, 2015, *Freshly Expressed Church: Lessons from Fresh Expressions for the Wider Church*, Cambridge: Grove Books.
Thomas, Norman E., 1995, 2003, *Classic Texts in Mission and World Christianity*, Maryknoll, NY: Orbis Books.
van Gelder, Craig and Dwight J. Zscheile, 2011, *The Missional Church in Perspective: Mapping Trends and Shaping the Conversation*, Grand Rapids, MI: Baker Academic.
Vatican Council II, 1965, *Ad Gentes: Decree on the Mission Activity of the Church*, Vatican City: Vatican Council.

2

(Why) We Need to Talk About Method

MARK POWLEY

Introduction

Two congregational plants were attempted by a young leader, but only one succeeded. The first, a new evening service, had a set of the factors we might associate with success: it started with a strong team in the target age, it built on established parish connections, and the charismatic worship style was suited to the leader. Broadly speaking, the methods were promising. The second plant was a mid-week project attempted by the same leader a few years later, but it didn't have the same factors in its favour. It had weak team affiliation. It was trying to grow in a context where there were few warm contacts. And throughout the process, the venue was entirely covered in scaffolding. Here is my question: *of the two plants, which one worked?*

When I asked this recently of a room of planters and pioneers, the answers were mixed. Understandably, people suspected a trick question. Maybe they wondered if I was holding back an 'X factor' that would make all the difference. Interestingly, quite a few people opted for the underdog scenario with the weak team, on the premise that God often works in unlikely ways. After all, if we could tell by a few simple conditions whether a plant would succeed, wouldn't we be excluding God from the process? Perhaps the Holy Spirit is our 'X factor'?

Well, the answer to the question is that the project with the strong team, close connections and relevant experience did much better than the second one. I know this because the young leader was me. And the reason I raise the question here is to highlight the issue of method. Effective methods do seem to make a crucial difference to the task of planting. But this fact may place us in something of a bind. If church planting depends on method, strategy and local conditions, where is the place for God? But if, on the other hand, the sovereign work of God is the key determinant, does it really matter what methods we use?

The present chapter seeks to address this challenge. It begins with a brief treatment of method, in particular highlighting the role of synergy: how to relate the work of God and humanity in the task of church planting. It continues by drawing on two main sources: the missionary logic of the Apostle Paul and the systematic theology of Hans Urs von Balthasar. In these theologies of extensive and passionate co-agency, we find a way through the impasse over method. I propose that we see church planting as an audacious divine–human partnership, the sacred craft of constructing a temple for the Holy Spirit. The advantage of this approach is to affirm human method, strategy, effort and creativity as vital elements co-opted into the very work of God; at the same time our method, being made visible rather than dismissed, can be held to account according to the pattern of Christ.

The problem of method

Method in church planting is already a matter of some contention. The means employed in starting new congregations are wide-ranging, so method in this context incorporates everything from general matters of missional approach, strategic planning and building community, to more specific entrepreneurial techniques like targeting groups, developing leadership potential, overseeing multiplication and growing financial and technological capital. All these are vital to the task of planting and consequential in determining the results. An interest in the technicalities of method therefore predominates in writing about church planting, which tends to have a 'how to' character, while ethical and theological concerns about method feature in critique of this genre.

We can begin with the problematization of method. A number of writers express concerns about church planting strategy in this connection. These might, for instance, relate to managerialism or the undue prominence of strategic planning. Guli Francis-Dehqani has argued that 'Language of vision and strategy risks ignoring the reality of frailty, brokenness, sin ... What we are called to is faithfulness' (Francis-Dehqani, 2022). Alison Milbank and Andrew Davison's widely noted critique of the Fresh Expressions movement uses a broader cultural lens, objecting that flexible and emergent new forms of church are liable to be eviscerated of the essential form of Christian faith, adopting instead the conventions of the surrounding culture. Hence, '"Fresh expressions" is a market commodity ... consumerism is a given and discrete fact into which one inserts the gospel' (Davison and Milbank, 2010, p. 128; see also John Milbank, 2008). Alan Roxburgh describes a 'technocratic revolution' in which 'The people of God are colonized and commodified with endless techniques that have little connection with a tradition that draws them into habits of discernment, place, prayer, and relationship' (2021, p. 51). Numerical growth as a key objective and measure of fruitfulness has come under repeated scrutiny. According to Eugene Peterson, 'The Church, when it has been alive, has never been popular. Never' (cited by Runcorn, 2008, p. 18). But now 'growth itself ... has been turned into the aim of the gospel' (Alison Milbank, 2023, p. 65). So why would we focus on arresting decline and stimulating growth? How can we be so bedazzled by technique? Andrew Root gives the predicament of the Western church a prophetic gloss: 'There are no human tactics or technologies, no religious mechanisms that can conjure up this God who is God' (Root and Bertrand, 2023, p. 92). Across this range of critical voices an identifiable and interlinked set of concerns arises – that the methods of church planting, in their efficient and readily replicated form, squeeze out the language and practices of faith, overlook the proper structure of ecclesial life and abandon the necessary vulnerability of discipleship.

These are important issues, some of which will be touched on later, but we should also exercise caution before rejecting planting methodology wholesale. If the methods of church planting constitute a de facto capitulation to market economics or worldly striving it is hard to see how they can be brought to the table without being dismissed as groundless. And yet can we really do mission without strategy, even if only implicitly? Must entrepreneurial initiatives be assumed to be irredeemable or set diametrically against careful listening and prayer? Are there not parallel risks in advocating only the methods and structures of previous generations, especially if these reflect a relatively singular cultural form? Milbank and Davison pose sharp questions of standalone fresh expressions, but they could pay more critical attention to the missional limitations and homogeneity of some modes of parish life, a point made tellingly by Michael Moynagh (2017, pp. 221–2).

At the very least, church planting methods should not be dismissed *tout court*. But the opposite, idealization of method, is also a danger. Without wishing to identify examples uncharitably, I have lost count of the number of times I have heard reference to 'the disciple-making methods Jesus himself used'. Likewise, the offer of 'universal principles that work regardless of context'. Here we are offered method shorn of troubling associations with Pelagian effort or human schemes. It is an ideal technique, rising pristine from the pages of Scripture. Far from being theologically problematic, it is incontestable.

But if methods are 'the very ways of Jesus' or 'taken from the book of Acts as a manual for church planting', how could they be subject to review? We are at risk of a tight and self-validating circle of hermeneutical reflection. Beginning with the mindset of our ecclesial network, we set out to read 'the methods of the early church' only to find our own ministry presuppositions affirmed. If our methods must be biblical as a point of confessional principle, and if what we find in Scripture is beyond critique, there is pressure to handle Scripture in a way that simply reflects our methods back to us. Hence, in guides claiming to engage comprehensively with Acts, we may read relatively little about temple worship, common ownership of goods or positive engagement with philosophy – despite these being demonstrably features of Luke's work – but plenty about discipleship values, leadership delegation and small groups in household units. If this selectivity of coverage is amplified by priorities in practice, the cycle may only continue.

A related analysis is offered by Christian Schwartz in his Natural Church Development model. According to Schwartz, successful church growth has two poles, both of which are vital. The organic pole relates to the spontaneous, unplanned aspects of church life; the technical pole relates to structure, strategy and planning. Some seek the growth of the church through entirely organic means – this Schwartz calls 'hyper-organic'. At the other extreme lies being 'hyper-technical', a widespread temptation: 'From clericalism to sacralism, from dogmatism to church growth technocracy ... they have in common the hyper-technical thought pattern ... utterly convinced that their formulae, dogmas, institutions, or church growth programmes will have a similar magical effect' (2002, p. 89). Schwartz's heuristic is a broad one, but it is still instructive. Our discussion of church planting method can easily fall into dismissiveness on the one hand or self-justification on the other.

There is one further approach worth mentioning here that perhaps more subtly deflects attention from church planting methods, which is to downplay sociological factors so as to highlight the work of God. Human contributions are relativized by the much greater work of God, with the result that method is not so much shielded from critique as removed from the limelight. As one leader expressed it to me, 'At core the church is God's work alone, not ours.' The textbook approach offered by Craig Ott and Gene Wilson, for instance, presents church planting as 'Essentially a spiritual undertaking, done primarily by spiritual means. Jesus is the real church planter ... But God works through ... well prepared and informed servants ... who make use of every available means' (2011, pp. 8, 11). Here, God and humans are like oil and water – the primary task is spiritual, but there are practical tasks at the lower level, and here planters may use 'every available means'. Arguably, this configuration of divine and human aspects can function as a form of methodological defence, even if only inadvertently. In the first place, if the primary agent is God then to criticize the ministry could be to criticize the work of God. And in the second place, methods are construed in these accounts as almost incidental. To focus on human and cultural conditions, or express concern about their configuration, could be seen as a distraction from matters of spiritual substance.

But this is insufficient. The theological risk here is that we undervalue the dignity of creative human contributions. Planning and strategy, the dispositions and gifts of the planter, the uniqueness of the local context with its conditions and possibilities – all these are redemptively significant and materially consequent. This is not a purely theological issue: the visibility and accountability of method in public ministry is also a matter of pastoral ethics. An overriding emphasis on 'God's work alone' could obscure crucial elements of the process such as socio-economic realities and the flows of power. If God is the key actor, what about the social status of the planter, the role of financial support, the power of cultural fit and psychological appeal? 'We don't really do anything special, we just pray and preach the gospel', says the articulate young man with a family, linked to a wealthy network known for its intensive spirituality! In such language, method is being occluded and perhaps quietly placed beyond critique. As a result, it becomes less critically visible and therefore less accountable.

Where does this leave us? Critics of church planting are right to ask for theological and social accountability. We should not reduce ecclesial life to sheer technique or baptize methods that do little more than reinscribe consumerism. But advocates are right to hold out for a sense that there is a gift in the practice of planting. And, understandably, they want to identify the work of God in a process that often feels fragile and costly. We therefore need an integrated account that can interrogate method without denigrating it and trace the work of God in church planting without idealizing it. My contention in this chapter is that crucial to such an account is an adequate theology of synergy. Why so? Properly synergistic discourse offers an approach to method that is both richer and more transparent. It does not disparage or downplay sociological and strategic factors; in fact, it embraces them. Synergy recognizes the human dimension as the arena for the co-work of God, not in order to naïvely accept all methods, but precisely to discern among them the characteristic form of Christ. Schwartz's twin-pole model has already pointed us towards a creative *via media*. In order to pursue this line of enquiry further we now turn to the letters of Paul.

Paul and method

One cannot read Paul for long without coming across an appeal for vindication: 'You remember our labour and toil ... You are witnesses, and God also, how pure, upright, and blameless our conduct was towards you believers' (1 Thess. 2.9–10); 'we are not peddlers of God's word like so many; but in Christ we speak as persons of sincerity, as persons sent from God and standing in his presence' (2 Cor. 2.17). Paul writes with the practicalities of ministry rarely far from view and defends himself as if his methods are under constant scrutiny. Why doesn't he mandate the works of the law? Why not accept contributions from Corinth? Why did he cancel a visit? What is the point of raising a collection? Does his written style differ from his preaching? Why is he so often rejected and persecuted? Why is he sending back Epaphroditus? How will he get to Spain? We could almost conceive his entire epistolary oeuvre as an extended apologetic for his missionary method. In all the chaos of itinerant ministry under imperial rule, and even allowing for the rhetorically loaded nature of Paul's self-justifications, he seeks to somehow make his missionary strategies visible to his congregations. Paul wishes his method to be accountable as an act of transparency before God (2 Cor. 12.19). He defends it, and sees God working powerfully through it, but he is also unabashed about its humanity. Paul is not generally embarrassed about the tools of his church planting trade – his costly journeys, his artisanal networks, the practice of self-supporting labour, preaching and mentoring, the communication technology of the epistle, his use of financial support and so on. All this is crucial to the 'craft' of temple construction, something he considers the holiest task imaginable.

1 Corinthians 3.5–17 is, of course, a *locus classicus* for church planting, but its specific relevance here is its exploration of synergy. Schwartz points out that, at the level of metaphor, both organic and technical language is used by Paul (2002, pp. 84–5). This can be illustrated as follows:

Organic	Technical
I planted ...	*I laid a foundation ...*
... but God gave the growth	*... Each builder must choose with care how to build on it*
Uncontrollable outcomes (see 1 Cor. 15.35–41)	Particular givens: one shared foundation
Disavowal of significance: *neither the one who plants nor the one who waters is anything*	Claim to significance: *like a skilled master builder*

On the one hand, Paul is happy to lead with organic language, through the metaphors of planting and seed but also the general sense of an iterative, open process. When he returns to this metaphor to teach about the resurrection, he reflects on the capacity of a seed for transformation and surprise – the 'bare seed' must die, and only God can give the 'body' that will be, which has a glory all of its own (1 Cor. 15.35–41). These statements are consonant with Schwartz's organic pole. Although they suggest human activity – planting and watering – the emphasis is on what only God can do: 'neither the one who plants nor the one who waters is anything' (1 Cor. 3.7). This serves Paul's main purpose in these chapters: he means to undercut Corinthian factionalism.

But Paul also alludes to the technical. His use of the building metaphor provides a contrast between the life that only God can give and a building that only emerges through human work. The image of a foundation implies a substructure already given in a way that determines future outcomes. Planting doesn't capture a sense of accountability – the seed grows regardless of the planter, just as the gospel can even be preached by enemies (Phil. 1.17–18). But building does allow for scrutiny of method. There is a clear distinction between different qualities of construction, culminating in the *full visibility* of eschatological judgement ('the work of each builder will become visible, for the Day will disclose it', 3.13). And there is a warning for the one who 'destroys God's temple' (3.17). This is why 'each builder must choose with care how to build' (3.10). Paul's construction metaphors also include a counter-balancing appeal to personal authority: 'like a skilled master builder (*architektōn*) I laid a foundation ... no one can lay any foundation other than the one that has been laid; that foundation is Jesus Christ' (3.10–11). Rhetorically, the two claims of this section are in tension – Paul is not anything/Paul is a master builder – but methodologically they could be read in creative juxtaposition. Planting involves both the 'divine' organic pole and the 'human' technical pole. In favour of this interpretation we may note his framing language: Paul and Apollos are God's co-workers (*synergoi*) (3.9) – labouring 'as one' (3.15) as they work for, and even *with*, God; see the comments of F. F. Bruce on this passage and 1 Thessalonians 3.2 (1982, p. 61). The Corinthians are, in the same breath, 'God's field, God's building' (3.9). Paul deliberately holds together the organic and the technical, and makes explicit his audacious claim of co-work, literally *synergy*, with God.

All this gives us a basic biblical indication to develop – Paul's practical missiology acknowledged the ultimate role of God, but was also willing to articulate the contribution of his own apostolic efforts. As a result, Paul's methods become 'visible'. That is, they are capable of being checked against the gospel of Christ, a matter for rational defence in his letters, and open for others to adopt. It is not necessary to deduce from this one passage a comprehensive theology of divine–human cooperation in the task of church planting, but there are certainly materials we can use to think further.

Developing the notion of synergy

At this point, I want to introduce the work of Hans Urs van Balthasar. Writing mainly in the context of post-war European Catholicism, Balthasar was a giant of systematic theology. He had no direct church planting credentials to speak of, but was a ceaselessly creative theologian and founded a new lay order. His relevance here is in the particular approach he takes to synergy, extending the insights of a movement that became known (disparagingly at first) as *nouvelle théologie*.

Balthasar sought an account of Christian life that gave full-blooded affirmation to the role of humanity but in such a way as to magnify, rather than diminish, the glory of the Lord. Whenever he touched on questions of method, technique and agency, he was sensitive to the explanatory power of the natural sciences, yet he maintained throughout that God is at work in the church. Interestingly for our purposes, he warned that churches face a dual danger: 'either dissolving into the purely pneumatic, which has no solid structure or stability, or of understanding themselves in purely sociological terms, which does not do justice to the presence of the living Christ organising his body' (1987, p. 72). Schwartz could scarcely have put it better himself.

Synergy, for Balthasar, is not simply a theological observation but a Christological principle axiomatic to all truly Christian thought. If Jesus Christ had to be fully human and fully divine – here retrieving a key emphasis of Maximus the Confessor – then all our speaking about the church's life must reflect the human and the divine together, not compartmentalized in neatly demarcated areas, but vitally enmeshed in a mutual act of giving and redemption. This is Balthasar's exposition of the significance of Mary. God's act of salvation does not simply descend from heaven; it is implanted in Mary: 'her (orthodox and "orthopractical") Yes contributes to making the Word's incarnation possible' (1990, p. 69). As for Mary, so for us and our methods. Humanity, filled with the presence of God, can become a carrier of the divine. And if created matter, like the womb of Mary and the physical body of Jesus Christ, is capable of bearing God, then our methods and plans *in all their humanity and imperfection* can be the vehicles of divine presence and love.

The importance of this principle should not be understated. We are apt to see the human and divine in competition. Our working assumption seems to be that if something is really a work of God then humans should play a diminished role. Likewise, human strategy and energy displaces the divine, leaving no room for the Spirit. The roots of this way of thinking are deep. It can be traced to the natural/supernatural divide so endemic in modern thought. It reflects the Protestant desire for the distinguishable *sola*, only giving glory to God. It meshes with church growth revivalism and the demands of charismatic exceptionalism – to seek a demonstration of power that is undeniably divine rather than human. But Balthasar refused this distinction emphatically. We don't need to play our strength off against God's. Even John Valentine, whose recent treatment of church planting seeks to keep these things in balance, has written of the 'supernatural' constitution of the church, operating 'not because of our abilities or skills or backgrounds' but through 'a power at work in our church plants which is greater than the most powerful forces in the universe' (2023, p. 43). Balthasar, however, reflects more the Thomist position articulated by Andrew Davison as the conviction that 'the absolute distinction between God's action and my action ... means they do not compete – they are "not in the same space" – and can therefore overlap' (2013, p. 157). The point at issue is that the power of God in church planting may be better expressed as *different in both kind and order* than the other powers of creation, rather than simply of greater magnitude, and this fact enables it to operate freely *through* our abilities, skills and backgrounds (for a profound exploration of this dynamic in a Christological frame, see Rowan Williams, 2018, pp. 219–25). Thoughtful strategy on the one hand and surrendered prayer on the other, focused energy and vulnerable faith, pressing on and letting go – they are not in opposition but belong together as part of a truly shared endeavour. Balthasar even wrote to Karl Barth on this point: 'I cannot understand why ... you refuse to allow that creaturely freedom is taken up into the freedom of grace. Not as something "competing" with God ... but rather as a creaturely possibility ... capable of being elevated' (Letter from 1940, cited in John Betz's Introduction to Erich Przywara, 2014, p. 104).

This is not to be understood as a simple concurrence – divine oil floating on top of human water. It is not just that God is at work 'at the same time' or even 'in a spiritual dimension or realm'. Rather, we act in God as God acts through us, so that the result is a 'double and reciprocal *ekstasis*' – a mutual self-outpouring (Balthasar, 1982, p. 122). As we move out of ourselves in faithful service and witness, God too is moving outwards so that we are united in the very process of acting together. Of course God's work is primary, but the distinction becomes increasingly imperceptible.

This goes beyond synergy as a form of dual description; it is holy partnership as a form of love. It returns us to the most profound statements by Paul about his apostolic and planting ministry: 'I worked harder than all of them – though it was not I, but the grace of God that is with me' (1 Cor. 15.10); 'it is no longer I who live, but it is Christ who lives in me. And the life I now live in the flesh I live by faith in the Son of God, who loved me and gave himself for me' (Gal. 2.20); 'we are ambassadors for Christ, since God is making his appeal through us' (2 Cor. 5.20).

This is how synergy allows us to identify the human without minimizing the divine. It sees that the priority of God's initiative is not reduced by full recognition of strategy and method. Indeed we not only *allow* for human contributions but *value* them as signs that can point beyond themselves, instances of divine glory shining through created means, human self-extension that participates by grace in the *ekstasis* of God.

Implications of synergy in practice

It only remains to suggest a couple of practical connections with the task of church planting: two gifts of synergy.

The *first gift* is to affirm the potential holiness of entrepreneurial ministry. Here synergistic thinking speaks to the realities of planting. Take the experience of a brand-new plant, launching in a local venue. The team arrive early, taking what until 4:30 that morning was a nightclub and transforming it into a space for divine worship. The stage must be set up, chairs put out, banners erected outside. Ingredient by ingredient, the team create and curate a space in which church emerges. The whole thing is an exhausting weekly work of love. Older planters may reflect sagely about slowing down and leaving room to find God's blessing, but in the early days it simply may not feel possible. Despite the real risks of burnout, in such seasons of energy and extension we may indeed know ourselves to be co-working with God. There is precedent for this: all Paul's greatest expressions of synergy occur when he is most spent.

We know that Paul saw his enterprising apostolic work in profoundly cultic terms: preaching the gospel in new places is 'priestly' (Rom. 15.16); he is 'poured out' as a sacrificial libation through his ministry (Phil. 2.17); and the 'building' for which he laid a foundation is nothing less than 'God's temple' (1 Cor. 3.16–17). Priest, sacrifice, temple builder – these are active and costly but also *sacred* roles. John Milbank has encouraged us to see ecclesial life and liturgy as: 'A co-operation between human and divine work, which is nonetheless entirely the work of God ... Here a collective human action invites the divine descent' (Milbank, 2015). Milbank is elsewhere critical of evangelical conversionism (2008). But could we not see in church planting a contemporary expression of the missionary endeavour of Paul? Could we even see its tasks along Milbank's lines as a distinctively human work that invites the inhabitation of God? Each plant is a specific *poiesis* – a creative work that can uniquely reflect God; each planter is the practitioner of a sacred craft (building here on the insight of Christian Selvaratnam, 2022). Arguably not enough has been made of this link between church planting and temple construction. Critics could ponder its significance more deeply; practitioners could honour the sacramental nature of planting more explicitly.

To take this reflection one stage further, church planting today is not simply the recovery of a long-lost spiritual charism, it is the alignment of earthly elements in a newly generative configuration. Entrepreneurialism, strategic management, global networks, contemporary culture and digital media – these are social and technological resources from previously untapped sources. True, at their worst they collude in a shallow mimicry of consumer culture. But that judgement alone would be unfair. At their best, they represent a contemporary instance of the wealth of nations being brought into the holy city, enriching the life of the church in increasingly plural ways. Obviously, this requires careful discernment. In practice, church revitalization through a grafting team often leads to a 'rewiring' of local ecclesial life. In an Anglican context, the geographical givenness of the parish and the architectural heritage of the building remain in place, but new people, new values and goals and new social networks create genuinely novel possibilities. A dramatic intervention like this can indeed turn out to be imperialistic imposition, but in other cases (or even at the same time) it can be a breath of fresh air, connecting with people from a diversity of backgrounds and ages untouched by the previous iteration. There are no guarantees; the process is fraught with risk. But sacred ministry always carried this weighty responsibility as part and parcel of its incredible promise.

A *second gift* of synergy, crucial in light of the above, is to enable discernment through the form of Christ. I have argued that the desire for Christian ministry to undeniably display the power of God can be misleading – such sheer power would be beyond accountability. Contrary to the hopes of some, we cannot identify experiences that are 'raw God' (Welby, 2015); but we can discern what is *recognizably* God. Discernment is not simply a matter of noticing moments of divine intervention but of learning to recognize Christ in the patterns and products of our ministry. An implication of this is that the work of the Spirit is never to be judged on magnitude alone. This speaks against pragmatic opportunism. It is not sufficient to see what works and bless it on the basis that it must already be anointed. It is not sufficient to treat the local church as a tool for replication via geometric models of growth. The Holy Spirit is not a nondescript force or an indeterminate principle of life. He is known and glorified as a divine person with a distinctive character of love. His work is made visible in a restored human teleology of worship and the common good. And the Spirit makes real the form of Christ in the uniqueness of our diverse human contexts – we should therefore make plenty of room for creativity, difference and unpredictable trajectories. No spiritual work can be reduced to power or numbers; these are only signs contributing to a greater picture in which Christ's face must be discerned.

While our methods can be recognized and affirmed in their humanity, this does not mean they are exempt from scrutiny. On the contrary, it is precisely because we can identify human contributions that they are open to evaluation. Paul gives us a template for this through his image of the 'foundation'. Christ gives us the shape, the form, of church (which suggests a position between the fixed pattern of traditionalism and hyper-Protestantism in which form is divorced from content and reduced to pragmatic concerns). How to recognize this form? We might begin with a simple Pauline outline of the ways Christ is mediated to us: *the gospel of Christ* – receiving and sharing the good news of peace with God; *the mind of Christ* – a perspective determined by his death and resurrection; *the Spirit of Christ* – the Spirit's gifts and character in our community; *the love of Christ* – orientated to people and place in service; *the body of Christ* – connected by Eucharist and by the tradition being handed on. Even this rudimentary sketch illustrates that methods which are imperialistic or isolationist fall short. Likewise approaches that lack the flexibility of grace or the vital dynamism of mission. Yet on this expansive ground we can still imagine a whole vibrant, complex and truly mixed ecology growing. Synergy does not mean underwriting mere pragmatism; Christ provides not only its logical basis, but also a living measure for healthy and ongoing discernment.

My argument in this chapter is that, in any theology of church planting, method belongs at the table, not off the table. Our method cannot help but speak of our humanity; but it *can also* speak of Christ. This is why we need to talk about method – to celebrate it as a truly human participation in the missional life of God, and to calibrate it with the ways of Christ. In order to do this, our methods need to be visible, accountable and open to change. This is the contribution a practical theology of planting, such as this book, must make.

References

Balthasar, Hans Urs von, 1982, *The Glory of the Lord: A Theological Aesthetics. Vol. 1. Seeing the Form*, trans. E. Leiva-Merikakis, San Francisco, CA: Ignatius Press.

——, 1987, *Truth is Symphonic: Aspects of Christian Pluralism*, trans. G. Harrison, San Fransisco, CA: Ignatius Press.

——, 1990, *Theo-Drama: Theological Dramatic Theory. Vol. 2: Dramatis Personae: Man in God*, trans. G. Harrison, San Francisco, CA: Ignatius Press.

Bruce, F. F., 1982, *1 & 2 Thessalonians*, Waco, TX: Word.

Davison, Andrew, 2013, *The Love of Wisdom*, London: SCM Press.

—— and Alison Milbank, 2010, *For the Parish: A Critique of Fresh Expressions*, London: SCM Press.

Francis-Dehqani, Guli, 2022, Chelmsford Diocesan Synod Presidential Address, cited in 'There is an alternative to Vision and Strategy', *Church Times*, 18 November 2022.

Milbank, Alison, 2023, *The Once and Future Parish*, London: SCM Press.

Milbank, John, 2008, 'Stale Expressions: The Management-Shaped Church', *Studies in Christian Ethics* 21(1), pp. 117–28.

——, 2015, 'What is Radical Orthodoxy?' University of Freiburg, http://www.unifr.ch/theo/assets/files/SA2015/Theses_EN.pdf (accessed 8.09.2019).

Moynagh, Michael, 2017, *Church in Life: Innovation, Mission and Ecclesiology*, London: SCM Press.

Ott, Craig and Gene Wilson, 2011, *Global Church Planting: Biblical Principles and Best Practices for Multiplication*, Grand Rapids, MI: Baker.

Przywara, Erich, 2014, *Analogia Entis: Metaphysics: Original Structure and Universal Rhythm*, trans. John R. Betz and David Bentley Hart, Grand Rapids, MI: Eerdmans.

Root, Andrew and Blair D. Bertrand, 2023, *When Church Stops Working: A Future for Your Congregation beyond More Money, Programs, and Innovation*, Grand Rapids, MI: Baker.

Roxburgh, Alan J., 2021, *Joining God in the Great Unraveling*, Eugene, OR: Cascade Books.

Runcorn, David, 2008, *The Road to Growth Less Travelled: Spiritual Paths in a Missionary Church*, Cambridge: Grove Books.

Schwartz, Christian A., 2002, *Natural Church Development Handbook: A Practical Guide to a New Approach*, 4th edn, Moggerhanger: British Church Growth Association.

Selvaratnam, Christian, 2022, *The Craft of Church Planting: Exploring the Lost Wisdom of Apprenticeship*, London: SCM Press.

Valentine, John, 2023, *Jesus, the Church and the Mission of God: A Biblical Theology of Church Planting*, London: Apollos.

Welby, Justin, 2015, 'Revolutionary Love', Lambeth Lecture, 4 March 2015, https://www.youtube.com/watch?v=1L8PgA-Kkzo.

Williams, Rowan, 2018, *Christ the Heart of Creation*, London: Bloomsbury.

3

Telling Stories for Transformation: Theodrama and Discipleship Formation in Church Planting Contexts

HELEN MILLER

Flexible church

In *Disclosing Church* (2020), Clare Watkins explores research undertaken at a Messy Church in Croydon, which meets monthly for a short all-age service that includes a Bible story, games, crafts and a meal. This format is consistent with Messy Churches across the UK, whose aim is to create churches that are hospitable to families who find Sunday services inaccessible or unappealing. Nearly 20 years after its founding, Messy Church remains one of the most prominent and widely adopted forms of fresh expressions (Watkins, 2020, p. 132).

Messy Church is, however, just one example of how those in established churches, alongside church planters, are thinking creatively about what church can and should look like in particular contexts. Michael Moynagh calls these endeavours 'new-contextual church' (2012, p. x), which he describes as having the following distinctives: a focus on those outside the church; a prioritizing of discipleship; and intentional adaptation to a particular context. In *Flexible Church* (Morris, 2019), I amend Moynagh's term, using the language of 're-contextual church' to refer to those seeking to form churches that are hospitable and accessible to the those they seek to serve. I chose 're-' instead of 'new' to emphasize the contextual nature of all churches, since all churches adapt, either intentionally or unwittingly, to the context in which they are located. Indeed, among those seeking to re-imagine church in contemporary contexts, there is often a desire to correct what is seen as an over-assimilation of the church into the culture of the past (Morris, 2019, p. 7).

Forming innovative expressions of church plays an important role in the church's call to 'make disciples of all nations' (Matt. 28.19) and, indeed, all nationalities and people groups within one nation. However, just as jazz improvisers need to understand the nature of jazz to be harmonious and not cacophonous, so too ecclesial innovators need to understand the nature of church in order to be faithful expressions of Christ's body in their context. As John Stackhouse (2003, p. 9) provocatively maintains, 'When we, the church, are confused about who we are and whose we are, we can become anything and anyone's.' In *Flexible Church*, therefore, I aim to outline an ecclesiology that has the flexibility to support adaptation into new contexts and the stability to ensure faithfulness to Christ. My conclusion is that churches are best able to be faithful expressions of Christ's body in their context if they acknowledge, and respond rightly to, various tensions.

These tensions include, first, the church's nature as both inherited and innovative. Churches are to be anchored in Jesus' salvific work, as recorded in Scripture, and evaluatively alert to the church's testimony to this work through history (inherited). Churches are also called to be responsive to the Spirit's guidance in the present and adapt critically and creatively to cultural change (innovative).

Second, I argue for both structure and spontaneity in churches' relationships and organization. This is to avoid stagnation, which occurs when structures are too rigid and resistant to change, and dissipation, which results when too much is left to informality and spontaneity such that, over time, people drift way.

Third, I maintain that churches must be both contextual and counter-cultural, adapting to their context to aid people's comprehension of the gospel, while living distinctively in those areas in which wider cultural norms are contrary to the ways of Christ.

Fourth, churches are called to live in both the 'now' and 'not yet' of Christ's kingdom, which was inaugurated at Christ's first coming and will be consummated on his return. This involves an expectation that Christ's work is manifest in the here and now alongside recognition that the fullness of the kingdom awaits Christ's return.

Fifth, churches need to maintain a right conception of God's transcendence and immanence, which, as explored below, has implications for how discipleship formation is construed and facilitated.

God's transcendence and immanence

Regarding God's transcendence and immanence, Stanley Grenz and Roger Olson (1993, p. 11) assert that:

Because the Bible presents God as both beyond the world and present to the world, theologians in every era are confronted with the challenge of articulating the Christian understanding of the nature of God in a manner that balances, affirms and holds in creative tension the twin truths of divine transcendence and the divine immanence.

Where the balance is wrong, the temptation is simply to 'pull harder' on the opposite side of the tension. However, such attempts at rebalance risk exacerbating the misconception that God's transcendence and immanence are somehow opposed; as if the more transcendent he is, the less immanent and vice versa. Kathryn Tanner traces this misconception to the influence of dualistic Greek philosophy on aspects of modern theology. Within dualistic conceptions, divine transcendence is understood as distance and separation. Aristotle's unmoved mover, for instance, sets the cosmos in motion while remaining far beyond it. Tanner notes, however, that seeing transcendence as distance and separation fails to account for God's otherness; God is immanently and intimately involved in his creation because, as the transcendent Creator, he is distinct from his creation and therefore not bound by it (2013, pp. 144–55). Paul writes in 2 Corinthians 4.6, 'For it is the God who said, "Let light shine out of darkness", who has shone in our hearts to give the light of the knowledge of the glory of God in the face of Jesus Christ.' God's nature as Creator is the foundation for understanding both his transcendence and immanence. It is as the transcendent Creator that God is immanently involved in the lives of his creatures.

God's sovereignty and human agency in discipleship formation

Seeing God's transcendence as according to, and not contrary to, his immanence has implications for a further tension that churches, and church planters, need to maintain: the tension between God's sovereignty and human agency in people's conversion and discipleship. Biblical texts such as John 15.1–8, regarding abiding in Christ, and Galatians 5.13–25, the fruit of the Spirit, indicate believers' dependence on Christ and his Spirit for their growth as disciples. As Grant Macaskill contends, only through the indwelling presence of Christ by his Spirit are people able to love God and neighbour (2013, p. 307). *Participatio Christi* (participation in Christ) precedes and is requisite for *imitatio Christi* (the demonstration of Christlike character).

Believers' dependence on Christ and his Spirit for their growth does not, however, exclude activity. Believers are united with Christ through faith in his salvific work which, as Macaskill contends, is an 'active quality', 'even though the very faith itself is presented as a gift and as an outworking of the Spirit's presence' (2013, p. 300). This paradox is resolved by reference to God's transcendence. Between created beings, if one gives another receives. As Creator not creature, God transcends such zero-sum reciprocity. Believers have active agency in their relationship with God, but this agency takes place in an overarching context of dependence; their ability to give to God is, itself, a gift from God (Morris, 2019, p. 83). How, then, can this active agency in discipleship growth be best conceived and encouraged? As evidenced among the Messy Church leaders whom Watkins engaged with, how ecclesial expressions 'make disciples' is a central question for those thinking creatively about how to engage with their local communities (2020, p. 133). My argument in this chapter is that the concept of 'theodrama' can help church planters guide and inspire those they work among to take an active role in their own discipleship while recognizing their dependence on the triune God for their growth.

Theodrama

Wesley Vander Lugt notes that the term 'theodrama' was first coined by Hans Urs von Balthasar in the 1970s (2014, p. 14). Balthasar's key theological question is the relationship between God's free sovereign action and human agency (Polanco, 2017, p. 427) – in Balthasar's terminology, 'How does the absolute liberty of God in Jesus Christ confront the relative, but true, liberty of man?' (1993, p. 117). Balthasar sees the metaphor of drama as particularly suited to answering this question since, as Karen Kilby notes, in theodrama, 'God is the author, the director, and also the chief actor' but, through Christ's work, his followers are called and empowered to play a genuine role (2012, ch. 3; cf. Balthasar, 1988, p. 18). Balthasar's aim in his five-volume *Theo-Drama* is therefore, as Lugt summarizes, 'to explore the drama of God's infinite being and redemptive action that frames every finite drama' (2014, p. 5).

Before Balthasar coined the phrase 'theodrama', the concept of drama had long been drawn on by theologians and ethicists and had proved fruitful for reflecting on right living (Lugt, 2014, p. 14). The formative power of story and drama is well known. Jesus' parables are exemplary in this regard. So too are the many proverbial tales that help form people's identities and their understanding of right and wrong. As Alasdair MacIntyre (2007, p. 216) maintains:

It is through hearing stories about wicked stepmothers, lost children, good but misguided kings ... sons who waste their inheritance on riotous living and go into exile to live with the swine, that children learn or mis-learn both what a child and what a parent is, what the cast of characters may be in the drama into which they have been born and what the ways of the world are. Deprive children of stories and you leave them unscripted, anxious stutterers in their actions as in their words. Hence there is no way to give us an understanding of any society, including our own, except through the stock of stories which constitute its initial dramatic resources.

Indeed, such is the formative power of narrative that MacIntyre contends, 'I can only answer the question "What am I to do?" if I can answer the prior question "Of what story or stories do I find myself a part?"' (2007, p. 216). Since people's decisions and behaviour are formed by the stories that they align themselves with, reshaping these narratives prompts change. David, for example, sees the sinfulness of his adultery and murder when the prophet Nathan reframes his actions through a parable about a rich man who steals his neighbour's lamb (2 Sam. 12.1–14).

This reshaping of the narrative(s) by which people live to reform thinking and action lies at the heart of theodramatic approaches to Scripture. Lugt defines theodrama as 'the drama of God's communicative action in dynamic interaction with his creation' (2014, p. 5). As this 'drama' becomes the dominant narrative by which a person interprets their life, they are inspired and equipped to be a faithful participant (or 'performer') in that drama. The language of drama is preferable to narrative, Lugt argues, since 'while a narrative framework emphasizes understanding a story from the past, a theodramatic framework highlights our present participation in a drama extending from the past into the future' (2014, p. 7). Nevertheless, understanding the drama's storyline is essential for faithful performance in it. Therefore, Lugt and Trevor Hart contend that the goal of 'theatrical theology ... is to resource fitting participation in the theodrama in dynamic interplay with accurate perception of the theodrama' (2014, p. xiv).

Probably the best-known example of a theodramatic approach to Christian praxis, though he does not use the term, is N. T. Wright's analogy of a Shakespearian play whose fifth and final act is partially missing. Wright argues that an experienced group of actors could immerse themselves in the first four acts, get to know the characters, and then improvise the rest of the fifth act in a way that is faithful to what has come before (1992, p. 154). So too, Wright argues, the Bible can be seen as a five-act play, with the last act partially missing. These five acts are creation, fall, Israel, Jesus and the church (1991, p. 19). Through immersing themselves in Scripture, Wright argues, believers are equipped to improvise the remainder of the fifth and final 'church' act.

Samuel Norman highlights the advantages of Kevin Vanhoozer's delineation of the five acts of Scripture as creation, Israel, Christ, Pentecost and church, and consummation (2022, p. 180). Norman contends that identifying consummation as the final act, not the church, is significant since it reminds the church that it 'does not have to work out the ending so much as to live in its light' (Vanhoozer, 2009, p. 174). Lugt outlines several other perspectives on what, and how many, the acts of Scripture should be. He notes, however, that the various iterations share a common structure: all highlight the movement of the biblical narrative from creation to new creation with the person and work of Jesus as the climactic and pivotal scene. Lugt's own approach is to play on the language of 'formation' to highlight the development between the different stages of the biblical narrative: Act 1 Formation (creation); Act 2 Deformation (fall); Act 3 Transformation Emerged (Israel); Act 4 Transformation Embodied (Jesus); Act 5 Transformation Empowered (church); and Act 6 Re-formation (new creation) (2014, p. 104). Regardless of exactly how the acts are configured, seeing Scripture through the metaphor of drama can contribute to discipleship formation in at least three ways.

Theodrama and discipleship formation

First, seeing Scripture as a drama helps to integrate orthodoxy (right beliefs), orthopraxy (right behaviour) and orthopathy (right loves) (Norman, 2022). One of the critiques directed at modernity's influence on the Western church is its elevation of right beliefs above right practice and right affection, with the movement from belief to action seen as unidirectional (Morris, 2019, p. 96). For instance, James K. A. Smith contends that the Western church 'has been duped by modernity and has bought into a kind of Cartesian model of the human person, wrongly assuming that the heady realm of ideas and beliefs is the core of our being' (2009, p. 76). While affirming the importance of ideas and beliefs, Vanhoozer contends that theatrical metaphors help overcome theory/practice dichotomies since conceiving of Christian faith as involvement in a drama inspires faithful action, alongside the pursuit of understanding (2014, pp. 21–2). For instance, while Wright's metaphor of the five-act play emphasizes the importance of improvisation in the church's performance, the presence of an overarching plotline sets the boundaries and goals of this improvisation. Improvisation is necessary but, as Nicholas Lash contends, 'What we may not do ... is to tell a different story' (1986, p. 44, quoted by Lugt, 2014, p. 90).

Lugt concedes that the language of 'performance' has connotations of hypocrisy and inauthenticity but observes that 'faking' is always a temptation for Christians (2014, p. 16).[1] A theodramatic approach shines light on this temptation and encourages believers towards genuine Spirit-empowered participation in Christ's ongoing work. Moreover, even when aspects of a believer's life and motives fail to align with their calling in Christ, 'performing' the part of a disciple is not adopting a fictional role, but seeking to live out the reality of who the Christian already is in Christ. As Lugt contends, 'Sanctification ... is not just becoming who we are *pretending* to be, but becoming who we *already are* in Christ and embracing this identity' (2014, pp. 135–6; emphasis original).

Second, the presence in Scripture of a coherent plotline, across a diversity of texts, points to the wisdom of the divine playwright who, as Lugt observes, enlists 'the participation of others in creating the script and performing the theodrama, while remaining sovereign over the entire process' (2014, p. 89). Thus, the paradox of God's transcendence and immanence is illuminated by conceiving of his role as both author and actor. Moreover, theodrama highlights believers' active role in their discipleship, while maintaining their dependence on the triune God.[2] Believers only participate faithfully in the divine drama as they are led and empowered by the divine author himself, through his Spirit. As Helen Collins notes, when engaging with Scripture, 'We do not read alone but with the risen Jesus through the Holy Spirit', who is the same Spirit who 'inspired, elected and sanctified the text to be Scripture for the church' (2020, p. 83). This same Spirit brings Christ's presence into a believer's life, granting them the 'mind of Christ' (1 Cor. 2.16). As Vanhoozer notes, Paul's affirmation of 'the mind of Christ' in a believer sits alongside his exhortation to '"Have this mind [of Christ]" (Phil. 2:5)' (2015, p. 148). This seeming contradiction (the need to aspire to something already gifted) reflects the believer's location in the theodrama *between* Christ's incarnation and return. 'For now we see only a reflection as in a mirror; then we shall see face to face' (1 Cor. 13.12, NIV). Within this 'now' and 'not yet' of a believer's formation in Christ, the 'Spirit's role in the drama of redemption is essential ... The Spirit is the theatrical "dresser" who clothes disciples with the righteousness of Christ ... The Spirit is the "giver of life" because he unites us to Christ' (Vanhoozer, 2015, p. 161).

Third, the metaphor of theodrama reminds churches that faithful biblical interpretation and faithful living occur in community. One-person plays do exist, but these are not an apt analogy for the drama of Scripture. Rather a company of actors are to pore over Scripture together, wrestling with its meaning and working out what it looks like to live rightly in response (Lugt, 2014, p. 10). Moreover, faithful performance is unlikely if a singular company isolates itself from others; rather, as Vanhoozer contends, 'Local theater (individual congregations) should draw upon the resources of regional theater (confessional traditions) and masterpiece theater (the ecumenical creeds)' (2009, pp. 181–3).

Given these contributions, how might theodrama be utilized to facilitate discipleship in church planting contexts? I will give two examples and then highlight one potential pitfall of adopting a theodramatic approach and explore how this might be mitigated.

Theodrama in church planting contexts

First, tell stories for transformation. Regarding the example included at the start of this chapter, Watkins notes that, while investigating how Messy Church makes disciples, there was a point in the research when the leaders wondered if they had unwittingly created a 'Jesus-less' church. The non-Christian mums who were interviewed expressed a desire for the same sort of activities and community building but in a non-religious space, indicating that they came despite the Christian content that was weaved into the activities and story time (2020, pp. 137–8). However, this was not the full picture. Not only was there evidence that the parents' attitudes towards the Christian faith were softening, but it was also apparent that their non-Christian children were being impacted by the songs and stories. One parent reported that their child now objected if the words 'God' or 'Jesus' were used disrespectfully at home. Another spoke of their child acting out the story of Jesus calming the storm while they were in the bath. The stories were sticking. Although the conclusion of the team was that the journey towards discipleship was longer and more complex than they had thought, through the biblical stories that they were telling they could see signs of change (2020, pp. 139–40).

Telling Bible stories is not just important in outreach, however, but also for encouraging perseverance and growth among existing disciples. Eugene Peterson notes how influenced Christians can be by their own transitory experiences and emotions. He argues that many Christians' beliefs about important matters such as forgiveness, prayer and judgement are based on their own subjective thoughts and recent experiences. This results in a faith that is too fragile to weather storms of uncertainty and grief. A narrow and self-focused perspective on faith is challenged by seeing the role that biblical characters play, with courage and faithfulness, or even fear and folly, in the unfolding of God's plan, particularly given these characters' inability to see the full picture of God's work. Peterson thus concludes that familiarizing oneself with the stories in Scripture is a powerful antidote for fleeting and fragile faith (2000, p. 166 as cited by Spangler and Tverberg, 2009, p. 74).

In addition to telling stories, church planters can use the metaphor of drama to facilitate discipleship. The impact of metaphors on behaviour is evidenced by Paul Thibodeau and Lera Boroditsky's research into how depicting crime as a beast or a virus impacts people's responses to it. They discovered that when crime was described as a virus, participants were keen to investigate the root causes and enact social reform to treat the problems. Conversely, when crime was described as a beast, participants focused on catching and jailing criminals and introducing harsher sentences (2011, pp. 1–3). Similarly, how people conceive of the Bible impacts their approach to it. If the Bible is seen as a self-help guide, its pages will be skimmed to find that which looks most beneficial for individual flourishing. If it is perceived primarily as a legal text, even poetry will be scoured for commands and stories reduced to morals. In contrast, presenting the Bible as a divine drama, with the church's role ongoing, encourages an approach to Scripture that encompasses its whole storyline and, as noted above, inspires faithful living in response. In practice, the word 'theodrama' is perhaps too technical to be used in church planting contexts. However, the popularity of Craig Bartholomew and Michael Goheen's *The Drama of Scripture: Finding Our Place in the Biblical Story* (2004), which is now available in twelve languages, illustrates the accessibility of the drama metaphor for believers across the globe. Moreover, introducing N. T. Wright's five-act play analogy, or analogies like it, can help people see that Scripture reveals a work of God that they are called to participate in.

Conceptualizing the Bible as a grand drama with God as the author and chief actor is particularly important in a secular context wherein, as Charles Taylor contends, for the first time in history, human flourishing without allegiance to anything or anyone external to the individual has become an ultimate goal (2007, p. 18). Within a secular outlook, the Bible and Christian faith can be seen as resources to help people pursue their individual flourishing, whether that be career success, emotional well-being, relational fulfilment or material wealth (Volf and Croasmun, 2019, ch. 6; cf. Morris, 2022, p. 77). In contrast, as Vanhoozer maintains, seeing Scripture as conveying a drama orchestrated by God challenges the human impulse to elevate oneself as the main character, reminding believers that they are the supporting cast. He contends: 'Spiritual formation and discipleship are about people coming to see the world, and themselves, in theodramatic terms, and to be so ravished by this vision that their heartfelt desire is to live for Christ and his kingdom rather than for oneself and one's fiefdom' (2015, pp. 168–69).

Notwithstanding these benefits, there are potential pitfalls in utilizing the metaphor of theodrama. Below, I identify one such pitfall and explore its mitigation.

Telling *the story* of Scripture

The power of stories and drama lies in their ability to evoke our imagination, enabling us to identify with the characters within it. Which character or characters we identify with is a subjective, and yet important, matter. It is tempting, for example, to identify solely with those presented most favourably. Indeed, part of Jesus' genius in his parables is how difficult he makes it for his hearers to do this. In the parable of the prodigal son, for example, the Pharisees and teachers of the law would not want to identify themselves with the younger rebellious son or even the father, who demonstrates the indignity of running to embrace a son who has dishonoured him. They are forced, therefore, through both elimination and resonance, to recognize that, in Jesus' story, they are the elder brother, whose apparent loyalty towards his father is deeply deficient. In relation to other parts of Scripture, though, it is tempting for people to identify with the positive characters and so be blind to the challenges that the texts bring. Conversely, others are designated the beasts, Babylons and Jezebels of today. How, then, might we mitigate the risk that, as we tell stories for transformation, we reinforce people's biases and maintain the status quo?[3]

We can tell *the stories* of Scripture in a way that points to *the story* of Scripture. This is the story that starts not with humanity but God, the transcendent Creator. More specifically, it starts with the triune God, as highlighted by John's assertion that 'In the beginning was the Word' through whom 'all things were made' (John 1.1a, 3a, NIV). For the New Testament authors, Christ is the beginning of the story, not just the middle and end.[4] It is the story that, through starting with God, conveys dignity on people, whom God makes in his image. It is the story that, through the Fall, highlights the deceitful corruption of sin that blinds people to their own evil and brokenness. It is the story that, through God's work in Israel, paves the way for its climax in the person and work of Jesus, illuminating the need for and overflow of grace that is received through Christ's death on the cross and resurrection to life. It is the story that reveals the church's role, as the 'pneumatic community' (Padilla, 2020, p. 346) under Christ's lordship, in the unfolding drama of God's plans and purposes for his world. It is the story that, though much of it remains unseen, has a pre-established end. Christ's kingdom will come, his will will be done on earth as it is in heaven.

I have entitled this chapter 'Telling Stories for Transformation'. A better title would be telling *the story* for transformation. Helping people familiarize themselves with the singular drama of God's revelation and work, with its central climax in Jesus Christ, is central to discipleship formation in church planting contexts. Going back, for instance, to the example of Messy Church that I introduced at the start, what conclusions might be drawn? In the middle of this chapter, I argued that the concern about creating a Jesus-less church may have been premature. Discipleship is a long and complex journey and, as I noted above, telling biblical stories seems to have had an impact. Perhaps, though, the concern still stands. The telling of isolated stories, when detached from the Bible's overall narrative, can induce moralism – 'Be more like David (at least in some respects) and less like Saul', 'Avoid grumbling like the Israelites in the wilderness', 'Be loyal like Ruth' and so on. While such lessons can be helpful, they overlook human beings' dependence on the saving work of Christ and the power of his indwelling Spirit for fulfilling their identity as those made in God's image.

I therefore encourage Messy Church leaders, and church planters, to point to *the story* of Scripture as they share biblical stories. For example, when telling David's story, ways in which his story points to Jesus could be highlighted. Jesus' perfection could be contrasted with David's sinfulness, David's need to seek forgiveness with Jesus' sacrifice to enable forgiveness, and the temporary nature of David's kingdom with Jesus' eternal reign.[5] When speaking of the Israelites' wilderness wanderings, referring to Jesus' wilderness temptations demonstrates that he succeeds where the Israelites fail. This highlights people's need for salvation and Jesus' unique ability to save. So too Ruth's story connects with Scripture's wider narrative. She is listed in Jesus' genealogy (Matt. 1.5). In addition, her inclusion as a Moabite within the covenant community prefigures the incorporation of those from every nation, tribe, people and language into God's family through Christ's salvific work. Her inclusion also points back to the promise given to Abraham that all nations would one day be blessed through him (Gen. 12.3). Helping listeners to make these connections, invites them into the drama of Scripture, highlighting God's sovereignty over the events of history even as he involves his people in his plans.[6]

Conclusion

My argument in this chapter is that 'theodrama' can help church planters guide and inspire those they work among to take an active role in their own discipleship while recognizing their dependence on the triune God for their growth. Seeing God as the author of and chief actor in the divine drama inspires faithful participation in God's ongoing purposes for his creation, while reminding believers of their dependence on Christ's Spirit for authentic performance. I therefore encourage church planters to think creatively about how they can share *the story* of Scripture in their contexts, pointing always to its climax in the person and work of Jesus and emphasizing God's wisdom and sovereignty in interweaving all the strands of Scripture to fulfilment in him.

Notes

1 This negative connotation of 'theodrama' highlights the power, and risks, of using metaphors. Janet Soskice defines a metaphor as 'that figure of speech whereby we speak about one thing in terms which are seen to be suggestive of another' (1985, p. 15). Regarding the 'theodrama' metaphor, a 'tenor' (God's revelation and interaction with his people) is spoken of in terms of a 'vehicle' (theodrama). Metaphors' communicative impact comes from the resolution of a semantic clash that occurs between the tenor and vehicle (Ricoeur, 2004, p. 254). The power of this impact comes from the wealth (and sometimes provocative nature) of the ideas that the metaphor invokes. As noted in this chapter, the metaphor of 'theodrama' recalls various concepts: the idea of God as the author and director of the drama; and the human response to God being something visible and acted out (or lived out). Lugt outlines other metaphorical associations too, such as the corporate nature of the 'company of actors' and the idea that the wider world learns about the 'theodrama' through watching the church's life. There is therefore richness and depth to metaphors. However, there is not unbounded breadth. When people coin or use metaphors, they do not intend for every possible element of the vehicle to be imported into people's understanding of the tenor (Ricoeur, 2004, p. 252). For instance, if Fred is called a fox, the communicator intends to convey that Fred is sneaky, like foxes, not that he is furry or has pointy ears. However, the coiner (or user) of a metaphor has limited control over which aspects of the vehicle the reader imports. It is therefore important to acknowledge negative connotations that the 'theodrama' metaphor might suggest and, as Lugt does, address these directly.

2 Lugt warns: 'The idea of playing a God-given role, however, can easily resemble the Stoic view of performance, which diminishes the free responsibility and improvisation of human actors.' He counters that Balthasar's presentation of theodrama preserves human responsibility (2014, pp. 134–5). The language of improvisation is important within this preservation since the analogy of a fully scripted play would be more susceptible to the Stoic conceptions that Lugt warns against.

3 A further issue requiring exploration is the appropriation of biblical narratives into the contemporary world. Samuel Ngewa, for instance, reflects on a sermon in which the necessity of tongues was preached. He notes: 'On reflection ... I wondered whether he was right to use a narrative to promise all of us the gift of speaking in tongues if we were truly saved' (2020, p. 297). Timothy Cargal highlights ongoing debates within Pentecostalism over the extent to which the descriptive narrative in Acts should be seen as prescriptive for the church (1993, p. 183). It is beyond this chapter's scope to explore this issue in depth, except to note the importance of church leaders and planters engaging with some of the many hermeneutical explorations that have been undertaken into how biblical narrative should be interpreted and related to today. Gordon Fee and Douglas Stuart's *How to Read the Bible for All Its Worth* (2014) provides a helpful entry-level text into relevant issues.

4 I am grateful to Mark Powley for his critique of Wright's 'five-act play' analogy (Powley, 2024). Powley argues that Wright's analogy 'is not sufficiently christological' since 'when the New Testament writers give "the big picture" of reality, they repeatedly start [not with creation but] in a different place', Christ. Christ is the beginning, not just the middle and end. Nevertheless, as Powley notes, this is revealed 'rather surprisingly' in the middle of the Bible's story. Therefore, although Powley's critique is compelling, the revelation of the true starting point in the middle of Scripture persuades me of the value of presenting the drama of Scripture in line with the canon's chronological order.

5 While it is probably too complex for children attending a Messy Church, the Bible Project's 'David the Priestly King' video provides an example of how the story of David can be told in a way that locates it in the wider narrative of Scripture. To explore the significance of David's story, Tim Mackie and Jon Collins both point back to the start of the Bible and forwards to Jesus, referring to some other key characters and events on the way (Mackie and Collins, 2021).

6 The approach that I am advocating accords with the redemptive-historic view of hermeneutics and homiletics that, as Bryan Chapell notes, is exemplified in Tim Keller's preaching and writing. Chapell (2018) maintains that 'context is part of the text' (p. 4). This context includes a passage's location in the Bible's overarching redemption story alongside its more immediate literary and historical context. Chapell argues: 'No aspect of revelation can be fully understood or explained in isolation from God's redeeming work that culminates in Christ's ministry' (p. 7). As Chapell clarifies, adopting a redemptive-historic approach does not mean crowbarring Christ into the text by tenuous connection or imaginative allegory. Rather, it involves recognizing that every biblical text is predictive of, preparatory for, resultant from, or reflective of Christ's work. This includes typology, wherein correspondence is seen between Old Testament characters, institutions and events, and those in the New Testament that 'more fully express salvation truths' (p. 10), most notably those that prefigure Jesus. However, as Chapell concludes, 'Christ-centered preaching ... does not seek to discover where Christ is mentioned in every biblical text but to disclose where every text stands in relation to Christ's ministry' (p. 7).

References

Balthasar, Hans Urs von, 1988, *Theo-Drama: Theological Dramatic Theory I: Prologomena*, trans. Graham Harrison, San Fransico, CA: Ignatius Press.

——, 1993, *My Work: In Retrospect*, trans. Brian McNeil, Kenneth Batinovich, John Saward and Kelly Hamilton, San Fransico, CA: Ignatius Press.

Bartholomew, Craig G. and Michael W. Goheen, 2004, *The Drama of Scripture: Finding Our Place in the Biblical Story*, Grand Rapids, MI: Baker Academic.

Cargal, Timothy B., 1993, 'Beyond the Fundamentalist-Modernist Controversy: Pentecostals and Hermeneutics in a Postmodern Age', *Pneuma* 15.2, pp. 163–87.

Chapell, Bryan, 2018, 'Redemptive-Historic View', in Scott M. Gibson and Matthew D. Kim (eds), *Homiletics and Hermeneutics: Four Views on Preaching Today*, Grand Rapids, MI: Baker Academic, pp. 1–29.

Collins, Helen, 2020, *Reordering Theological Reflection: Starting with Scripture*, London: SCM Press.

Fee, Gordon D. and Douglas Stuart, 2014, *How to Read the Bible for All Its Worth*, 4th edn, Grand Rapids, MI: Zondervan.

Grenz, Stanley J. and Roger E. Olson, 1993, *20th-Century Theology: God and the World in a Transitional Age*, Downers Grove, IL: IVP Academic.

Kilby, Karen, 2012, *Balthasar: A (Very) Critical Commentary*, Grand Rapids, MI: Eerdmans.

Lash, Nicholas, 1986, *Theology on the Way to Emmaus*, London: SCM Press.

Lugt, Wesley Vander, 2014, *Living Theodrama: Reimagining Theological Ethics*, Abingdon: Routledge.

—— and Trevor Hart, 2014, *Theatrical Theology: Explorations in Performing the Faith*, Eugene, OR: Cascade Books.

Macaskill, Grant, 2013, *Union with Christ in the New Testament*, Oxford: Oxford University Press.

MacIntyre, Alasdair, 2007, *After Virtue: A Study in Moral Theory*, 2nd edn, Notre Dame, IN: University of Notre Dame Press.

Mackie, Tim and Jon Collins, 2021, *David the Priestly King* [online video], The Bible Project, https://bibleproject.com/explore/video/david-priestly-king/ (accessed 20.12.2023).

Morris, Helen, 2019, *Flexible Church: Being the Church in the Contemporary World*, London: SCM Press.

——, 2022, 'A Wonderful Plan for My Life? Pete Ward's "The Gospel and Change" in Dialogue with Charles Taylor', in Helen Morris and Helen Cameron (eds), *Evangelicals Engaging in Practical Theology: Theology That Impacts Church and World*, Abingdon: Routledge, pp. 70–83.

—— and Helen Cameron (eds), 2022, *Evangelicals Engaging in Practical Theology: Theology That Impacts Church and World*, Abingdon: Routledge.

Moynagh, Michael, 2012, *Church for Every Context: An Introduction to Theology and Practice*, London: SCM Press.

Ngewa, Samuel M., 2020, 'Pneumatology: Its Implications for the Africa Context', in Gene L. Green, Stephen T. Pardue and K. K. Yeo (eds), *Majority World Theology: Christian Doctrine in Global Context*, Downers Grove, IL: InterVarsity Press, pp. 295–309.

Norman, Samuel, 2022, 'Theodrama: A Contemporary Application', in Helen Morris and Helen Cameron (eds), *Evangelicals Engaging in Practical Theology: Theology That Impacts Church and World*, Abingdon: Routledge, pp. 177–84.
Padilla, C. René, 2020, 'Power for Life and Hope', in Gene L. Green, Stephen T. Pardue and K. K. Yeo (eds), *Majority World Theology: Christian Doctrine in Global Context*, Downers Grove, IL: InterVarsity Press, pp. 338–50.
Peterson, Eugene H., 2000, *A Long Obedience in the Same Direction: Discipleship in an Instant Society*, 2nd edn, Downers Grove, IL: IVP.
Polanco, Rodrigo, 2017, 'Understanding von Balthasar's Trilogy', *Theologica Xaveriana* 67.184, pp. 411–30.
Powley, Mark, 2024, 'What's Wrong with Tom Wright's Five-act Play Biblical Theology?', *markpowley.com*, https://markpowley.wordpress.com/2024/02/13/whats-wrong-with-tom-wrights-five-act-play-biblical-theology/ (accessed 21.3.2024).
Ricoeur, Paul, 2004 (1977), *The Rule of Metaphor: The Creation of Meaning in Language*, trans. R. Czerny, K. McLaughlin and J. Costello, London: Routledge.
Smith, James K. A., 2009, *Desiring the Kingdom: Worship, Worldview and Cultural Formation*, Grand Rapids, MI: Baker.
Soskice, Janet M., 1985, *Metaphor and Religious Language*, Oxford: Clarendon.
Spangler, Ann and Lois Tverberg, 2009, *Sitting at the Feet of Rabbi Jesus: How the Jewishness of Jesus Can Transform Your Faith*, Grand Rapids, MI: Zondervan.
Stackhouse, John G., 2003, 'Preface', in John G. Stackhouse (ed.), *Evangelical Ecclesiology: Reality or Illusion?*, Grand Rapids, MI: Baker Academic, pp. 9–11.
Tanner, Kathryn, 2013, 'Creation Ex Nihilo as Mixed Metaphor', *Modern Theology* 29.2, pp. 138–55.
Taylor, Charles, 2007, *A Secular Age*, Cambridge, MA: Harvard University Press.
Thibodeau, Paul H. and Lera Boroditsky, 2011, 'Metaphors We Think With: The Role of Metaphor in Reasoning', *PLoS ONE* 6.2, pp. 1–11.
Vanhoozer, Kevin J., 2009, 'A Drama-of-Redemption Model: Always Performing?', in Stanley N. Gundry and Gray T. Meadors (eds), *Four Views on Moving Beyond the Bible to Theology*, Grand Rapids, MI: Zondervan, pp. 151–99.
———, 2014, *Faith Speaking Understanding: Performing the Drama of Doctrine*, Louisville, KY: Westminster John Knox.
———, 2015, 'Putting on Christ: Spiritual Formation and the Drama of Discipleship', *Journal of Spiritual Formation & Soul Care* 8.2, pp. 147–71.
Volf, Miroslav and Matthew Croasmun, 2019, *For the Life of the World: Theology That Makes a Difference*, Grand Rapids, MI: Brazos.
Watkins, Clare, 2020, *Disclosing Church: An Ecclesiology from Conversations in Practice*, Abingdon: Routledge.
Wright, N. T., 1991, 'How Can the Bible be Authoritative? (The Laing Lecture for 1989)', *Vox Evangelica* 21, pp. 7–32.
———, 1992, *The New Testament and the People of God*, London: SPCK.

4

Church Planting, Community and the Triune God of Grace

JOSHUA COCKAYNE

Introduction

The title of this chapter is a reference to the Scottish theologian James B. Torrance and his 1994 Didsbury lectures, *Worship, Community and the Triune God of Grace*. In exploring Torrance's account of trinitarian worship, I will argue that we can learn important lessons about the theology and practice of church planting. More specifically, I suggest, much of our language and theology of church planting is thought of in 'practically unitarian' terms (to borrow a phrase from Torrance), with little attention paid to the actions of the persons of the Trinity in the midst of planting. It is common to talk of planting as our response to the work that God has done, or as our fulfilment of the great commission to *go and make disciples*. This way of thinking regards human beings as the primary agents at work in the life of the church. Contrastingly, a trinitarian theology of planting regards all church planting as a gift of participating in the ongoing work of the Trinity in the world; church planting is a means of participating in the ministry of Christ by the power of the Spirit in making known the love of the Father. The resulting view of church planting holds that the primary task of the planter is not one of strategy, but of discernment; asking where Christ continues to build his church today and participating in this life through the Spirit.

Torrance's critique of unitarian worship

Let's start by considering Torrance's argument. To begin, he describes two conceptions of worship, the first of which he describes as 'the most common and widespread', and which he dubs the 'unitarian' view. On this view of worship:

> We go to church, we sing our psalms and hymns to God ... No doubt we need God's grace to help us do it. We do it because Jesus taught us to do it and left us an example as how to do it. But worship is what *we* do ... In theological language, this means that the only priesthood is our priesthood, the only offering our offering, the only intercessions our intercessions. (Torrance, 1996, p. 20; emphasis original)

Torrance argues that this view of worship is unitarian in practice (even if its participants ascribe to the doctrine of the Trinity), since the ministry of the Trinity does not feature in our descriptions of worship and plays no role in our practice of our worship. He writes that such a view 'has no doctrine of the mediator or the sole priesthood of Christ, is human-centred, with no proper doctrine of the Holy Spirit, is too often basically non-sacramental, and can engender weariness' (Torrance, 1996, p. 20).

Contrastingly, on the 'trinitarian model', worship is not primarily thought of as something we do but rather, as Torrance puts it, is:

> the gift of participating through the Spirit in the incarnate Son's communion with the Father. It means participating in union with Christ, in what he has done for us once and for all, in his self-offering to the Father, in his life and death on the Cross. It also means participating in what he is continuing to do for us in the presence of the Father and in his mission to the world ... Is not the bread which we break our sharing in the body of Christ? ... Our intercessions and mission to the world, are they not the gift of participating in the intercessions and mission of the 'apostle and high priest whom we confess' (Heb 3:1)? (Torrance, 1996, pp. 20–1)

Rather than the *weariness* of human-centric worship, in which worship is always a human response to a divine work, the trinitarian perspective thinks of worship itself as a gift of participating in something that is already ongoing. It takes seriously the author of the epistle to the Hebrews' claim that Christ is a high priest who has offered a once and for all sacrifice for us, and continues to intercede for us at the right hand of the Father (Heb. 7.25). It emphasizes Paul's claim in Romans that the 'Spirit intercedes with sighs too deep for words' (Rom. 8.26). A trinitarian view of worship recognizes what is already ongoing in the ministry of the Godhead and invites us to be participants, rather than the primary agents of worship.

The pastoral and practical force of this theological claim is made movingly when Torrance recounts an encounter with a pastor on a beach in California, who is struggling to pray while his wife is in hospital dying from cancer. The pastor tells Torrance that he lacks the faith to pray for his wife to be healed. Torrance recounts:

> What did I say to him? Did I tell him how to find faith, how to pray – throw him back on himself? No I did not. I said ... In Jesus Christ we have someone who knows all of this. He has been through it all – through suffering and death and separation – and he will carry you both through it into resurrection life ... I said, 'None of us knows how to pray, but the Spirit knows all about us. He knows all about you and is interpreting your desires and your groans and your longing to know how to pray.' (Torrance, 1996, pp. 44–5)

Summarizing this encounter, Torrance reflects:

> in a pastoral situation, our first task is not to throw people back on themselves with exhortations and instructions as to what to do and how to do it, but to direct people to the gospel of grace – to Jesus Christ, that they might look at him to lead them, open their hearts in faith and prayer, and draw them by the Spirit into his eternal life of communion with the Father. (Torrance, 1996, p. 45)

In emphasizing the secondary nature of our agency in the life of the church, the trinitarian model of worship allows us to see that worship and prayer are primarily gifts of grace, not works to strive after.

Ecclesiology and participation

While Torrance's claims concern the practice of worship in the church, the implications of his discussion apply to ecclesiology more generally, I think. It is not uncommon to hear the kind of language Torrance describes as 'unitarian' with reference to church ministry in general, and church planting in particular. For example, I was recently attending a clergy training on church leadership. The speaker presented us with two models for thinking about leading in the church, which were accompanied by some diagrams to help illustrate the point (see Figures 1 and 2). The first of these, call it the 'clerical model', thinks of everything in the life of the church having to go through the leader; in effect the priest or the leader stands in the place of Christ and brings Christ into the life of the community. While Christ is present, it is only insofar as the leader makes Christ known. The speaker in this seminar wanted us to see (and rightly so, in my view) that the leader's role in the church was not *dis-*

tinct from the other members of the church; rather the priest stands as one of many parts in the body of Christ (see 1 Cor. 12.18–20). Thus, the second model, which I'll call the 'community model', thinks of *all* ministry (ordained or lay) as part of the church, over which Christ is the only authority.

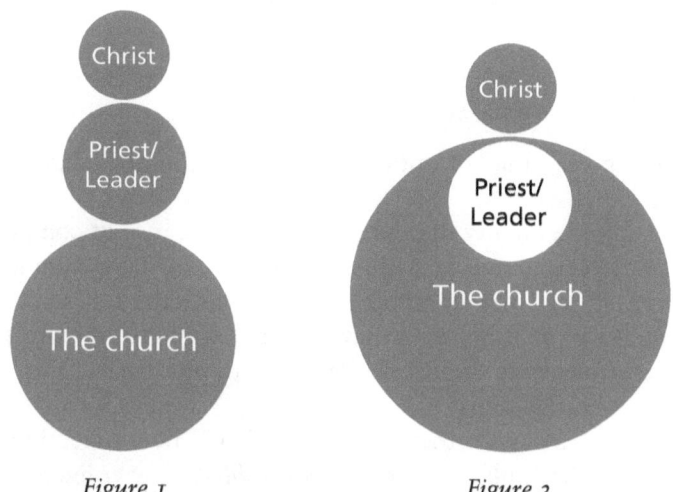

Figure 1   Figure 2

It would not be difficult to find these two models in the context of church planting, nor in the church planting literature. Now, the problem with these ways of thinking about church leadership is not so much the sentiment that priestly or leadership ministry is one gift among many in the church. I think this much can be inferred from Paul's discussion of the body of Christ in 1 Corinthians 12. Rather, the preoccupation with our own leadership betrays an implicit ecclesiology that looks very much like Torrance's unitarian view of worship. While God might provide us with some guidance and grace while we plant churches, in both models of leadership, the church that is planted and grown is a work of human beings responding to God. The diagrams themselves highlight this assumption – it is you and I who are the primary agents at work in the church, trying our best to do the work of God, and living out Christ's commands on his behalf.

Perhaps I am being uncharitable; the purpose of the session in question was not to reflect deeply on the nature of the Trinity and its relation to ecclesiology, but to argue for a shift in our view of church leadership. However, a cursory glance through much of the literature on church planting would suggest that these two models quite fairly represent the implicit ecclesiology of many. In a recent book I read on church planting (I won't tell you which), throughout the book it was common for the author to talk about 'my church' and 'your church'; to use language such as, 'When *you* plant a church be sure to do x, y, z …' and even went as far as saying that church planting requires 'hard work, strategy, leadership … and a whole lot of prayer', as if it were one need among many. Or consider Stefan Paas' summary of the pragmatic reasons many authors give for planting churches:

> Church planting is supposed to further the growth of the church by a set of interrelated reasons, such as:
> - extending the range of options for people who are religiously interested;
> - increasing the quality of churches' supply because of competition;
> - creating access to unreached people groups and new immigrants;
> - keeping up with demographic shifts and growth;
> - having lower thresholds for newcomers because of the more flexible character of young churches. (Paas, 2016, pp. 7–8)

Such arguments are not difficult to find, either. The implication of these claims is that church planters primarily *establish* new congregations; we do this in order to keep up with demographic shifts, extend the range of options, create access to unreached people, and so on. The emphasis is squarely on what *we* do. In Torrance's vocabulary, this is to think of church planting in practically unitarian terms – the only priesthood is *our* priesthood, the only intercessions are *our* intercessions and the only church planted is *our* church.

What the unitarian models of church planting fail to see is that our agency is not the primary activity in the church. Rather, as Tom Greggs puts it:

> Although the church shares in many – if not all – of the characteristics of other organizations, its primary existence is ultimately distinct from every other expression of human sociality. The church comes into being as an event of the act of the lordship of the Holy Spirit of God who gives the church life. (Greggs, 2019, p. 2)

The church is fundamentally the activity of the persons of the Trinity, in which we as church leaders and church planters are given the gracious gift of participating.

We can see this point vividly in Paul's famous image of the body of Christ in 1 Corinthians 12. If the church were primarily a work of human activity, his words on church unity would read as such: 'Just as the body is one and has many members ... so it is with *the church.*' Instead, notice how Paul finishes this sentence: 'Just as the body is one and has many members ... so it is with *Christ.*' In other words, the unity of the community of the church comes not from any human organization or structure, but only from the work of the Holy Spirit, who's activity brings about a unity in Christ. In Gordon Fee's words, 'spiritual unity' cannot be 'forced' on to the church through human structures and designs, as if unity were 'simply another human machination' imposed by human beings onto the 'common life' of the church (Fee, 1987, p. 607). Instead, the unity found in the church can only be understood as arising from the work of the Spirit in the community. Thus, it would be a mistake to think that this claim is a merely a metaphor to describe a certain kind of activity. As Richard Hays puts it:

> Exegetes have long debated whether the designation of the church as 'the body of Christ' is for Paul a mere metaphor or a mystical reality. The truth is that this is a false dichotomy; Paul would probably not understand the terms in which the problem is posed. Certainty 'body of Christ' is a metaphor; just as certainly, Paul believes that this metaphor illumines the truth about the church's union with and participation with Christ. The church is not merely a human organization; rather, it is brought into being by the activity of the Holy Spirit, which binds believers into a living union with the crucified and risen lord. (Hays, 2011 pp. 113–14)

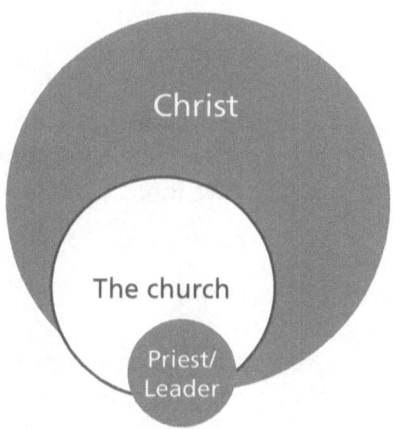

Figure 3

Thus, in contrast to the two unitarian models we have considered, a better model looks like the 'participation model' (see Figure 3). This model of ecclesiology sees participation in the life of the church primarily as a *gift*. It emphasizes that the church is a work of the Holy Spirit, who draws us into the community of faith to constitute the one body of Christ – it is not *our* ministry but Christ's. While there is not scope here for a full exploration of what 'participation in the life of Christ' may consist in, it is important to see that by 'participation' I mean more than 'joining in with God' or 'doing the things Jesus asks us to do'. Andrew Byers, in his work on ecclesiology in John's Gospel, explores the kind of unity that Jesus ascribes to the disciples in his high priestly prayer, *that they may be one as the Father and the Son are one* (John 17.11). Byers writes that the unity prayed for here 'certainly entails a participation in Jesus' mission and activity', but it must 'extend beyond a call to social harmony or a functional imitation Jesus' earthly ministry' (Byers, 2017, pp. 198–9). Jesus is making an ontological claim about the identity of those who are found in Christ. Byers writes: 'Beyond a task-orientated or functional unity, Jesus prays that this new social entity [i.e. the church] will actually share in his pre-existent divine glory' (Byers, 2017, p. 152). The church's identity is fundamentally *in* Christ, in union with Christ, not merely a human organization that responds *to* Christ.

Participation and church planting

So what difference might this theological shift make to the practice of church planting? The worry many may have is that I have offered a theological technicality that makes no real difference to the ministry of planting. Indeed, regardless of which ecclesiology is implicit in planting, one will surely have to strategize, plan, think about demographics and context. One will have to decide whether to employ a community or clerical model of leadership. So let's conclude by considering some of the implications for planting. I will offer three.

1. All strategy is a work of discernment

The first thing to note is that if the church is primarily a work of the Trinity, and not a work of human beings, then the task of planting new communities is not a kind of *creation* but a kind of *participation*. If this is the case, then decisions about vision, strategy and planning are primarily about listening; seeking to find out where the Spirit is at work in our communities and participating in this work. As Edwin van Driel writes:

> If Christ constitutes the church, and not we ourselves, we will have to understand our congregations and their mission differently ... If God establishes the church, then any process that aims to re-vision a congregation's future must start with God. 'Strategic planning' must be first and foremost a process of *discernment*. (Van Driel, 2020, pp. 60–1; my emphasis)

Note that Van Driel does not endorse a doing away with *strategic planning*, but a reframing of strategy as a kind of prayer. The question is not whether the church prays *or* strategizes. Indeed, if we look through the pages of Acts, we see the early church expanding with strategy and purpose as they are led by the Holy Spirit (see the summary of Paul's missional strategy in McGinnis 2022, ch. 2). This means that church planters will need to be trained well in how to understand context, to lead teams, to write five-year plans – as Christian Selvaratnam (2022) has recently argued, there is a 'craft' to church planting that is comparable to the kind of skill picked up by artisans over long periods of training in context.

But if strategy is primarily a means of discernment, then it is simply impossible to engage in this task without prayer. This means that the aim of church planting might not necessarily be to find the most need, or to find the most attractive way to package the gospel for a new context. There are many skills we can learn from marketing professionals and business planners that could build effective organizations, but planting that comes detached from the ministry of the trinity is not really *church* planting at all; it is merely a kind of organization building.

2. The life of the planter is a supernatural life

This point leads helpfully on to the second: the life of planting is a supernatural life. Writing in 1946 (there truly is nothing new under the sun!) on the prayer life of the parish priest, Evelyn Underhill stated:

> The vocation of the Christian minister is a supernatural vocation; and how can he fulfil it, unless he lives a supernatural life? Much is now being said about evangelism; but before we get effective evangelism, we have to get effective evangelists. Evangelism is useless, unless it is the work of the one devoted to God, willing and glad to suffer all things for God, penetrated by the attractiveness of God. New machinery, adaptations and adjustments, are not the first need of the Church of England; but more devoted, adoring, sacrificial souls. (1946, pp. 144–5)

If the ministry of starting new Christian communities is one of discerning the movement of the Spirit today, then we must take seriously the need to inhabit the supernatural life. There are challenging questions for those who are in the ministry of church planting. Asked how things are at Holy Trinity (my own context), my instinctive (and honest) response was to say: 'Very busy!' As Eugene Peterson provocatively argues, this word – busy – is an adjective, which when attached to any pastoral ministry is 'an outrageous scandal, a blasphemous affront'; Peterson writes that, 'The word *busy* is the symptom not of commitment but of betrayal. It is not devotion but defection' (1993, p. 17). As he goes on to say, 'Hilary of Tours diagnosed our pastoral busyness as ... a blasphemous anxiety to do God's work for him' (1993, p. 17). If we want to do more than 'dispense mimeographed handouts that describe God's business', Peterson thinks, we have to become unbusy; we 'cannot be inwardly rushed, distracted, or dispersed. In order to pray I have to be paying more attention to God than to what people are saying to me; to God than to my clamoring ego' (1993, p. 20).

It is important to see that this emphasis on spirituality is an outworking of the Trinitarian claims made about the nature of the church; as Michael Gorman puts it:

> To be sent as Jesus was sent is to be in a relationship of mutual indwelling with the Sender such that the works one does are the works of the indwelling one ... Like Jesus, disciples are in a relationship of mutual indwelling ... But ... since they are not God by nature, the disciples need to depend on Jesus ... by constantly abiding and praying. (Gorman, 2018, pp. 131–2)

Moreover, it follows that if we want to teach and equip those who plant churches, then we must help them to build patterns of devotion and adoration not just strategies and skills – in the words of the old idiom: 'If you wish to build a ship, do not divide the men into teams and send them to the forest to cut wood. Instead, teach them to long for the vast and endless sea.' The ministry of planting as participation begins with fervent intercession, prayer walking and reflective prayer.

3. *It is not our job to plant the church*

Last, an emphasis on church planting as participating in the life of the Trinity offers to shift our own sense of importance in the process of church planting. In the midst of growth reports, accountability structures and church planting conferences spotlighting the success stories of rapidly growing ministries, it can be easy to develop a sense of our own importance in building the church. Craig Barnes puts the point well: 'Nothing is more threatening to the souls of those in a minister's care than a messianic illusion that tempts the pastor to take over for Jesus Christ. Pastors save no one ... We are never more, or less, than witnesses' (Barnes, 2020, p. 122).

Not only can this emphasis fend off the worry of ego-planters, who serve only to build their own empires, but it can also provide a sense of release for those engaged in the task of planting. I vividly recall teaching a class on pastoral care to a room full of student pastors and reiterating this point that they cannot replace the pastoral ministry of the good shepherd; at best they can *witness* to the good shepherd. One of the students was visibly moved by this reflection, and when I followed up he told me that he had felt a weight of burden lift from him in realizing that he could not save his students from their mental health problems and broken lives. For this pastor, this wasn't an excuse to pull back from pastoral ministry, but an invitation to view his ministry through a different lens.

I know from first-hand experience that in the task of church planting, many of these burdens feel heightened, especially if you are the one carrying the ministry through its early days and fulfilling many roles at once, while the community begins to form. The reminder that we cannot plant the church, but that we can merely participate in the work of Holy Spirit in building the body of Christ, provides a sense of perspective to frame what we deem 'failure' and 'success'. In Scott Hagley's words, 'The church, united with Christ, participates in this way of life in the power of the Spirit, but never out in front of Christ' (Hagley, 2020, p. 105). A trinitarian model of church planting will never allow the planter to get *out in front of Christ*; we must see our work through the lens of the activity of Christ, always seeking to discern and follow where Christ is already leading.

Conclusion

There is surely much more that could be said about the practical implications of the ecclesiology that is implicitly adopted by a church planter. My hope is that I have shown that theology really matters to this conversation. If our view of the church remains practically unitarian, to borrow Torrance's phrase, we risk building a church formed around human best efforts and structures, and risk the weariness of planting out of a sense that God needs us to plant his church. A trinitarian model of planting, by contrast, encourages us to see that planting is primarily a gift of grace; it is the gift of joining in with the ministry of Christ in the world, through his Holy Spirit.

References

Barnes, M. C., 2020, 'The Mission of God in Pastoral Care', in Van Driel (ed.), *What is Jesus Doing?*.
Byers, A. J., 2017, *Ecclesiology and Theosis in the Gospel of John*, Cambridge: Cambridge University Press.
Fee, G. D., 1987, *The First Epistle to the Corinthians*, Grand Rapids, MI: Eerdmans.
Gorman, M. J., 2018, *Abide and Go: Missional Theosis in the Gospel of John*, Eugene, OR: Wipf & Stock.
Greggs, T., 2019, *Dogmatic Ecclesiology: Volume 1: The Priestly Catholicity of the Church*, Grand Rapids, MI: Baker Academic.
Hagley, S., 2020, 'A Present Witness: Incarnation, Participation, and the Spirit of God', in Van Driel (ed.), *What is Jesus Doing?*.
Hays, R. B., 2011, *First Corinthians*, Louisville, KY: Westminster John Knox Press.
McGinnis, D., 2022, *Missional Acts: Rhetorical Narrative in the Acts of the Apostles*. Grand Rapids, MI: Wipf & Stock.
Pass, S., 2016, 'Why Church Planting in Europe? On Authorizing a Common Evangelical Practice', in Miranda Klaver, Stefan Paas and Eveline van Staalduine-Sulman (eds), *Evangelicals and Sources of Authority*, Amsterdam: Amsterdam University Press, pp. 184–205.
Peterson, E., 1993, *The Contemplative Pastor*, Grand Rapids, MI: Eerdmans.
Selvaratnam, C., 2022, *The Craft of Church Planting*, London: SCM Press.
Torrance, J., 1996, *Worship, Community, and the Triune God of Grace*, Milton Keynes: Paternoster Press.
Underhill, E., 1946, *Collected Papers of Evelyn Underhill*, London: Longmans, Green & Company.
van Driel, E. C. (ed.), 2020, *What is Jesus Doing?: God's Activity in the Life and Work of the Church*, Downers Grove, IL: InterVarsity Press.

5

Who is Doing the Planting? Understanding Human Agency while Keeping the Focus on the Work of the Spirit

JAMES BUTLER

Introduction

The adjective 'church planting' and the noun 'church planter' have an implied agency. In church planting literature this agency is regularly given to human subjects. Two recent church planting books written by self-identified 'church planters' are helpful examples. Selvaratnam uses 'church planter' for 'those who start new churches and those who revitalize or renew existing churches using church planting methods' (Selvaratnam, 2022, p. 108). Similarly, for Valentine, a church planter is the leader (Valentine, 2023). For both Selvaratnam and Valentine, and in church planting literature more widely, prayer and the work of the Spirit are named as central and yet so often the emphasis is on the human subject, the church planter, and the role of the Spirit is assumed but ill defined. One solution to this might be to make a clearer turn to *missio Dei* theology, that mission is first God's mission, which the church is called to participate in, along the lines encouraged by *Mission-shaped Church* and Fresh Expressions (Archbishops' Council, 2004). This theology has been popularized in the fresh expressions movement by the phrase often attributed to Rowan Williams, the Archbishop of Canterbury at the time: 'finding out where the Holy Spirit is at work and joining in' (Kim, 2012). *Missio Dei* theology appears to explicitly foreground divine agency and position human agency in a role of discerning and participating. And yet when it comes to expressing this in the actual practice of mission and church planting it often remains equally nondescript. A model that has gained particular traction in fresh expressions is Moynagh's 'loving first journey'. In this model, listening comes first leading to loving and serving, forming community, discipleship, church forming and doing it again (Moynagh, 2012, pp. 208–9). Even though Moynagh is explicit that this is not his intention, such a linear process easily leads to the implication that listening is a first step and once Christians know what to do they can act. The tasks of discerning and participating become separated and human agency easily becomes prioritized when it comes to action.

I am arguing in this chapter that much more careful theological work needs to be done. It is vital to not just name the Spirit's work as central, but actually be able to articulate how the Spirit's work is central and account for the relationship between divine and human agency in mission and church planting. Rather than seeking a blueprint theology (Healy, 2000), describing the relationship in the abstract, I will develop a practical theology of participating in the *missio Dei* based on the lived experience and practice of four missional communities. By engaging with the lived and messy practice of mission in everyday life, I propose that there are theological resources to enable an account of discernment and participation in the *missio Dei* that will hold divine and human agency together in practice. As I will demonstrate, by focusing on the lived spirituality of these missional communities, an integrated account of agency in the *missio Dei* is offered that integrates practices of prayer and discernment with mission by basing them in a mission spirituality that becomes the foundation of a theology of agency in the *missio Dei*. In doing so I will respond to the question about 'Who is doing the planting?' by offering a more collaborative account, which while prioritizing the work of the Spirit, resists drawing distinct lines between human and divine agency. I will conclude the chapter by naming some of the implications for an ecclesiology of church planting from such an account of agency; one that is dynamic, provisional and Spirit-led.

Identifying a missional spirituality in practice

The four missional communities in the qualitative research engaged with were chosen because they were actively involved in social action within their local community and were actively seeking to build Christian community as they did this.[1] All four had a charismatic evangelical background and all were questioning and challenging this background in different ways as they engaged in mission. I am using the term missional community in a broad sense, not as part of a particular movement but as a term to include the huge variety of groups and communities seeking to be faithful in their locality as Christians. I see these operating in what Doornenbal has called the 'emerging missional milieu' (Doornenbal,

2012). While they would not necessarily see themselves as church planting, they certainly fall within the kinds of fresh expressions communities promoted by Moynagh and offer helpful insights into the theology of starting such communities (Moynagh, 2012). Rather than try and give a short summary of each community, or to try and summarize the research in a paragraph, in this section I will offer snapshots of the four communities to give a sense of their practice at the same times as drawing out key observations for developing an account of agency in the *missio Dei*. By looking at the lived practice of these missional communities, of how they develop their inherited charismatic evangelical spirituality to help them experience God in the midst of social action, I will develop an account of mission that integrates discernment and participation.

Prayer

It is not a coincidence that all four of these missional communities began in prayer. The 24/7 Prayer movement was gaining prominence around the time that these communities were beginning (2005–10) by encouraging a chain of non-stop prayer, with churches and groups signing up for a week of prayer and to fill a 'prayer room' for one week of one-hour slots. As the 24/7 Prayer movement developed they found themselves drawn into practices of mission and justice, particularly in developing missional communities called boiler rooms (Greig, 2003). All four missional communities had been influenced by 24/7 Prayer and run prayer rooms. Eastbark[2] missional community had come into being as the result of a local 24/7 Prayer week. Ben, part of the leadership team, felt that having the prayer room as the 'main thing' demonstrated their desire for 'God to be the centre of it'. Jenny, also part of the leadership team, explained that at the beginning, they tried not to direct the community but encouraged people to pray in the prayer room and 'just see what God did'. They talked about 'fumbling through different challenges' and how messy it was but when you look back: 'It makes perfect sense and I could put it in a nice story line for you but at the time it didn't feel like we were going anywhere.' At the time of the research the pattern of the community was weekly meals where they ate and prayed together. Individuals would pray in the prayer room weekly, and they had more intensive weeks of prayer together a few times a year.

They describe their social action as an 'overflow' from the prayer room, particularly their work in the local school where they had an after-school café and supported many young people, including some at risk of exclusion. They felt their prayer pushed them out into the community, and that what they experience 'comes back to the prayer room and directs [their] prayers'. While at first glance this might sound like a separating of prayer and action – retreating to pray and then going out to act – it is actually far more integrated. Prayer is taken into everyday life. They set up prayer rooms wherever they go and they pray with and for people and places when they are in them. When I spent time with them it was clear that prayer had become the instinctive response to challenges. Prayer becomes a place of integration and, rather than separating discernment and participation, draws them together; discernment is happening within participation and participation becomes part of the ongoing patterns of discernment.

Learning to see God in mission

Something similar could be seen in the way Lynwood missional community operated. They looked quite different from Eastbark, as they were focused on the collection and delivery of furniture and other items from those who wanted to donate to those in need. And yet similar patterns of prayer permeated their work. They met for an hour of prayer every Monday, they prayed whenever the van went out to collect or deliver furniture and, just like Eastbark, prayer became the instinctive response in both challenges or celebrations: praying when they had mislaid something, praying when the computers went down, and thanking God when someone donated the furniture that was needed. As Ben in the Lynwood community described, this was 'prayer in action'. What Lynwood also demonstrated clearly was the way they experienced God in mission. Tony is explicit about this:

> In Lynwood you can actually see, feel, and be part of the Lord God Almighty working – and that for me is spine-tingling [...] When you pray and something happens immediately, and it happens better than you'd imagined it's quite ... yeah!

Alice, who led the Lynwood community, described how she prayed over the furniture:

> Sometimes as I'm walking round the hut, if I'm walking round and I'm praying about stuff that's in and where it's got to go I'll get a real sense [that] I've got to pray over a piece of furniture or something for God to reveal to me his plans for that and that can be very real – that can be like – I've got to stop here – 'Where's this wardrobe going Lord?'

She sees God as intimately involved in the details and practicalities of work. Her charismatic evangelical practices of prayer are being translated into the work they are doing. She could experience God within the social action like she did in charismatic evangelical worship. Rachel described how they expected God to interrupt them to keep them 'aligned' and 'in tune' with what he was doing. Interruptions might come through people turning up unexpectedly, phone calls out of the blue, surprise encounters on the van or external factors that disrupted their plans. They also talked about sensations, feelings, or words and pictures in prayer times. All these things were identified as God interrupting them and leading them to where they needed to be and were carefully considered and prayed about. Tony commented: 'You want to see God at work? I'll show you God at work – if you have got the commitment and the eyes to see – because you can see everything at Lynwood and see nothing – but you need spiritual eyes to see it.'

At Lynwood, the prayer and the community helped people to have those 'spiritual eyes', to learn to 'see' God at work and to learn to discern that. Within these accounts human action is always seeking to actively participate. Discernment is not a first step before participating, but an ongoing pattern and one that continually directs participation and comes out of participation.

Creating space for God

Hilchester missional community had a slightly different way of talking about their mission. Just like Eastbark and Lynwood, prayer was important, and the community began with weeks of 24/7 prayer and committing to regular meals and prayer times together. They were based on a deprived estate on the edge of a reasonably affluent town. They talked about 'creating space for God' through their mission and social action. Similar to Eastbark, this meant having space for prayer within their mission activities, whether this was a time of reflection before their football games with young people or prayer spaces within their community activities or schools work. Hilchester did have stories, along the lines of Lynwood, of surprise encounters, interruptions and the way God guided them, but they also saw how human agency could take the lead at times while always discerning God. Charlie, who was leading the youth work, used the phrase 'creating space for God to move', which was about freeing space in his week to be responsive, but also being aware that as he did things God could use them. He talked about the opportunity they had to foster a young person from their community for a short time.

Another example was the way they were open about their faith with the young people and 'Seeing God represented well in this community, so that people whatever their perspective can [say], "Well I've seen that God is good – I may not believe in him but I see he's good."' Becky, one of the of the founding members of Hilchester missional community told me about a lady she met who was a spiritualist whom she invited along to the Monday night meeting saying that she 'will probably be another person who for a long time there is a connection and a care and we will see what God does with it'.

Again, Hilchester demonstrated an integrated sense of their work in relation to God's mission. Rather than a step of discerning and then participating, discernment took place in the midst of participation, and their own participation might open up opportunities to see and discern God together. By stepping out and doing things, taking opportunities as they arose, they anticipated that God would do something with what they offered. Charlie talked about it in terms of good stewardship of what they had been given, and how all they did was not in their own strength, but in trusting in God and trying to follow God's will.

Collaborating with God

The fourth community in the research was Airbury, who ran a drop-in space that had been used at different times by homeless people, mums after school drop-off, people with mental health issues and people who were lonely and wanted community. They had become known as a group who would support people and help signpost them to provisions around the town. Similar to the other communities they had begun by seeing themselves as a prayer room in the town, and still had a regular pattern of prayer. They had a small but growing community who met once a month on a Friday lunchtime for communion and a meal, and who met to eat together on Sunday evenings. Their spirituality had moved further away from charismatic practices than the other groups and was more focused on what they described as 'finding God in the desert'. They felt a better theology of suffering was needed than what charismatic evangelicalism could offer. They were frustrated by the charismatic evangelical churches they had been part of which, from their perspective, 'Just prayed and did sod all about that and expected God to be the answer to their prayers when God was expecting them to be the answer to those prayers.' They had developed quite a complex way to understand how they participated in mission. Claire, who led the community, described this in an entry in her blog:

We are lately seeing that our work together is about working like archaeologists, dusting off the dirt that is covering the inner beauty of someone and helping it to be revealed. Everyone has something beautiful inside, and for some it's been covered over deeply for a long time, so the work is painstaking, but is actually the work of the Holy Spirit, so all we do is see the leads and follow them, as we can.

Claire talks about how the work of the Spirit and human action overlap and are identified together. They are working with and, by some mystery, even doing the work of the Spirit as they patiently care for others. Towards the end of the quotation she reverts to describing this as the Spirit acting and the human following, but the lived reality she is describing is far more integrated. It is perhaps better described as collaboration than simply following. An act that is both a human act and a divine act.

Discovering a mission spirituality

What these snapshots of the four missional communities reveal is an emerging mission spirituality within their practice. They have taken their charismatic evangelical spirituality and extended it to help them make sense of their engagement in mission as a community. By using the language of 'extending' I am particularly thinking of the ways in which charismatic evangelical practices have been adapted to make sense of their mission engagement, for example Alice in Lynwood praying around the furniture. Typical places to identify charismatic evangelical spirituality would be in their worship and in 'ministry time'. Steven describes charismatic evangelical 'times of worship' as 'periods of sustained sung worship, with a group of musicians leading the congregation in a succession of modem songs' (Steven, 1999, p. 128) and he describes intimacy as the goal of charismatic worship (p. 163). This sense of being close to God and experiencing God can be seen in the account of the missional communities, only here that sense of encounter now comes through the engagement in mission. The practice of ministry time sheds further light on charismatic evangelical spirituality. An individual is prayed for by others who might place a hand on them. Pytches' account of prayer ministry helps to illuminate the practice:

> Those ministering should always keep their eyes open and observe what God is doing ... Those ministering can bless and honour what God is doing for his people. Lay a hand lightly upon the person under the power of the Holy Spirit, using words such as 'We bless you, Lord for

what you are doing in this person', 'We honour the work of the Holy Spirit in this person now, Lord' or 'Increase your power Lord, upon this person' ... Those ministering should seek for 'words of knowledge' or other gifts of the Spirit, to show them what more God wants to do. (Pytches, 1985, p. 275)

The Holy Spirit is seen as the primary agent of ministry time, and those praying seek to participate in that work. There are clear resonances with the practice of ministry time and the ways in which the missional communities engage in mission, keeping the Spirit as the primary agent and seeking to see what God is doing and to discover how they are to participate. The communities can be seen adapting and extending these practices to help them make sense of their experience of mission. For example, Andrew, the leader of the Hilchester missional community, turned around the common charismatic evangelical phrase 'discern what God is doing and to bless that' (Pytches, 2002, p. 256), saying that they were trying to 'bless and then see what God does with that'.

What I want to emphasize is that the missional communities have developed a mission spirituality that is coherent with their experience and history. In thinking about participating in the *missio Dei*, a clear emphasis on discerning the Spirit is certainly helpful, but the point is that in seeking to discern the Spirit they have found practices and postures that make sense to them. Their engagement in mission takes place through their own spirituality and Christian tradition, which is then adapted, changed and extended as they engage in their context. While there is a tendency in mission and church planting literature to move away from vision and strategy towards tools and practices, what this shows is that the focus needs to go further on to developing a mission spirituality of discernment and participation that makes sense to the community, not imported as practices from outside. It also makes sense of the messiness of life and discernment and the embeddedness of such discernment in everyday life.

A practice-engaged and prayer-based account of participation in the *missio Dei*

My argument is that discernment and participation are integrated into the community life through their developing mission spirituality. Through extending and adapting their charismatic evangelical spirituality, discernment and participation are not separate tasks, but become overlapping and interrelated practices and postures. This integrated mission spirituality enables a more mysterious understanding of the relationship between divine and human agency where clear distinctions are difficult.

This account of human and divine agency within the *missio Dei* based in a mission spirituality indicates the need for a pneumatology of mission. Such accounts are available although perhaps less common than might be expected. A particular example is 'Together Towards Life' (TTL), produced by the Commission on World Mission and Evangelism of the World Council of Churches (2012). TTL reflects on how 'Life in the Holy Spirit is the essence of mission' and how 'spirituality gives the deepest meaning to our lives and motivates our actions' (2012, p. 3). Although spirituality was at the heart of TTL, five years later in the next meeting in Arusha, there was a concern expressed about this emphasis on the Spirit and how the centrality of Christ was becoming lost (Bevans, 2018). Within the Arusha Call to Discipleship document there was a desire to reassert the role of humans in the *missio Dei* and to be more explicit about the uniqueness of Christ, which was done through the language of discipleship (CWME, 2018). I have argued elsewhere that the introduction of the language of discipleship changes the missiology and is not in keeping with the affirmation of spirituality and the agency of the Spirit in TTL (Butler, 2023). My own proposal here, through the lived theology of these missional communities, suggests a way that the emphasis of TTL on spirituality can be maintained, and in fact be made more central.

Beginning the account of human and divine agency within a mission spirituality enables a starting point of integration rather than dis-integration (Watkins, 2020, pp. 42–3). The accounts of the missional communities demonstrate that their prayer practices embody this integrated understanding.[3] These missional communities began in the prayer room, praying individually and together. Each missional community testifies to the ways that prayer shaped them both in the earlier stages of developing the missional community and in an ongoing way. Rather than seeing prayer as a stage in the process of developing a missional community, it is the thing that centres them on God. This is what Cocksworth argues about prayer in relation to theology.

By working with the fourth-century monk Evagrius' short treatise *On Prayer*, Cocksworth explores how theology and spirituality can be understood as integrated. He takes Evagrius' assertion that 'prayer is the mind's conversation with God' (Evagrius, *On Prayer*, p. 3, quoted in Cocksworth, 2018, p. 35) and argues that rather than seeing this as fitting a back-and-forth between God and the one praying, it is rather a 'messy "polyphony" of voices' (Cocksworth, 2018, p. 36) and that prayer is better understood as being 'caught up in the Son's eternal conversation with the Father' (p. 37). Just like the experience of the missional communities, rather than prayer seen as a discrete activity or 'momentary performance, Evagrius saw prayer as a continuous unceasing event' (Cocksworth, 2018, p. 38), integrating formal prayer with the wider life of a monk. Cocksworth continues: 'True prayer was reached when the entire Christian life is set to and ordered by the rhythm of the pray-er's uninterrupted dialogue with the divine' (p. 38). This is why, for Cocksworth, prayer matters for theology, because 'Prayer is the site where the divine and the human meet' (p. 39). While Cocksworth's focus is on the integration of spirituality and theology, his account of prayer sheds light on why and how prayer is significant in understanding divine and human agency in the *missio Dei*. He states that 'the human activity of prayer becomes more expansively about being caught up by the Holy Spirit into the prayer of the praying Son before the Father' (p. 77). These developing Trinitarian insights provide a lens to see mission, the *missio Dei* and the practice of the communities as integrated. The ongoing practices of prayer and discernment developed in the missional communities, embedded in the everydayness and messiness of life, are ways of participating not just in eternal conversation of father and son, but also in the work of the Spirit in the world. In this account of prayer the ability to draw clear lines between divine and human agency, and indeed between words and actions, is lost; prayer is being attentive to the divine conversation happening in us and 'keeping company with' God or, as Cocksworth sums it up, as 'union' (p. 37). Even the act of prayer cannot be seen as a solely human act because 'God not only gives prayer to the pray-er as "gift" but even prays "in" the pray-er (p. 37).

According to Cocksworth, prayer is the place where divine and human meet, where the human is caught up in the divine and the work of the Spirit. Prayer is less a discrete activity and more an unceasing event integrated in all of life. Prayer, and the mission spirituality developed from this prayer, becomes a place of integration – not a discrete practice that prepares the Christian for mission, but the way in which discernment and participation become a posture and continual practice of mission. The practices of mission are always open to the movement of the Spirit, who draws the Christian into the prayer of the Father and Son, and draws them into the engagement of the *missio Dei* in the world. Through the lived experience and lived theology of the missional communities, the place of integration of divine and human agency is not found in a universal theological model or idea, but in a spirituality of discernment and participation that engages with the messiness of everyday life and discernment.

A practical theology of participation in the *missio Dei*

What the close attention to these missional communities has revealed is that the integration of divine and human agency takes place within the prayer-based practices of everyday life of the communities. It is in the particular, the contextual and the embodied that participation in the *missio Dei* makes sense. Too often in mission the question is about what needs to be done. Much time and energy is spent deciding on action and convincing others to join in that action. This may be done in the context of prayer, but is often experienced as a tension of trusting God and needing to act. By instead focusing on a spirituality, one that is coherent with the experience and background of those participating, this is experienced in a much more integrated way. After all, if, as TTL affirms, 'mission begins in the heart of the Triune God and the love which binds together the Holy Trinity overflows to all humanity and creation', then participation needs to be understood both as based in the Spirit and in mystery (CWME, 2012, p. 2). The patterns of discernment and participation are not stages, but through the prayer-based mission spirituality, are lived as different sides of the same coin. The *missio Dei* is not seen as some fixed expression, but as always open to being shaped, changed, interrupted and refocused by the work of the Spirit in the world. Similarly, participation is not some predefined act, but in the participation by humans, mission is also shaped and changed. What is the Spirit and what is human becomes difficult to define clearly, and an overlap between the two begins to emerge. The theological basis is not a clever theological device, but an expansive and Trinitarian understanding of prayer; a pattern of participation first learnt through prayer, but as Cocksworth, through the work of Evagrius, demonstrates, one that is increasingly a 'continuous, unceasing event'.

Through a mission spirituality of discernment and participation that is based in prayer, open to the interruption and guidance of the Spirit and shaped by the dynamics of prayer, both communal and individual, an integrated account of divine and human agency is possible. Through this mission spirituality a continual pattern of discerning and participating is developed that keeps the community open to the surprises and encounters of everyday life and faith and to the work of the Spirit in, through and around them.

Who is doing the planting?

Picking up the question of agency in church planting, this practical theological account of the *missio Dei* gives a complex answer to the question of who is doing the planting. It is the Holy Spirit who plants, and yet through the mystery of the triune God's action in the world, humans are draw into that work, as those who participate and collaborate with God. To maintain this properly complex account of divine and human agency what is needed is a mission spirituality that is able to engage with the messiness of everyday life and account for the difficult, confusing and never finished process of discerning and participating. For the missional communities, this was built on a charismatic evangelical spirituality of prayer, experience and encounter, but the point is that the mission spirituality developed needs to be one that is coherent with the spirituality of the group participating in the planting.

This account of divine and human agency in mission also suggests a different account of mission ecclesiology. From this integrated view of divine and human agency, it would be better to think about the church as coming into being in the world through the collaborative and interrelated work of the Spirit and Christians, than as a thing that is fixed in a particular place. Perhaps digging deeper into horticultural references might enable this, but if as Ward has suggested, the church can be better understood as liquid, perhaps new metaphors can helpfully move us to appreciate this reality of divine and human action together (Ward, 2013). Church planting in this view needs to be seen in much more dynamic ways, a participation in the flow and life of the Spirit; being drawn into a calling to be church in the world, always growing in holiness and maturity in Christ. I will leave the reader to decide the extent to which 'church planting' and 'church planter' remain helpful terms, but my hope is that this practical theological account of the *missio Dei* might give better language for describing the interrelated nature of divine and human agency, and focus attention away from strategies, or even particularly practices towards developing a mission spirituality.

Notes

1 More detail can be found in my PhD thesis (Butler, 2017).

2 All names of communities and individuals are pseudonyms to protect their identity.

3 Kwiyani (2019, pp. 85–6) makes a similar point about the ways African Diaspora Churches bring an integrated sense of prayer to mission.

References

Archbishops' Council, 2004, *Mission-shaped Church: Church Planting and Fresh Expressions of Church in a Changing Context*, London: Church House Publishing.

Bevans, S., 2018, 'Transforming Discipleship and the Future of Mission', *International Review of Mission* 107.2, pp. 362–77.

Butler, J., 2017, *Exploring the Lived Theology of Small Missional Communities: Uncovering Charismatic Practices and Beliefs to Enable Sustained Engagement in Social Action*, doctoral dissertation, Durham University.

———, 2023, 'Human Agency in the Missio Dei and the Problem of Discipleship', *International Review of Mission* 112.1, pp. 110–24.

Cocksworth, A., 2018, *Prayer: A Guide for the Perplexed*, London: T&T Clark.

Commission on World Mission and Evangelism, 2012, 'Together towards Life: Mission and Evangelism in Changing Landscapes (TTL)', WCC, available at: https://www.oikoumene.org/en/resources/documents/commissions/mission-and-evangelism/together-towards-life-mission-and-evangelism-in-changing-landscapes (accessed 26.04.2019).

———, 2018, 'The Arusha Call to Discipleship', *International Review of Mission* 107.2, pp. 542–6.

Doornenbal, R. J. A., 2012, *Crossroads: An Exploration of the Emerging-Missional Conversation with a Special Focus on 'Missional Leadership' and its Challenges for Theological Educational*, Delft: Eburon.

Greig, P., 2003, *Red Moon Rising*, Lake Mary, FL: Survivor.

Healy, N. M., 2000, *Church, World and the Christian Life: Practical-Prophetic Ecclesiology*, Cambridge: Cambridge University Press.

Kim, K., 2012, *Joining in with the Spirit: Connecting World Church and Local Mission*, London: SCM Press.

Kwiyani, H., 2019, 'Can the West Really Be Converted?', *Missio Africanus Journal of African Missiology* 4.1, pp. 77–96.

Moynagh, M., 2012, *Church for Every Context: An Introduction to Theology and Practice*, London: SCM Press.

Pytches, D., 1985, *Come Holy Spirit: Learning to Minister in Power*, London: Hodder & Stoughton Religious.

———, 2002, *Living at the Edge: The Autobiography of David Pytches*, Bath: Arcadia.

Selvaratnam, C., 2022, *The Craft of Church Planting: Exploring the Lost Wisdom of Apprenticeship*, London: SCM Press.

Steven, J., 1999, 'Worship in the Spirit: a sociological analysis and theological appraisal of charismatic worship in the Church of England', PhD thesis, King's College London (University of London).

Valentine, J., 2023, *Jesus, the Church and the Mission of God: A Biblical Theology of Church Planting*, London: Inter-Varsity Press.

Ward, P., 2013, *Liquid Church*, London: Wipf & Stock.

Watkins, C., 2020, *Disclosing Church: Generating Ecclesiology Through Conversations in Practice*, London: Routledge.

6

'Don't offer help ... ask for it': Towards an Ethics of Church Planting in Conversation with Aquinas

BETH HONEY

Introduction

The experience of church planting and pioneering on the margins is often significant – significant in its impact on our theological reflection, in spiritual encounters and in the potential impact on the context. For many of us it is a lifelong vocation, and it has become a higher priority in recent decades within the denominational churches. It is a privilege to be in such situations and be part of the activity of church planting in these contexts and of the prayer, planning and process. We cannot underestimate the impact it has on us to be part of the transformation that we see in the lives of others, and our own.

But what if our own activity is not the most important aspect of church planting? What if the questions we ask of others and our willingness to receive help is the most important decision we make? Power dynamics will always be at play in the offering and acceptance of activity and help and the cultural and contextual exchanges in the processes and establishment of church plants and pioneering in the places and spaces considered in this chapter. We may have to be willing to lay down our sense of 'making a difference' and even 'seeing God at work'.

This chapter will consider these questions and dynamics not only from the standpoint of pragmatism, but from ethical reflection on the *good* that exists in areas on the margins that often experience suppressed potential. As we plant and pioneer and seek union with God in such places, what if we consider the beauty that can be noticed and even called forth as we choose to embrace vulnerability?

In the following pages, alongside painting some pictures of suppressed potential released in the context of urban outer estates, and those that are more rural and isolated, the resources of New Thomism will be explored as an ethical standpoint for the union with God that supports the development of integrated discipleship. The ethical foundations offered by Aquinas offer a significant standpoint for a *good* posture for planting and pioneering on the margins. This chapter will also challenge us to consider some of the obstacles to sustainable leadership of church planting within our current church structures. As we begin to lay down our understandings of our own roles in the narratives of the stories of church planting and pioneering, new stories can be told, and new voices heard.

Posture, power and potential

We are shaped by church planting as much as we shape the world by it – it is ultimately an act of God but the actions we take while planting are significant. The posture we take displays so much about the power dynamics that are in operation. We are agents of this, and we need to take responsibility for where we *have* been and *are* complicit with excluding others from the story of planting and from sharing the potential sustainability of communities and their leadership. For us to take these actions ethically we need to begin to be honest about what we may have prevented from growing and flourishing through our actions so that we notice what is *good*.

If we were to consider a more radical integrated approach to discipleship within church planting and refusing a *them and us* from the outset, sustainability may become more attainable, even as any church plant is seeded, nurtured and seen to grow in fruitfulness in front of all sets of eyes and not only those given or claiming the power and authority to make strategic decisions. In practical terms, this could mean simply involving all in the consultation process, from information gathering, team building to establishment of any project. In ecclesiological and theological terms, it asks us to consider who we engage as part of our 'teams' and our 'churches' from the outset of any new venture.

We have a significant history of church planting in the UK as denominational churches and free churches, but we also have theological resources and traditions to draw on in our reflection on our current practices that have perhaps not been brought to bear on that history. This chapter reflects on my experience of being involved in two significant periods of leading and being part of new worshipping communities in the UK context in very different places (outer estate in an urban context and now scattered and rural) – both marginal places or places of suppressed potential.

I have also spent time reflecting on the first of these contexts alongside modern interpretations of a Thomist ethic to consider how we can church plant and develop discipleship in an ethical way from our foundations and not only our practice. How do we find the good, the skills and abilities, the treasure that is here, and in ourselves and build on that? What is already here and to be noticed? This theological reflection is in conversation with a natural law ethic, or a eudemonistic understanding of seeking union with God in a place. How do we seek the beauty of God while dwelling in this place? How do we understand the integration of discipleship in these contexts? How do we embrace vulnerability and asking for help instead of our tendency to always offer it?

Many of our church planting models, approaches and postures ask us to make plans that may look more like meeting needs in a place of suppressed potential, however well-meaning and Christlike or even contextually appropriate that may seem. Who decides what is appropriate or has those conversations – and who is in the room? If we are honest, it is not often those who are already living in those areas in those conversations when decisions are being made. And if we continue to be honest, these conversations remain largely homogeneous and not very diverse. There remain significant barriers to the inclusion of diverse voices being represented in the places of influence and authority.

In areas on the margins, be they urban or rural, there will always be a power dynamic in church planting that tends towards the heroic. Olthuis has highlighted that to make self-sacrifice a value in itself is a paradigm of power, where the choice is self-seeking or becoming other-directed (Olthuis, 1997, p. 144). If we begin with everything that we will do, even if it is *our* listening, *our* responses, *our* invitations, then we miss both the actions of God, but also the good that is to be noticed and the treasure that is to be found. What if our posture is more about the integration of our own discipleship within church planting; integration between our actions and our own desire to know God, and between all of those involved in the process?

It is a significant commitment to refuse to use exclusive language or lean into a separation from the outset, but instead to speak about integration and to allow everyone intrigued to know any intentions in any project or possibility 'in' in order to make their own decisions about what they may or may not want to contribute to or be part of. I notice now how in my practice this has become second nature, and within any planning it is vital that it is an oral process and not only a written one – so important in areas on the margins. That opens the whole of the community to everyone and most importantly it allows it to be shaped by everyone, even as it is being shaped by God. Olthuis goes on to suggest that, if set in the context of seeking union with God, this can be the first move towards mutuality: 'The dance of mutuality is always drenched in vulnerability and risk because it is a non-coerced meeting of two free subjects in the wild spaces of love' (Olthuis, 1997, p. 147). The integration of discipleship thus begins with this 'mutual dance' among the agents of change, but continues with the integration of grace and nature, a fusion, in the understanding of the virtues that are so essential to an understanding of Aquinas.

Aquinas – grace infused

Discipleship is an anachronistic word in a discussion of Thomas Aquinas. However, the discussion of this area of how to live well, or how to live a virtuous life, falls in a Thomist integration of Aristotelian and Augustinian narratives of human goals. In new Thomism, Porter and those who have followed have found in Aquinas a way to see grace fulfilling nature. Porter also tentatively suggests that it is perhaps blinkered to not recognize the effect of the infusion of grace in those who display virtues without necessarily identifying themselves as part of the Christian church. She recognizes that this raises many theological questions, and yet by suggesting this, Porter recognizes the freedom of grace to work in nature (Porter, 2005, p. 398).

An integrated discipleship demands that we do not separate the story of God from the works of God, but by focusing on the person of God, the whole of our humanity in its strength and weakness is included in his grace. Faith is not a separate category, but for Aquinas there is always *more* on the way to *beatitudo*; God is there for us to discover and then encounter ever more intimately:

> So we start knowing our human goal only in general as something very good, and we desire it in the way we know it ... But in the end, when we know perfectly and distinctly, we discriminate our human goal from other goods; and then we desire the highest good as it really is, that is, as a spiritual good. (Aquinas, 1993, p. 320)

In any area of suppressed potential, it is not therefore enough to create an alternative community in the church that changes society through example and service: integrated discipleship seeks to embed actions and words within everyday life in a way that changes and develops culture, seeking to value what is already good and to order that which is disordered. Porter argues a Thomist ethic will seek out Christlike values that are seen in nature, thus allowing the moral conversation to be owned outside of the (potentially) narrow community of the church (Porter, 2005, p. 333).

In this way, as I have argued above, all are involved from the outset in both the organization and planning of any church planting activity, and therefore in any discipleship. In areas of suppressed potential, discipleship begins from the outset as conversations of faith and 'why' are often integrated, as there is often an inbuilt suspicion and questioning of authority and activity that has built up over years of being let down by institutions. It is therefore a positive and essential aspect of church planting to have honest and open conversations including all involved about what is happening and what needs doing and why it may be happening from the very first possibilities.

Faith is thus part of all aspects of life, it is not an additional element of any community, but can be integrated at all levels and with all members of that community. The integration found in Aquinas provides a framework for the fundamental connection of everyday life and faith and a mode of discipleship that remains open for grace to reach all areas of that context; it is not only a community of faith that is transformed, but the culture and society around it, and grace is to be found in both.

In practice, this may look like waiting to be invited to initiate something new rather than offering it and asking for help from everyone. For example, in two very new explorations I am currently involved in, two of the main encouragers, networkers and innovators would not identify themselves as having faith or connecting with church. Yet the conversations we have had around faith and why they are interested in connecting with community and others in making such plans with others are significant.

It goes beyond pragmatism to listen to and include these voices; it is an ethical imperative as their voices and skills and abilities are grace infused and remain open to the dynamic of the *beatitudo*. There is no controlling power of the group as we now begin to gather, but a flow of grace that connects and integrates nature and grace with a gentleness and acceptance. The power dynamic is disrupted through the mutuality and humility of shared skills and knowledge and the creativity of shared endeavour; and projects such as community gardening, art for well-being, youth art and faith studio space, the non-judgemental drop-in listening spaces, shared meals and community vans all offer spaces for people to make, create and share around tables and in safe spaces. They are spaces that need careful and skilled curating and nurturing and yet they are beautiful and healing spaces at their best.

This is the possibility of mutuality and integration – not allowing an unequal power dynamic, but to open the conversation to all, and instead allowing grace to infuse nature and nature to be fulfilled in grace. The narrative and story of such a community becomes its driving force and momentum and the specific plans and outcomes thus follow on from these, as holy habits follow on from the pursuit of union with God. As we open the activity and actions of any church plant or worshipping community and invite others into shared activities by asking for help, then the celebration of all that is good in that community is opened up. It is not about something good being brought into that community, but about *good* being uncovered together.

This is both essential to the characterization of the infusion of nature by grace in the thought of Aquinas, and in the way in which the integration of discipleship emerges in areas on the margins. Aquinas can therefore inspire a significant vocation to union with God and a posture for planting and pioneering.

How much more open would our church planting models be if we considered encounter with God for all the focus and delight of any processes, strategy, papers, funding application, recruitment, mission action planning, house or van purchases, prayer meeting. What if we asked: How does each of these decisions allow and enable an openness to the greatest number of people having the possibility of an integrated encounter with God? By doing so we embrace *beatitudo* as our aim for all – our flourishing and completeness, beyond any them and us.

Safer vulnerability as sustainability

When we choose to dwell in a place and to seek out the good, and to ask for help, we are embracing vulnerability. We are choosing people not problems, people not projects, people not only possibilities. It is *all* about people and about relationships, but not in a mechanistic or programmatic way. The focus is union with God in a way that is about delight in developing community in an integrated way. We are of course vulnerable to how this will turn out.

Creating and curating spaces, both literal and in every way, to offer and receive grace is essential in such places – to not only be the host but also the guest; to listen and to speak; to be both the weak and the strong. This is essential to the health, well-being and flourishing of everyone involved. To continue to seek to dwell in areas of suppressed potential is not easy, whether they are places you can choose to live in or places you cannot choose to move away from. Leadership needs sustaining to enable and establish church planting and pioneering, for the ongoing development of healthy communities.

I am currently living in Cumbria – between Penrith and Carlisle – and working for at least part of my week with a charity and social enterprise called Restore. I am helping to develop a community within the Penrith area to create space for exactly this. We host and enable others to host groups within a large charity shop in Penrith town and are now seeking to take this space out on the road to isolated villages. We are seeing many lonely and isolated people drop into this space and make it their own, and help lead the groups now, alongside a flourishing and bustling shop.

The groups have space for reflection in different ways and connect with a rhythm of relationship and chaplaincy, and after less than a year a growing number of people see this as their main point of contact with faith, creativity and spirituality. I believe this has come about in part due to this giving away of power and asking for help, and this continues to develop in depth and reach in this context.

The importance of where we dwell and where we choose to spend our time and our hours and days is vital. 'Dwell' is a significant word here and I am using it rather than the word 'live'. When we 'dwell' we intentionally invest in our relationships, in how we spend our time, our money, our investments. We can live somewhere, and still spend our free time, our money, our leisure time and all our attention elsewhere. We can even 'dwell' somewhere that we don't live by taking a significant interest in its well-being and care. But how we then treat the people around us in terms of respect is even more essential. If we never ask for help that respect may not be given. Asking for help is one of the ways that someone knows that we trust them. It then becomes a genuine relationship and not a client–service provider relationship.

Vulnerability is ironically our superpower and our way of not being the ones in the room or the place who have all the answers. Asking for help is not a gimmick but born out of actual need. It does take some risk to admit to our vulnerabilities and to do so in ways that are safe for ourselves and for others, but this reflects a community of integrated discipleship. It can be as simple as asking to borrow something we lack, and to be honest when we have something worth borrowing. Or in our case, when living on an outer estate in Derby, throwing a gardening rather than a garden party when we first inherited a large garden and being honest about our abilities to keep a large garden.

We can notice the good in ourselves and the need as we do in others. Then at least we will not be doing more damage and we may well be able to have some honest conversations about the place we are all at before the God who we all need. Suffice to say that recent conversations about the well-being and risk of those in the front line of ministry (and I am sure this applies to the front line of any profession or vocation that is constantly caring) puts any reflection about vulnerability and community back in the forefront of our thoughts, and indeed prayers. This can also extend to healthy and safe places of inclusion and signposting so that no one community is all things to all people – we need to connect communities too so that they keep boundaries and good spaces when people need them.

It is not by accident that in both contexts that I have had the privilege of seeing a community grow and develop there has been a focus on creativity, play and well-being. Many of those who are involved in those groups are rediscovering curiosity and a space to explore the goodness and creativity of God. Play is something that is an end in itself, and this will speak of a God who is in himself enough. For Aquinas, Kerr has noted 'there is a human desire for knowledge which is rooted in *wonder*' (Kerr, 2002, p. 78; emphasis original). This knowledge is in the context of a creature–Creator relationship that is often yet to be fully realized, and participated in, through encounter. There is also a specific vulnerability to play – and not needing to be active and to be serving, which is difficult and takes time for those more used to serving to embrace.

Church planting, especially on the margins, will only really take root if it is allowed to be vulnerable. This vulnerability means that we need to have our safeguards, in the fullest sense, in place so that we have space and freedom to be able to play and see the true integration of discipleship flourish. We have nothing to lose, and everything to gain as we relearn how to 'play' with God in a part of their world that the Church of England (and other churches) have largely become disconnected from. We are seeing some moves to redress this, and yet we are in such early stages still, and I fear that we have not yet grasped the true beautiful fruit that is growing in these parts of God's garden.

If we shy away from allowing this vulnerability, we will not truly see new leaders grown and develop from the margins. We will be satisfied with churches that have been imported and colonized from other parts of our country and cultures, and our cities, rural and coastal communities that the church has retreated from will remain places that are underrepresented in terms of the integrated discipleship this chapter is concerned with. We may be able to count some redistributed numbers who move into places to 'serve', but offering help, not receiving it, and not seeing significant sustainable communities grow.

We are also perhaps being tempted to ask the wrong questions of such contexts at times, rather than celebrating what is genuinely growing. I believe that we do need different models, and yet we need to be aware that those that tend towards the more powerful stances and postures will read and be understood in more marginal places in certain ways, and potentially not release the tentative leaders who could sustain young developing fruit. It is a significant and ongoing need to consider the development potential of these leaders and how to help them grow where they are being planted. If we ask the wrong questions, we may be tempted to uproot young plants or neglect them or undernourish them at key points in their growth.

There are experimental and growing programmes emerging among the training institutions, but what a thought that we could soon have church planting and leadership streams at NVQ levels accessible to those who are seeking qualifications at Levels 2–4, and apprenticeships. We need to think more radically and put things in the hands of those who are in estates and allow new shapes and forms to grow and not expect them to look the same. What if we truly ask for help from those who are seeing growth in other denominations, or in other parts of the world, or even those who work in other sectors who find they have engagement?

The 'why' of planting and pioneering – union with God

The beauty that can be noticed in places like Derwent and Penrith, and which a Thomist ethic points us to, is a significant integration. This is about integrated discipleship in terms of the integration of nature and grace, and the integration of human beings with their ultimate end in relationship with their Creator. This allows the healing and the transformation to good of what is already ordered to good. This apprehension of God is not a replacement of what has been known before, but instead a realization that God is already present in experience. Worship in this context is about noticing the presence of God. As Aquinas has described it:

> For a body is said to fill place inasmuch as it excludes the co-presence of another body; whereas by God being in a place, others are not thereby excluded from it; indeed, by the very fact that He gives being to the things that fill every place, He Himself fills every place. (*ST* I. 8.2)

Noticing the presence of God may therefore be about noticing the good in ourselves and in the context we live within, as well as directly noticing the actions of God through grace. It is a pleasure to have a rhythm in the shop in Penrith for all who visit, of all faiths and none. 'What are we grateful for today, and what do we still seek support with?' We notice the actions of grace in our lives and in the world around us, together. What we discovered through the context of Derwent Oak has always been and continues to be a place to stop and notice and reflect on what is by nature good, as well as a place to receive grace for healing, and the reordering of the internal and external life.

Being part of both communities and taking time to reflect with Aquinas has embedded in me the rhythm of asking for help and not only offering it. As I continue in the vocation of developing and enabling new things, I seek to keep this rhythm going. So some simple rules – no new projects or groups without new leaders or ideas from others. The hope in this way of working is to have a posture of church planting that it is light weight on any leaders as it always shared, values vulnerability as it is integrated in its discipleship from the start, creates grace-filled communities of welcome and is sustainable as the circle is wide from the start, and leadership is inclusive.

The ethical foundations within a Thomist understanding of grace-infused nature sees the transformation of culture and society through the integration of discipleship and the ultimate union with God. For this ethic of church planting to be rooted, perhaps we will need to trust those we have not yet trusted and ask for help from those we as yet have not asked, knowing that they too are on a path to union with God. But our own discipleship will be all the freer for it – our own *beatitudo* – what a relief – a necessary relief where we can ask for help and not only offer it.

References and further reading

Restore

www.restorecumbria.co.uk.

Derwent Oak

https://www.churchofengland.org/about/fresh-expressions/out-small-acorns-derwent-oak-grew.

Aquinas

Summa Theologica (ST), http://www.ccel.org/ccel/aquinas/summa.pdf.
Aquinas, 1993, Commentary on book 4 of Peter Lombard's *Sentences*, Oxford: Oxford University Press.
Distinction 49.1, in *Selected Philosophical Writings*, Oxford: Oxford University Press, 1993.

Secondary

Kerr, F., 2002, *After Aquinas: Versions of Thomism*, Oxford: Blackwell.
Olthuis, J. H., 1997, 'Face-to-Face: Ethical Asymmetry or the Symmetry of Mutuality?', in *Knowing Other-wise: Philosophy at the Threshold of Spirituality*, ed. J. H. Olthuis, New York: Fordham University Press.
Porter, J., 2005, *Nature as Reason: A Thomistic Theory of the Natural Law*, Cambridge: Eerdmans.

Reflections on Part One

One of the oft-repeated critiques of church planting is that it prioritizes human innovation and strategy over and above the work of God. For instance, in his discussion of the obsession with 'innovation' in the North American Church, Andrew Root depicts the declining church as grasping for the practices of business in order to resuscitate a dying human institution. Contrastingly, Root writes, 'Our church forefathers and mothers may have done some innovative things, but they were never seeking innovation itself' (Root, 2022, p. 64). In fact, Root argues, if we look to the history of the Western Church, reference to 'innovation ... is almost always derogatory. Only in our contemporary moment has innovation become an overwhelmingly positive term' (Root, 2022, p. 20). The problem is not the presence of things that are new, for Root, but that the pursuit of innovation as the end of the church is a gross distortion of what the church is. Similarly, in her reflections on church planting in the Church of England, Alison Milbank maintains that we appear to have forgotten that the church is not a human institution, but rather a 'divine society', a 'mystical union ... of all those who have, are or will be joined to Christ in baptism' (Milbank, 2023, p. 4). Participating in the mystical life of Christ is not merely a metaphor to explain something important about the church's identity; it 'is the language of actual metaphysical incorporation' (2023, p. 5), Milbank thinks.

Notably, the essays in the first part of the book take as a given the worries that Milbank, Root and others articulate, that the work of the church must be grounded in the mission of God in the world. This much is assumed. Where substantial disagreement is found is how practitioners are supposed to engage in and with the mission of God. What ought to take priority? A proper grappling with church polity and institution, as Collinson supposes in his engagement with Milbank's work? The collaborative and joint agency of strategy, planning or theodrama, as Miller and Powley have claimed? A better posture (Honey)? Or a more robust engagement with spirituality, as in Cockayne's and Butler's arguments? To point out the need for the priority of divine agency is relatively straightforward. But to know where and how to prioritize this is where things get more complex.

Perhaps the answer lies in some combination of these responses – a proper wrestling with the importance of *missio Dei* for the context of leading new churches must surely lead to changes in our posture, our spirituality, our engagement with strategy vision, and wider church polity. The Anglican *via media* might tempt us to answer: 'Yes and Amen!' to all of the conclusions drawn by our contributors to these chapters. But to do so would be to ignore the fault lines underlying the nuanced positions articulated in these chapters.

For instance: What is the role of divine and human agency in the ministry of the church? Is human agency secondary and merely participative, derivative of acts of divine agency? Or are human agents empowered to collaborate with God through church structures and communities? These lead to some more practical, concrete questions: Is our human capacity to discern the work of God bound up with the institutional church? Or can God's mission be discerned locally, congregationally, perhaps even individually? These are theological questions the church has disagreed upon and, indeed, have been issues that have led to major schism and division.

Moreover, these theological questions have profound importance for the ministry of planting new churches. They raise questions about who or what can authorize the starting of new churches, the locations of these churches and the direction these churches can take. Our answers to these questions will also impact on the everyday decisions of church planting: Who can preach and preside in this context? Which liturgies can be used? Who can be designated a 'leader'? Where does money come from and how can it be spent? We cannot sensibly answer these practical questions without first attending to the theological questions of authority, discernment and ecclesiology raised in these chapters. The danger of missing the fact that these are fundamental theological differences is that we continue in disagreement only at the level of praxis and become ever more polarized and siloed as a result. At the very least, recognizing the depth of our disagreements helps us to understand one another better, giving space for one another's responses and – perhaps – finding if not so much common ground, then some ways of sharing space in our differences.

In this way, although a volume such as this is not well placed to resolve age-old theological disagreements on the authority of the church, or the means of God's relationship to human agency, we do believe that in noting fault lines, it might help us become more attentive to their implications. We also hope this work might be generative of further research that continues to develop these important questions, with rigour and attention to the significance of theology for the work of starting new churches.

References

Milbank, A., 2023, *The Once and Future Parish*, London: SCM Press.
Root, A., 2022, *The Church After Innovation: Questioning Our Obsession with Work, Creativity, and Entrepreneurship*, Westmont, IL: Baker Academic.

PART TWO

Praxis: Theological Method for New Churches

7

Leveraging Indigenous Theologies for Church Growth in Light of the Emergence of World Christianity

PAUL AYOKUNLE

Introduction

The call for recognizing indigenous theologies could not be more appropriate and urgent than today, with Christianity continuously booming among diverse non-Western cultures and regions. Indeed, over the last hundred years, the centre of gravity of Christianity has shifted from the global North (North America, Europe, Australia, Japan and New Zealand) to the global South (the rest of the world, especially Africa, Asia and Latin America), with unprecedented growth in the latter (see Kwiyani, 2014). For instance, in 1900 Africa, there were only nine million Christians while 300 million were present in Europe (Zurlo, Johnson and Crossing, 2021). By 2021, over 600 million Christians were now in Africa and a much lower figure of about 500 million in Europe – a difference in excess of 100 million. This sort of watershed in the history of World Christianity, Ola notes, is only comparable to the Protestant Reformation of about 500 years ago (Ola, 2019). It is only fair for the voices of those who now demographically represent the Christian faith to receive as much attention and affirmation in theological circles and church growth endeavours as their Western counterparts.

To solidify its argument for the validation of indigenous theologies for church growth, this chapter presents the *omolúàbí*-shaped ecclesiology (OSE),[1] an African approach to church showcasing the riches and potential benefits of grassroots theologies for church growth if it is to fly. The OSE builds upon the norm-setting dimension of personhood among the Yoruba people of south-western Nigeria (Akintoye, 2014). The Yoruba concept comes to the fore to suitably represent an African indigenous theology in the chapter for at least two reasons. First, I am of Yoruba ethnicity, so I am considerably familiar with key concepts within the culture. Second, *omolúàbí* as a moral aspect of personhood in Yoruba cosmology perfectly dovetails with the common theme of *ubuntu* in discussions of African identity (Nussbaum, 2003; Antwi, 1996; Shutte, 1993). One may even conceive of the *omolúàbí* framework as an elaborate Yoruba rendition of *ubuntu* social ethics and ideology because of their non-dismissible similarities.

The need for indigenous theologies in church planting and growth

I understand that even though non-Western regions now host most of the world's Christians, intellectual, economic and political dominance remain in the West (Phiri, 2022). Yet to continue to theologize and do missions from Western paradigms with little or no recognition of other voices is unhelpful for the body of Christ and church growth in particular, for at least two reasons. First, the practice sustains the empire mission model that sees church growth and planting proceed from an elevated position of power (in terms of culture, wealth, nationality, literature or other positional advantages), consciously or unconsciously. Since the hotbed of Christianity has often been the centre of empires (beginning with the Jewish dominance and then the Roman, British and American empires), it has been the case that mission agents advance to other cultures with the power and advantages of the empire, including dominant theological standpoints and church planting models (Phiri, 2022). They often fail to see God already at work among the unprivileged recipients to lead them to partner with him however he wants. Consequently, they unconsciously establish churches that must theologize and do church like them to be authentic – a result of the subtle pride that comes with power (1 Tim. 6.17).

In the end, the new plants struggle to grow since they are unfamiliar with the foreign concepts about God and the church from the privileged mission agents. Indeed, as the Irish missionary to the Gold Coast (present-day Ghana) James McKeown (1900–89), who planted the Church of Pentecost in Ghana, observes: 'It would be difficult to grow an English oak in Ghana. A local species, at home in its culture, should grow, reproduce and spread; a church with foreign roots was more likely to struggle' (Christine, 1989). However, where there is room for indigenous theologies to emerge, the people will be more inclined to better comprehend the faith they have received and find it easier to proselytize. Plus it is in every culture contributing their own theological reflections that the church can truly mature into the full stature of Christ (Eph. 4.13) since God has incarnated his truth in different cultures that it both affirms and seeks to transform.

Second, retaining Western theological hegemony, for instance, without much appreciation of perspectives from the non-Western worlds, despite the explosion of the church in such regions, slows down the realization of God's multi-ethnic agenda[2] for his church, as Revelation 7.9 suggests.[3] It is in every culture listening to one another as they theologize without the sense of a teacher–student relationship from any, that the church would dwell together more honestly in unity. This is the way new plants in indigenous communities can feel included in the multi-ethnic body of Christ as they become members. Of course, the idea of inclusion is inherent in the concept of Catholicity, one of the four basic marks of the church.[4] The implication of inclusion, and thus multi-ethnicity, is that supremacy mindsets or other acts of marginalization would reduce in the church, whether along racial lines, social class or any other caste. The church, despite its diversity in composition, would then be closer to attaining 'the unity of the faith and of the knowledge of the Son of God, to maturity, to the measure of the full stature of Christ' (Eph. 4.13). It is in the atmosphere of unity that church growth is more prone to happen. Indeed, as the Psalmist wonders, 'How very good and pleasant it is when kindred [regardless of their differences] live together in unity!' (Ps. 133.1). In this state of oneness, as he concludes in the third verse, 'the LORD ordained his blessing.'

Third, where indigenous theologies also find a place in church planting and growth endeavours as with the prevailing voice of Western theologies, the church would be able to show the increasingly multi-ethnic societies of the world how diversity can be advantageous rather than problematic. This is the church being 'the light of the world' indeed (Matt. 5.14). Yes, the church can be the institution governments observe to learn how to handle their multi-ethnic societies to harness the blessing of racial and cultural diversity. However, if new church plants, for instance, are already being established to conform to *foreign* theologies in their contexts, rather than being allowed to evolve with their own ways of conceptualizing God, I wonder how the churches can then show the world profitable ways of engaging with diversity. Therefore, one cannot possibly overemphasize the advantages of embracing indigenous theologies in our church planting and growth efforts.

Omolúàbí-shaped ecclesiology

In this section, I present the *omolúàbí*-shaped ecclesiology.[5] I briefly discuss the African ecclesiology in relation to church growth to reveal some of the potential gems of indigenous theologies when they find a louder voice and receive a wider embrace.

The OSE derives from the African (Yoruba) concept of *omolúàbí* to formulate a theology of the church for growth. This sort of productive dialogue between the Yoruba moral dimension of personhood and Christianity is not forceful because the 'African moral system has a religious foundation' (Mbiti, 1969). In fact, *omolúàbí* values broadly overlap the attributes constituting the 'fruit of the Spirit' in Galatians 5.22–23.[6] The *omolúàbí* principles also form a cultural portrayer of 2 Peter 1.5–7, which lists some necessary additives to the lives of believers in Christ.[7] As a preliminary to understanding the OSE, in the following conversation I summarize the *omolúàbí* construct and its key principles.

The omolúàbí *concept*

Many African cultures' moral sense of identity implies that an individual is not considered a person by just being human, but by necessarily acting in ethically acceptable manners and in tandem with social responsibilities within society (Ikuenobe, 2016). The *omolúàbí* concept is a highly valued philosophical and cultural construct concerned with the moral aspect of identity among the Yoruba (Olanipekun, 2017). The social scientists Grace Akanbi and Alice Jekayinfa rightly submit that 'the end of Yoruba traditional education is to make every individual "Omoluabi"' (Akanbi and Jekayinfa, 2016, pp. 13–19; see also Akinyemi, 2015). Philosophically and culturally, *omolúàbí* represents someone who possesses good virtues. The concept provides a yardstick for determining the morality or immorality of any act in society (Adebowale, 2019). To refer to someone as *omolúàbí* is to recognize and affirm that such a person is well cultured, mannered, honourable and respectful – a well-behaved person (Osoba, 2014). An *omolúàbí* embodies all virtues that facilitate the sound expression of wisdom, knowledge and skills for his or her betterment of society by necessity (Adebowale, 2019). The following virtues are foundational for *omolúàbí*, among other desirable qualities.

Relational savvy

Omolúàbí showcases a sound understanding of the workings of relationships so that they are beneficial to everyone involved (Adeniji-Neill, 2011). Maintaining harmony in all relationships, whether at work, school or home, is essential to an *omolúàbí* in attaining individuality, identity or self-actualization (Payne, 1992). Therefore, an *omolúàbí* operates by two guiding principles in social relationships: *àjobí*, meaning blood relations, and *àjogbé*, which translates as co-residence (Akinwowo, 1983). To an *omolúàbí*, everyone relates together from the viewpoint of 'shared humanity'. Harmony in social relationships also extends to the spirit world since African cosmological understanding accommodates the interaction of the spirit world and the physical world (Nel, 2019). Hence, *omolúàbí*s maintain equilibrium in their relationship with the spirit world.

Inú rere

The second fundamental virtue of *omolúàbí* is *inú rere* (goodwill, having a clean and good mind towards others), which is both a moral and mental quality (Abimbola, 1975). *Inú rere* pushes *omolúàbí* to give easily to the community in deeds and actions (Adeniji-Neill, 2011). It readily finds expression in the principle of hospitality, which creates 'the desire for, a welcome without reserve and without calculation, an exposure without limit to whoever arrives' (Derrida, 2005). To emphasize the importance of *inú rere* evident in hospitality and benevolence, the affirmation of personhood among the Yorubas does not occur without considering deeds linking individuals with their families, friends, community and others (Adeniji-Neill, 2011). In essence, *inú rere* is responsible for the love, care, kindness and concern that an *omolúàbí* shows towards other people instead of overly focusing on himself or herself.

Cultural integration

Omolúàbí is culturally aware and integrated (Adeniji-Neill, 2011). The uncultured is an *omo lásán* or *omokómo*, suggesting a worthless child. *Omokómo* is socially unincorporated, culturally deviant, or a misfit in the community or set-up (Oyeneye and Shoremi, 1997). Chief among the implications of being cultured is to have *iteríba* (respect) (Abimbola, 1975). An *omolúàbí* has self-respect (including recognition and setting boundaries) and honour for others, including parents, elders, other authority figures, peers and even younger ones (Adeniji-Neill, 2011). *Ìwàpèlé* or *iwàtútù* (gentleness or gentle character) also comes to the fore as a vital element of being cultured. *Ìwàpèlé* expresses itself in 'being mindful of the individuality of others, treating others gently and being tolerant and accommodating of the peculiarity of the existence of others' (Dada, n.d.). An *omolúàbí*, who has high regard for culture, demonstrates *ìwàpèlé* in communications, business, musical constructions, religious actions and other aspects of life (Bewaji, 2004).

Ọ̀rọ̀ síso

The spoken word (*ọ̀rọ̀ síso*) is so significant among the Yorubas that it forms another key characteristic of *omolúàbí* (see Abiodun, 1987; Opefeyitimi, 2016; Abimbola, 1975). *Ọ̀rọ̀*, meaning 'words', can convey disrespect or hurt to others when used frivolously or unguardedly. *Omolúàbí* has this understanding and therefore uses *ọ̀rọ̀* with dexterity. It is admirable for *omolúàbí* to demonstrate intelligent use of *ọ̀rọ̀* by engaging Yoruba proverbs (*òwe*) in communication. Indeed, without *òwe*, 'speech flounders and falls short of its mark, whereas aided by them, communication is fleet and unerring' (Owomoyela, 2005). An *omolúàbí* is that cultured person who can 'optimise the efficaciousness of speech', leveraging proverbs amid other communication tools and consequently demonstrating cultural appreciation and awareness.

Ìwà

The fifth hallmark of *omolúàbí* is *ìwà* (character). Even in *omolúàbí*'s etymology, *ìwà* is central (Abimbola, 1975). *Ìwà* can either make one more valuable when exhibiting *ìwà rere* (good character/moral goodness) or less desirable when demonstrating *ìwà buburu* or *ìwà ibaja* (bad/terrible character). Good character may not be the sole determinant of personhood, but it certainly attracts a lot of admiration for the Yorubas. In fact, they often link good character and *ewà* (beauty). For them, moral goodness acts as the 'normative necessary condition for a person to be truly and strictly considered beautiful, and to be a person in the robust sense' (Ikuenobe, 2016, p. 7). Bad character, however, receives condemnation and reduces an individual's personhood or humanness to the level of 'ordinary things' such that one attracts the tag *èniyàn lásán* (worthless fellow) or *eranko* (animal) (Fayemi, 2009, p. 2). As the African philosopher Ademola Fayemi concludes, *ìwà* is the 'fulcrum of human personality'.

Isé and akínkanjú

Another set of connected central qualities of *omolúàbí* is *isé* (hard work) and *akínkanjú* (courage/bravery) (Adeniji-Neill, 2011). *Omolúàbí* puts a lot of care and effort into work because, without a strong work ethic and diligence, a person attracts the tag of *òle* (lazy/indolent person), making other *omolúàbí* qualities meaningless (Dada, n.d.). Indeed, Yorubas hold that *isé l'ogun ìsé, eni ti ko sisé yio jale*. This popular saying literally translates as 'Hard work is the panacea for poverty; whoever does not work hard will become a thief or robber.' *Isé* and *akínkanjú* virtues ensure that an *omolúàbí* courageously navigates tough times and develops *ìfaradà* (fortitude) to endure and rebound when knocked down (Oyebade and Azenabor, 2018). Rightly so: life is not a bed of roses and can be unpredictable. As such, without the extra virtue of *akínkanjú* to support *isé*, it may be difficult to remain hardworking or exhibit other core qualities of *omolúàbí*. *Akínkanjú* is opposed to 'escapism, self-condemnation, abandonment and indulgence in vices to circumvent life obstacles' (Oyebade and Azenabor, 2018).

Òtító

Òtító (truth), integrity and honesty are a compendium of related, basic characteristics of *omolúàbí* (Abimbola, 1975). Integrity conveys a sense of wholeness or completeness from the Latin word, *integras* (Montefiore and Vines, 1999). Likewise, *omolúàbí* exhibits coherence and consistency in principles, values, thoughts, speech and actions. *Omolúàbí* is honest, straightforward, incorruptible, truthful and accountable (Dobel, 2016). Thus, he or she becomes 'a good and dependable person who stands above board at all times' (Akanbi and Jekayinfa, 2016). *Omolúàbí*'s integrity and *òtító* reflect in his or her private and public endeavours that such an individual does not indulge in or support fraudulent activities (Oyerinde, 1991). Truth and integrity are central to being an *omolúàbí* because, ultimately, they are the 'stuff of moral courage and even heroism' (Brenkert, 2004).

What *omolúàbí*-shaped ecclesiology would look like

I believe that the church can enhance its growth through the interaction between *omolúàbí* principles and ecclesiology. The resultant indigenous ecclesiology would have the following expression.

Recognition of and harmony with the Spirit

Perhaps OSE's spiritual emphasis is its most crucial element. Just as an *omolúàbí* is conscious of the participation of the spiritual world in the physical, engaging OSE would imply that the church recognizes the influence and necessity of the Holy Spirit in its life. The church cannot be 'unidimensional' in its orientation, as with the Western interpretation of life events, but multifaceted, acknowledging spiritual reality alongside the physical (Ayokunle, 2021). African Pentecostals are confident that church growth is spiritual and passionately demonstrate this belief in the supernatural, in alignment with the African world view. Thus, it should not be strange that Pentecostalism has taken over the face of Christianity in Africa (Kwiyani, 2014). The global church can learn from *omolúàbí*'s multidimensional world view. In practical terms, OSE's supernatural emphasis would imply that the church believes, permits and projects the Bible teachings on divine healing, angels, visions, miracles, prophecies, dream interpretation and other spiritual possibilities through the Holy Spirit's power. Then the church can truly begin to 'live by the Spirit, [and] ... be guided by the Spirit' (Gal. 5.25).

Also, OSE would insist that the church maintain peace and fellowship with the Holy Spirit. This 'communion of the Holy Spirit' (2 Cor. 13.13) will more than likely require a vibrant prayer life since prayer is a vital channel to 'truly connect with God [or His Spirit]' (Omartian, 2009). Unity with the Holy Spirit will also see a church mature in the fruit of the Spirit and grieve him less every day (Eph. 4.30). Such a church will experience more productivity as it deploys various growth strategies, for the Holy Spirit remains the enabler of biblical church planting and growth principles (Gibbs, 1986).

Relational awareness

OSE expects that the church operates with a rich knowledge of relationship dynamics. Being the church in this way would undoubtedly help its social growth. Living by the *omolúàbí* ethos of *ìwàpèlé* and *ìteríba* would translate to congregants respecting themselves regardless of age, social status, race or other classifications. By implication, the youths would find it more convenient to contribute to the church's development without being disdained or silenced. The adults would also enjoy the benefits of learning from the younger generation besides the opportunity to pass down their much-needed wisdom in an atmosphere of respect for individuality. Consequently, the cross-pollination of ideas and learning would increase, culminating in church growth.

Relationship dynamics awareness would also mitigate conflicts and misunderstandings in the church, as more forbearance would characterize social interactions. The other's attitudes, behaviour and actions would filter through the consciousness that pluralistic cultures comprise the church. As such, the tendency for offences would reduce. Leaders and members would engage more effectively without distrust, bitterness, anger, hypocrisy, pride or prejudice as they respect relationship etiquette and boundaries and operate in love with one another. Congregants, regardless of their divide, would also be able to serve more lovingly together as they apply the social principles of *àjobí* and *àjogbé*. Indeed, highhandedness would find faint expression in the church that models *àjobí* and *àjogbé*. As with the early church, everyone would live as comrades and a true family. Luke describes the brotherly love of the early church thus: 'There was not a needy person among them, for as many as owned lands or houses sold them and brought the proceeds of what was sold. They laid it at the apostles' feet, and it was distributed to each as any had need' (Acts 4.34–35).

Stress on social ministry

OSE would mean that the church gets involved socially in the life of its members and community. It would not measure its growth by spiritual contributions only. Rather, it would equally be aware of and deliberately seek to address its members' needs and social justice. This imperative for the church's social engagement derives from *omolúàbí*'s virtues of hospitality and benevolence – both offshoots of *inú rere*. The leaders of a socially involved church will be cautious to prevent their professional backgrounds' formality from impeding the church's social commitments. Indeed, there is the tendency for ministers with professional experiences to style their congregations as business environments, preferring their highly skilled membership to which they focus most of their efforts, including social ministry.

OSE is opposed to such bias and segregation, which prevents social interaction and opportunities for congregants to meet one another's material and immaterial needs. Instead, the *omolúàbí*'s goodwill implicit in OSE would ensure that church leaders put away preferences in administering the church and its resources. By implication, the body of Christ would be open to all and show concern and care, even to the marginalized. As in Luke 4.18, the poor, prisoners, blind, oppressed and other overlooked groups in society will find aid through the church's social services. As the church becomes more intentional in its social engagement, especially beyond its congregants to strangers, it would begin to live up to its expectation as 'the light of the world' (Matt. 5.14) instead of a shining light to itself. The acts of love would open up possibilities for the recipients to join the church, increasing its numerical strength.

Excellent leadership

OSE also demands effective leadership, that pastors keep evolving through *isé* (hard work) and *akínkanjú* (courage) to remain relevant in a fast-developing and changing world. More specifically, church leaders may need to add to their ministerial training, both formally and informally. David not only led the Israelites by integrity or personal charm but also with skills (Ps. 78.72). The Covid-19 pandemic has exposed the need to acquire some technological expertise, an unusual field for many church leaders. Learning an unfamiliar skill would likely require *iteríba* (humility and respect) from the pastors since the facilitators may be young professionals or pew members. Leaders must similarly extend training or discipleship to their congregations. Only after investing in training their church members would pastors be ethically correct to expect improved lifestyles, patterned after Christ, from them. A methodical discipleship process is helpful in this regard. The systematic training would be in addition to ministers' exemplary lifestyles modelling Christ's life to their congregations, just as trainers do with their trainees.

OSE would also ensure that through excellent leadership, delivered on the platform of *isé*, leaders apply themselves to the thorough and consistent study of the Scriptures and other helpful materials for their ministries. Doing the above would align with Paul's advice to Timothy to 'Study to shew thyself approved unto God, a workman that needeth not to be ashamed, rightly dividing the word of truth' (2 Tim. 2.15, KJV). Demonstrating *akínkanjú* would also imply pastors courageously speaking out when they feel helpless, lonely, depressed or discouraged. Asking for help would no longer look like a sin or abomination. Of course, when ministers have support systems, they will be fresh. The church will enjoy them at their best and, thus, also enjoy better nourishment and growth.

Holistic salvation

OSE seeks a comprehensive or holistic salvation experience. Just as *omolúàbí* provides a system for validating personhood from a moral viewpoint in Yoruba culture, Christian identity would only be more meaningful, recognized and whole with a complementary ethical life. Titus 3.8 affirms the same truth that Christians must not be lacking in moral goodness or 'good works'.[8] While the advocacy here is not for perfectionism, it would only be awkward for anyone to claim membership in the church and yet be morally deficient. James re-echoes it this way: 'But someone will say, "You have faith and I have works." Show me your faith without works, and I by my works will show you my faith' (James 2.18).

To church leaders, holistic salvation would, for instance, translate to a balance in presenting God's ability and desire to provide for his people as Jehovah Jireh (Gen. 22.14) so that such negative tags as the prosperity gospel would become extinct (see Hunt, 2000; Heuser, 2015; Gbote and Kgatla, 2014). Indeed, God has pleasure in the prosperity of his servant (or people) (see Ps. 35.27). Humanity's excesses in revealing this truth should not result in the total rejection of God's power and eagerness to supply all needs (including material). Moreover, this dimension of God cannot but be particularly emphasized in regions without adequate social amenities or other physical needs. Africans do not even consider a religion (or God) meaningful that does not meet their multifaceted needs besides the salvation of their souls (Ayegboyin and Ishola, 2013). In essence, Jesus' moderate lifestyle would be the yardstick for presenting God's willingness to prosper his people. Indeed, Jesus is the pinnacle of *omolúàbí* and 'the pioneer and perfecter of our faith' (Heb. 12.2).

Holistic salvation also concerns spoken words. OSE suggests that church leaders demonstrate tact in using words for their communications and sermon delivery to be more positive and less offensive. The dexterity with words stems from *omolúàbí*'s grasp of *òrò*. Paul also understands the importance of sound speech and lists it among the crucial qualities young men must exhibit in Titus 2.6–8. Indeed, pastors must never forget that words are delicate; they must always proceed with discretion to achieve their intended purposes and minimize offences (Rapp, 2002). In all, where holistic salvation marks a congregation, the church would experience growth. The necessity of complementary moral life to spiritual experience for affirming Christian identity will result in more spiritually mature Christians. These congregants would make the church attractive to outsiders through their moral goodness, thus leading to a numerical increase for the church.

Conclusion

The recognition and affirmation of indigenous theologies are, indeed, important and helpful for *missio Dei* (the mission of God). In the same way that 'God so loved *the world* that he gave his only Son' (John 3.16), he has revealed himself within different cultures and people. No culture is more loved or privileged over others for exclusive access to God's wisdom. Neither is any group of people the sole curator or steward of God's revelations. The variety in creation and its complementary design, attest to God's love for diversity and the wholeness that comes from interdependencies. No matter how seemingly trivial or massive the insight is, the church must begin to acknowledge sound theological reflections from all cultures. Validating some and looking down on others or attempting to make them conform to the dominant voices reduces the chances of the church to know God more wholesomely and deeply, and to grow. Indeed, the OSE hints at how resourceful indigenous cultures can be in theologizing and for church growth, if and when they find wings to fly. Indigenous theologies are necessities for advancing God's mission as the church continues to seek ways to contextualize the Christian faith so that it may be more productive to its recipients. The emancipation of indigenous theologies is inevitable and urgent.

Notes

1 While I am aware of the more comprehensive meaning it has in theological discourse, I have applied the term 'ecclesiology' loosely in this chapter to refer to the lifestyle of the church, a way of doing or being church. I have taken this approach to avoid any theological argument that may be associated with the concept and retain the focus of the chapter. Also, I developed the *omolúàbí*-shaped ecclesiology as part of my doctoral research at Liverpool Hope University as a means for promoting church growth and realizing multi-ethnic congregations.

2 In a broad sense, a multi-ethnic church connotes a gathering of believers in Christ, where members come from various backgrounds without one culture asserting itself over others.

3 'After this I looked, and there was a great multitude that no one could count, from every nation, from all tribes and peoples and languages, standing before the throne and before the Lamb, robed in white, with palm branches in their hands' (Rev. 7.9).

4 See Archbishops' Council, 2004. Catholicity refers to 'the universal scope of the church as a society instituted by God in which all sorts and conditions of humanity, all races, nations and cultures, can find a welcome and home'. See more in Avis, 2000.

5 Again, I developed the *omolúàbí*-shaped ecclesiology as part of my doctoral

research at Liverpool Hope University as a means for promoting church growth and realizing multi-ethnic congregations.

6 The qualities are 'love, joy, peace, patience, kindness, generosity, faithfulness, gentleness, and self-control'.

7 Here Peter notes: 'For this very reason, you must make every effort to support your faith with goodness, and goodness with knowledge, and knowledge with self-control, and self-control with endurance, and endurance with godliness, and godliness with mutual affection, and mutual affection with love' (2 Pet. 1.5–7).

8 'I desire that you insist on these things, so that those who have come to believe in God may be careful to devote themselves to good works; these things are excellent and profitable to everyone' (Titus 3.8).

References

Abimbola, W., 1975, 'Iwapele: The Concept of Good Character in Ifa Literary Corpus', in W. Abimbola (ed.), *Yoruba Oral Tradition: Poetry in Music Dance and Drama*, Ibadan: University of Ibadan Press.

Abiodun, R., 1987, 'Verbal and Visual Metaphors: Mythical Allusions in Yoruba Ritualistic Art of Orí', *Word & Image* 3.3, pp. 252–70.

Adebowale, B. A., 2019, 'Aristotle's Human Virtue and Yorùbá Worldview of Ọmọlúàbí: An Ethical-Cultural Interpretation', available at https://www.researchgate.net/publication/331382642_omoluabi/link/5c76a4e3a6fdcc4715a11dd3/download (accessed 14.10.2020).

Adeniji-Neill, D., 2011, 'Omoluabi: The Way of Human Being: An African Philosophy's Impact on Nigerian Voluntary Immigrants' Educational and Other Life Aspirations', *Africa Migration* 5, https://africamigration.com/issue/dec2011/Omoluabi-Dolapo-Addeniji-Neill.pdf (accessed 08.08.2024).

Akanbi, G. O. and A. A. Jekayinfa, 2016, 'Reviving the African Culture of "Omoluabi" in the Yoruba Race as a Means of Adding Value to Education in Nigeria', *International Journal of Modern Education Research* 3.3, pp. 13–19.

Akintoye, A. S., 2014, *A History of the Yoruba People*, Dakar: Amalion Publishing.

Akinwowo, A., 1983, *Ajobi and Ajogbe: Variations on the Theme of Sociation*, Ile-Ife: University of Ife Press.

Akinyemi, A., 2015, *Orature and Yoruba Riddles*, New York: Palgrave Macmillan.

Antwi, D. J., 1996, 'Koinonia in African Culture: Community, Communality and African Self-Identity', *Trinity Journal of Church and Theology* 6.2.

Archbishops' Council, 2004, *Mission-shaped Church: Church Planting and Fresh Expressions of Church in a Changing Context*, London: Church House Publishing.

Avis, P., 2000, *The Anglican Understanding of the Church: An Introduction*, London: SPCK.

Ayegboyin, D. and A. S. Ishola, 2013, *African Indigenous Churches: An Historical Perspective*, Bukuru, Nigeria, African Christian Textbooks.

Ayokunle, S. O. A., 2021, *Communities of Faith in Diaspora: Elements and Liturgy of Worship*, Ibadan: Baptist Press.

Bewaji, J. A., 2004, *Beauty and Culture: Perspectives in Black Aesthetics*, Ibadan: Spectrum Books.

Brenkert, G. (ed.), 2004, *Corporate Integrity and Accountability*, Thousand Oaks, CA: Sage.

Christine, L., 1989, *A Giant in Ghana: 3,000 Churches in 50 Years – The Story of James McKeown and the Church of Pentecost*, Chichester: New Wine Press.

Dada, S. O., 'Aristotle and the Ọmọlúwàbí Ethos: Ethical Implications for Public Morality in Nigeria', Gainsville, FL: University of Florida Center for African Studies, available at https://news.clas.ufl.edu/aristotle-and-the-omoluwabi-ethos-ethical-implications-for-public-morality-in-nigeria/ (accessed 08.08.2024).

Derrida, J., 2005, 'The Principle of Hospitality', *Parallax* 11.1, pp. 6–9.

Dobel, J. P., 2016, 'Integrity in the Public Service', *Public Administration Review* 50.3, pp. 354–66.

Fayemi, A. K., 2009, 'Human Personality and the Yoruba Worldview: An Ethico-Sociological Interpretation', *Journal of Pan African Studies* 2.9.

Gbote, E. Z. M. and S. T. Kgatla, 2014, 'Prosperity Gospel: A Missiological Assessment', *HTS Teologiese Studies/ Theological Studies* 70.1.

Gibbs, E., 1986, 'The Power Behind the Principles', in C. P. Wagner (ed.), *Church Growth: State of the Art*, Carol Stream, IL: Tyndale House Publishers.

Heuser, A., 2015, 'Religio-Scapes of the Prosperity Gospel: An Introduction', in A. Heuser (ed.), *Pastures of Plenty: Tracing Religio-Scapes of the Prosperity Gospel in Africa and Beyond*, Frankfurt: Peter Lang.

Hunt, S., 2000, '"Winning Ways": Globalisation and the Impact of the Health and Wealth Gospel', *Journal of Contemporary Religion* 15.3, pp. 331–47.

Ikuenobe, P., 2016, 'Good and Beautiful: A Moral-Aesthetic View of Personhood in African Communal Traditions', *Essays in Philosophy* 17.1.

Kwiyani, H. C., 2014, *Sent Forth: African Missionary Work in the West*, Maryknoll, NY: Orbis Books.

Mbiti, John S., 1969, *African Religions and Philosophy*, Oxford: Heinemann Educational Books.

Montefiore, A. and D. Vines (eds), 1999, *Integrity in the Public and Private Domains*, London: Routledge.

Nel, M., 2019, 'The African Background of Pentecostal Theology: A Critical Perspective', *In Die Skriflig/In Luce Verbi* 53.4, pp. 1–18.

Nussbaum, B., 2003, 'African Culture and Ubuntu Reflections of a South African in America', *World Business Academy: Perspectives* 17.1, pp. 1–12.

Ola, J., 2019, 'Strangers' Meat is the Greatest: African Christianity in Europe', available at https://www.academia.edu/41993424/_Strangers_meat_is_the_greatest_treat_African_Christianity_in_Europe (accessed 08.08.2024).

Olanipekun, O. V., 2017, 'Omoluabi: Re-thinking the Concept of Virtue in Yoruba Culture and Moral System', *Africology: The Journal of Pan African Studies* 10.9, pp. 217–31.

Omartian, S., 2009, Foreword to E. M. Bounds (ed.), *Power through Prayer*, Chicago: Moody.

Opefeyitimi, A., 2016, 'Ayajo as Ifa in Mythical and Sacred Contexts', in J. Olupona and R. Abiodun (eds), *Ifa Divination, Knowledge, Power, and Performance*, Bloomington, IN: Indiana University Press.

Osoba, J. B., 2014, 'The Nature, Form and Functions of Yoruba Proverbs: A Socio-Pragmatic Perspective', *IOSR Journal of Humanities and Social Science* 19.2, pp. 44–56.

Owomoyela, O., 2005, *Yoruba Proverbs*, Lincoln, NE: University of Nebraska Press.

Oyebade, O. and G. Azenabor, 2018, 'A Discourse on the Fundamental Principles of Character in an African Moral Philosophy', *African Journal of History and Culture* 10.3, pp. 41–50.

Oyeneye, Y. O. and M. O. Shoremi, 1997, 'The Concept of Culture and the Nigerian Society', in O. O. Odugbemi (ed.), *Essentials of General Studies*, Vol. 2, Ago Iwoye: CESAP.

Oyerinde, O. A., 1991, '"Omoluabi" – The Concept of Good Character in Yoruba Traditional Education: An Appraisal', *Andrian Forum* 4, pp. 190–203.

Payne, M. W., 1992, 'Akìwowo, Orature and Divination: Approaches to the Construction of an Emic Sociological Paradigm of Society', *Sociological Analysis* 53.2, pp. 175–87.

Phiri, Lazarus, 2022, 'Mission Without Empire', *Mission Shift* [podcast], Campus Crusade for Christ International, available at https://www.cru.org/communities/city/episode/ep6-mission-without-empire/ (accessed 08.08.2024).

Rapp, Christof, 2002, 'Aristotle's Rhetoric', in E. N. Zalta (ed.), *The Stanford Encyclopedia of Philosophy*, Stanford University: Center for the Study of Language and Information.

Shutte, A., 1993, *Philosophy for Africa*, Rondebosch, South Africa: UTC Press.

Zurlo, G. A., T. M. Johnson and P. Crossing, 2021, 'World Christianity and Mission 2021: Questions about the Future', *International Bulletin of Mission Research* 45.1, pp. 15–25.

8

From the Margins to the Mainstream? Four Questions for the Theology of Church Planting

ANDY WIER

Introduction

In 2022, Church Army's Research Unit (CARU) published the report *Paid Pioneers: From the Margins to the Mainstream* to coincide with its 25th anniversary. Founded in 1997 and led by Revd Dr Canon George Lings until his retirement in 2017, CARU have been studying pioneering, church planting and what subsequently became known as fresh expressions of church for over a quarter of a century. As its subtitle suggests, the *Paid Pioneers* report reflected on the changing landscape of pioneering and considered whether it is moving 'from the margins to the mainstream' of church life. In focusing on experiences of paid pioneers, it drew attention to the fact that many Anglican dioceses and other denominations have begun to financially invest in pioneering and church planting in a way that would have been unthinkable in previous decades. Though this could be interpreted as a sign that pioneering and church planting are becoming more mainstream, the report also showed that the relationship between pioneers and the wider church is still sometimes an uneasy one. In view of this, it concluded by identifying four key risks with relation to pioneering and four corresponding key messages, which are summarized in Table 1 below.

Launched at a fringe event at the Church of England's General Synod, the *Paid Pioneers* report was written primarily for an audience of practitioners and decision-makers, not academics. And though it contained some theological insights and assertions, it was not an explicitly theological report (since its focus was reporting and summarizing the findings of recent empirical research). Within this chapter, I hope to begin to address this by exploring the implications of *Paid Pioneers* for the theology of church planting. This will be structured around the four risks and key

Table 1: Summary of *Paid Pioneers* (Church Army's Research Unit, 2022, pp. 8–9)

Risk	Key message for the wider church
Dismissing pioneering	Discern carefully which models of pioneering (e.g. grassroots pioneering, traditional church planting, social enterprise) are most appropriate.
Domesticating and stifling pioneers	Create space for risk-taking alongside appropriate accountability. Be careful not to impose over-simplistic performance management frameworks which can easily alienate pioneers.
Decoupling evangelism from pioneering	Look below the radar! Don't only take an interest in what you fund!
Dismiss unpaid forms of pioneering	Put the 'evangelism' back into 'pioneer evangelism' and train pioneer evangelists.

messages summarized in Table 1, with a section devoted to each. Each section will summarize the *Paid Pioneers* report's key arguments before going on to reflect theologically on these by identifying and beginning to explore a key question for the theology of church planting.

Church planting and pioneering in a mixed ecology

The *Paid Pioneers* report noted that the relationship between 'grassroots pioneering' and church planting based on a resource church model is currently a source of contention with some pioneers concerned that, in some contexts, the former is being quickly disregarded in favour of the latter. However, the report suggested that rather than thinking of grassroots pioneering and traditional church planting as mutually exclusive alternatives, it is better to see them as potentially complementary. Drawing on an example of mutually beneficial collaboration within a Church Army Centre of Mission, *Paid Pioneers* argued that there is considerable potential for grassroots pioneering and traditional church planting to complement each other or be creatively combined (Church Army's Research Unit, 2022, p. 18).

In reflecting further on this assertion, I wish to locate and examine it in the context of wider theological discourse and debate about the 'mixed economy' or 'mixed ecology' of church life. Within an Anglican context, the term 'mixed economy' was first used by Archbishop Rowan Williams after the 2004 publication of *Mission-shaped Church*, and has subsequently been employed to describe the possibility of fresh expressions and 'inherited' forms of church existing alongside each other in relationships of mutual respect and support (Müller, 2020, p. 37). But concerns about being unduly influenced by economic models have led to a shift in language and it is now more common for Anglican leaders to appeal to a vision of the mixed ecology of church life. This is evident particularly in the Church of England's *Vision and Strategy* for the 2020s. This listed becoming a church where 'mixed ecology is the norm' as one of three main priorities, and described the mixed ecology as 'the flourishing of church and ministry in our parishes, and in other communities of faith through things like church planting, fresh expressions of church, and chaplaincy and online' (Church of England, undated). As Archbishop Stephen Cottrell explained in a General Synod paper, this priority was also linked to the identification of 'two specific and deeply connected and bold outcomes': 'a parish system revitalised for mission' and creating 'ten thousand new Christian communities' (Church of England, 2021, pp. 1–2). Though within popular church discourse, mixed economy/ecology thinking is most typically associated with attempts to justify the co-existence of the parish system and the creation of new Christian communities, it also seems to reflect the implicit assumption that all manner of different forms of new Christian community (whether church plants, fresh expressions of church or other new communities linked to chaplaincy or online presence) should be able to flourish and thrive together. In this sense, the *Paid Pioneers* report's assertion that grassroots pioneering and traditional church planting can complement each other may be seen to implicitly reflect mixed ecology thinking. In view of this, I suggest that a theology of church planting needs to engage with the question: *Does the mixed ecology provide a theologically coherent vision in which fresh expressions of church, resource churches and parish churches can thrive and flourish? (Or is this pure pragmatism and Anglican fudge?)*

Proponents of the mixed ecology have put forward various theological arguments to support the co-existence of different forms of church. The FX website, for example, argues that the idea of the mixed ecology 'has its roots in God' and 'echoes the Trinity' because the mutual dependence of inherited churches and fresh expressions in the mixed ecology church parallels the relationship between Father, Son and Holy Spirit within the Godhead (FX, undated). And according to Archbishop Stephen Cottrell's 2021 General Synod report on the mixed ecology, this concept is also the outworking of a vision of a church 'focused on, and shepherded by, Jesus Christ' (Church of England, 2021, p. 2). This is informed by an engagement with the work of Andrew Walls, who writes: 'The Church must be diverse because humanity is diverse, it must be one because Christ is one' (cited in Church of England, 2021, p. 2) and by reflection on the letter to the Ephesians' description of a church characterized by cultural diversity and union in Christ. Drawing on a contribution to a previous Synod debate from Bishop Steven Croft, Cottrell also suggests that the mixed ecology has New Testament parallels in the relationship between the Jerusalem church and the Antioch church, as well as historical precedent in the longstanding co-existence of parish churches, religious communities, chaplaincies and daughter-church style church plants in the Church of England (Church of England, 2021, p. 2).

More critical voices, however, have suggested that the vision of the mixed ecology being held up as a 'panacea' (Thompson, 2022) for the church's ills ultimately lacks substance and coherence or risks conflating the ecological and the economic. The Anglican theologian and priest Anderson Jeremiah drew attention to this in a 2021 *Church Times* article which highlighted that, contrary to popular perception, 'mixed economy' and 'mixed ecology' mean two different things. The former he characterizes as 'a capitalist economic model, with a few bits of socialism' in which only 'the most efficient succeed'. The latter derives from the study of ecology and advocates 'a healthy ecosystem built on a diversity of organisms'. Jeremiah suggests that within contemporary debates about the mixed ecology church, some are presenting an 'economic' model as an 'ecological' one because ecological metaphors are 'more palatable' than economic ones. He also argues that much of the Church of England's 'mixed ecology' thinking is still driven by 'mixed economy' thinking associated with success, multiplication, growth and diverting resources away from 'unsuccessful' initiatives or 'limiting factors' (an economic expression) that are seen as a burden and impediment to the church's success (Jeremiah, 2021).

Though I would question any assertion that an emphasis on growth and reproduction only reflects an economic model (see Lings, 2017), Jeremiah helpfully highlights the need to pay closer attention to implicit assumptions, values and definitions and the risk of conflating the ecological and economic. Or to put it another way, his article exposes a potential gulf between the Church of England's 'espoused theology' (Cameron et al., 2010, p. 54) of the mixed ecology and an 'operant' theology embedded in practices that reflect assumptions of the free market. Returning to the question of the relationship between grassroots pioneering and resource churches, there is also the risk that despite the Church of England's official acknowledgement of the need for both within the mixed ecology, the dominance of economic models is leading to the rejection of slow-burn grassroots approaches to pioneering in favour of resource churches that reportedly provide a proven track record and quicker results. Indeed, it could even be suggested that concepts like the mixed ecology are being used to legitimize this, giving the impression of something organic while prioritizing economic models.

Funding, theology and power

The *Paid Pioneers* report noted that as pioneering has (in some ways) moved from the margins to the mainstream of church life, the wider church has rightly required the pioneers it has funded to be accountable. But the report also highlighted that the very high demands the church places on paid pioneers can often be a source of significant frustration and distress, which distracts them from pioneering. In view of this, it argued that the wider church needs to create spaces for pioneering that combine accountability with risk-taking – being careful to not impose over-simplistic performance management systems but building in regular, relational reviews (Church Army's Research Unit, 2022, p. 9).

In reflecting further on these issues, I want to suggest that more consideration needs to be given to the theological significance of churches' decisions and practices around funding. My interest in this dates back to the early 2000s when I worked in the community regeneration sector and the 'New Labour' government was investing millions of pounds in the 'regeneration', 'renewal' or 'transformation' of 'deprived' neighbourhoods. As a middle manager for a local authority, I managed some of these funds and subsequently went on to work as an independent consultant and bid-writer. These experiences provided a fascinating insight into some of the 'games' that organizations (including churches and faith-based organizations) sometimes play when engaging with large-scale funding programmes. A desire to reflect further on these issues was one of the catalysts for me commencing a professional doctorate in Practical Theology. As part of this I wrote an (unpublished) article in 2010 that used the metaphor of 'the funding game' as a way of exploring the theological significance of churches' decisions about funding.[1] Re-reading the article recently, I was struck that though some of the arguments were specific to the experience of churches accessing government funding, there were also some interesting connections to issues around denominational funding for church planting and pioneering.

One of the themes 'The Funding Game' explored was the power dynamic at work when churches or community organizations access government funds. It argued that, in accepting government funds and seeking to make themselves useful to government, recipients of public funding are becoming 'delivery agents of the State'. As such, they have become subject to the regulatory practices of government and complicit in the 'incorporation' of the third sector by government. There are interesting parallels between this language of 'incorporation' (of third sector organizations by government) and the *Paid Pioneers* report's vocabulary of 'mainstreaming' (of pioneers by the Church of England and other denominations). Both metaphors speak of including something as part of something larger, but in a way that is not completely benign. Though the relationship between grant-giver and grant-receiver may sometimes be naïvely interpreted and celebrated as pure gift, it is important to recognize that there is an inevitable power dynamic within funding relationships. Whether the parties involved are aware of this or not, grant-making often performs a regulatory function since the way large-scale funding programmes are designed and administered enables powerful institutions to direct the activities of grant recipients towards their own ends.

Through initiatives like the Strategic Development Fund (SDF), the Church of England has invested millions of pounds in church planting over recent years. According to a recent independent review, £82.7 million of SDF funding was awarded to projects 'starting new churches' between 2014 and 2021, with over half (£45.7 million) of this going to new resource churches (Church of England, 2022, p. 31). Though there have been various evaluations of SDF-funded activities during this period, many of them seem not to have been published or widely shared (Church of England, 2022, p. 43). And from the available evidence, it appears that such evaluations have focused primarily on pragmatic considerations like the achievement of 'outcomes' and identifying 'transferable lessons'. To date, there seems to have been very little theological reflection on the impact of the availability of SDF funding on contemporary church planting theology and practice. I therefore suggest that a theology of church planting needs to engage with the question: *What influence, for good or bad, are multi-million-pound funding programmes having on church planting theology and practice? What theological resources are available to better understand the power dynamics at play here?*

Within a Church of England context, a theology of church planting needs to recognize and reflect on issues of power. This includes acknowledging that much of the current investment in pioneering and church planting is being funded by the historic wealth of the established church. There are complex power dynamics at work here that are not always acknowledged within the espoused theology of contemporary Anglican church planters. To explore these issues further, it may be helpful to bring contemporary Anglican church planting practice into dialogue with the work of writers like Stuart Murray. Over the past three decades,

Murray has written numerous books on church planting (1998), post-Christendom (2004) and the Anabaptist tradition (2015). Much of his work explores what it means to be a church on the margins, eschewing the 'distorting influence' within Christendom of power, wealth and status on the Christian story (Murray, 2004, p. 21). Though there is not space here to fully explore these issues, it is important to engage with perspectives like this from beyond Anglicanism when exploring the power dynamics at work within church planting initiatives funded by the established church.

Small, fragile and mundane

The *Paid Pioneers* report studied the experiences of paid pioneers because this had been the focus of CARU's recently commissioned research projects. However, the report was at pains to point out that pioneering is not only about what paid or formally designated 'pioneers' do. Though paid pioneering often gets most of the attention, previous CARU reports have highlighted the significance of other 'below the radar' forms of pioneering. Our 2019 *Playfully Serious* report, for example, noted that the Messy Church movement is pioneering alternative forms of leadership, with Messy Churches primarily led by women, lay people and volunteers (Church Army's Research Unit, 2019, p. 8). In view of this, *Paid Pioneers* cautioned against overlooking unpaid forms of pioneering, urging the wider church: 'Look below the radar! Don't only take an interest in what you fund!' (Church Army's Research Unit, 2022, p. 9).

Other researchers have helpfully highlighted the importance of 'Listening to the voice of the lay planters' (Myriad and CCX, 2022) and the experiences of lay pioneers (Butler, 2022). However, I want to suggest that the distinction between paid and unpaid pioneering is just as, if not more important, than that between lay and ordained. All too often, it is only the work of paid planters and pioneers (whether lay or ordained) that gets recognized. If a theology of church planting is orientated only to these experiences and contexts, it is going to be unhelpfully skewed. Developing this idea further, a key question that I would like to begin to explore is: *How can a theology of church planting pay attention to the small, fragile and mundane?*

Smallness and fragility

In 2016, Church Army's Research Unit published *The Day of Small Things*, a detailed report that analysed fresh expressions of church (including church plants) within 21 of the 42 dioceses of the Church of England (Lings, 2016). The report title reflected one of the research's main findings: that the world of fresh expressions of church is one of 'young, varied and small communities' (p. 11) with only 9% having over 100 members (p. 9). The title was also an allusion to Zechariah 4.10 about not despising 'the day of small things'. As George Lings explained in the Foreword, the choice of title reflected the conviction that the Church of England's fresh expressions of church are 'one of the small things in our day which are signs of renewed hope'. Though it may be tempting to despise their relatively small size and fragility, Lings goes on to say that the use of the term 'the day' suggests something of a *kairos* moment, a season when something's time has come. As such, the report title invites the Church of England 'not to despise what is growing within its family, but has not yet been given sympathetic attention' (p. 9).

In my view, this continues to be a timely and pertinent challenge for all those concerned with the theology of church planting. As we have already seen, in the years since the publication of *The Day of Small Things*, a lot of the Church of England's financial resources have gone into the creation or development of larger resource churches. Whether or not this is a good thing has been the subject of much debate, which I do not wish to add to at this stage. But regardless of the pros and cons, I suggest that any denomination or diocese needs to be prepared to see beyond its flagship projects and strategic programmes and pay attention to what is happening 'below the radar'.

Mundane holiness

As well as paying attention to the experiences of smaller, fragile young churches, I suggest that a theology of church planting needs to recognize and engage with the ordinary and mundane. This flows out of a tension I have observed within many churches I have engaged with over the years between 'the heroic' and 'the mundane'. As I wrote in a 2015 Grove Book based on my doctoral research, 'our Christian subculture encourages us to think and act like heroes or superheroes', but I fear that the promotion of a hero culture in our churches risks uncritically reflecting the contemporary obsession with the extra-ordinary (Wier, 2015, p. 23). And in this regard, I have found Sam Wells' distinction between heroes and saints to be a helpful corrective: the hero is always at the centre of the story, but the saint is at the periphery of a story that is really about God (Wells cited in Wier, 2015, p. 23). A theology of church planting therefore needs to be wary of heroism and instead embrace a 'mundane holiness' (Bretherton, 2007, p. 227) that is open to seeing God at work within the 'ordinary, mundane, boring stuff of life' (Wier, 2013, p. 64).

Evangelism and church planting

The *Paid Pioneers* report suggested that there is sometimes a reluctance to talk about evangelism within contemporary pioneering. This was informed by the observation that evangelism was not explicitly mentioned in the espoused aims of various diocesan/denominational pioneer projects CARU recently evaluated and by our wider observations of the pioneering landscape over the years. For Church Army, however, any decoupling of evangelism from pioneering is problematic and (while affirming a holistic view of mission and concerns about culturally insensitive, unethical, or imperialistic forms of evangelism) the report went on to argue that the church needs to 'Put the "evangelism" back into "pioneer evangelism" and train pioneer evangelists' (Church Army's Research Unit, 2022, p. 30). This provocative conclusion clearly reflects Church Army's position and standpoint as an organization committed to doing, advocating, resourcing and enabling evangelism, but a key question this raises is: *What is the place of evangelism within a contemporary theology of church planting?*

While reflecting on this, I recently reread two important reports that were both published in 2004. That year, the Church of England published *Mission-shaped Church* (Archbishops' Council, 2004) and Church Army produced *Inside Out: The Report of Church Army's Theology of Evangelism Working Party* (Church Army, 2004). Revisiting these reports nearly 20 years on, I was struck by the strong sense of disconnection between them. *Mission-shaped Church* was about church planting and fresh expressions of church and said very little explicitly about evangelism. *Inside Out*, in contrast, focused on the theology of evangelism and did not say a lot about church planting. I do not want to overstate the significance of this observation since it could be argued that a commitment to evangelism was implicit in *Mission-shaped Church* and that *Inside Out* mentioned the development of 'new forms of church'. Nevertheless, I suggest that the lack of significant overlap between these two key texts is quite telling and illustrates the need to give more attention to the relationship between church planting and evangelism.

Within the world(s) of church planting and pioneering, a lot of attention is given to discussions about the relative benefits and limitations of different models, strategies and methods – for example within debates between advocates of 'serving first' pioneering and 'worship first' resource churches (Moynagh, 2012, pp. 206–8). But a theology of church planting needs to also engage with evangelism because without it church plants and new worshipping communities need to rely on transfer growth and pioneering community work becomes indistinguishable from secular community projects (Church Army's Research Unit, 2022, p. 19). Many church planters and pioneers, however, seem to find speaking about Jesus in contemporary mission contexts quite difficult. Christian Paas suggests that, for many practitioners, such 'speechlessness' may reflect a degree of embarrassment in relating a classic evangelical gospel predicated on the world's lostness to a secularized audience: 'If witnessing about Jesus is framed within an ontology of wrath, lostness and atonement that is no longer acceptable or intelligible to most people, then speaking about Jesus in any salvific sense may be experienced as embarrassing' (Paas, 2022, p. 328). A theology of church planting needs to recognize and engage with such difficult soteriological and missiological issues and not simply assume that, with the 'right' church planting model, evangelism will just happen. For Paas, this requires constructing a new soteriological narrative capable of 'connecting the various strands of soteriology and building strong and inspiring connections between the life and ministry of Jesus on the one hand and contemporary experience on the other' (p. 337). Though it may be possible to discern some of its possible 'building blocks' or 'contours' (pp. 337, 341), this emerging narrative is 'not yet fully developed or even coherent' (p. 339) so there is clearly further work to be done here.

Twenty years on from the publication of *Mission-shaped Church* and *Inside Out*, the relationship between evangelism and church planting still needs to be better understood. With this in mind, Church Army's Research Unit have recently launched a new stream of research on effective evangelism.[2] We look forward to collaborating with other planters, practitioners and theologians in exploring these issues over the years ahead.

Notes

1 'Publishable article' submitted as part of the Portfolio Work referred to in my doctoral thesis (Wier, 2013, p. ix).
2 For more details and future updates, visit churcharmy.org/our-work/research/.

References

Archbishops' Council, 2004, *Mission-shaped Church: Church Planting and Fresh Expressions of Church in a Changing Context*, London: Church House Publishing.
Bretherton, Luke, 2007, 'Mundane Holiness: The Theology and Spirituality of Everyday Life', in A. Walker and L. Bretherton (eds), *Remembering our Future: Explorations in Deep Church*, Milton Keynes: Paternoster.
Butler, James, 2022, 'Setting God's pioneers free?', *Ecclesial Futures* 3.1.
Cameron, Helen, Deborah Bhatti, Catherine Duce, James Sweeney and Clare Watkins, 2010, *Talking about God in Practice: Theological Action Research and Practical Theology*, London: SCM Press.
Church Army, 2004, *Inside Out: The Report of Church Army's Theology of Evangelism Working Party*, Sheffield: Church Army.
Church Army's Research Unit, *Playfully Serious*, 2019, Sheffield: Church Army's Research Unit, https://churcharmy.org/our-work/research/recently-completed-research/playfully-serious/ (accessed 09.08.2024).
Church Army's Research Unit, 2022, *Paid Pioneers: From the Margins to the Mainstream*, Sheffield: Church Army's Research Unit, https://churcharmy.org/our-work/research/recently-completed-research/paid-pioneers/ (accessed 09.08.2024).
Church of England, 2021, *General Synod GS 2238: Vision and Strategy*, https://www.churchofengland.org/sites/default/files/2021-10/gs-2238-vision-and-strategy-update.pdf (accessed 25.08.2023).
Church of England, 2022, *Independent Review of Lowest Income Communities Funding and Strategic Development Funding*, https://www.churchofengland.org/sites/default/files/2022-03/irls-final-report-2.pdf (accessed 25.08.2023).
Church of England, undated, *Vision and Strategy: A Vision and Strategy for the Church of England in the 2020s*, https://www.churchofengland.org/about/vision-and-strategy (accessed 25.08.2023).
FX, undated, *The Mixed Ecology*, https://freshexpressions.org.uk/what-is-fx/the-mixed-ecology/ (accessed 11.08.2023).
Jeremiah, Anderson, 2021, 'Mixed-Ecology Church: Why Definitions Matter', *Church Times* 23 July, https://www.churchtimes.co.uk/articles/2021/23-july/comment/opinion/mixed-ecology-church-why-definitions-matter.
Lings, George, 2016, *The Day of Small Things*, Sheffield: Church Army's Research Unit, http://churcharmy.org/wp-content/uploads/2021/04/the-day-of-small-things.pdf (accessed 09.08.2024).
Lings, George, 2017, *Reproducing Churches*, Abingdon: BRF.
Moynagh, Michael, 2012, *Church for Every Context: An Introduction to Theology and Practice*, London: SCM Press.
Müller, Sabrina, 2020, 'Towards the Acceptance of Diversity: A Brief History of the Mixed Economy of Church and Continental European Adaptations', *Ecclesial Futures* 1.1.
Murray, Stuart, 1998, *Church Planting: Laying Foundations*, Carlisle: Paternoster.
Murray, Stuart, 2004, *Post-Christendom: Church and Mission in a Strange New World*, Carlisle: Paternoster.
Murray, Stuart, 2015, *The Naked Anabaptist* (rev. edn), Scottdale, PA: Herald Press.

Myriad and CCX, 2022, *Listening to the Voice of the Lay Planters*, https://ccx.org.uk/content/listening-lay/ (accessed 25.08.2023).

Paas, Stefan, 2022, 'Soteriology in Evangelical Practice: A View from the Street', *Exchange: Journal of Contemporary Christianities in Context* 51.4.

Thompson, Robert, 2022, *'Resource Churches': When Planting Becomes Colonialism*, https://viamedia.news/2022/05/28/resource-churches-when-planting-becomes-colonialism/ (accessed 25.08.2023).

Wier, Andrew, P., 2013, 'Tensions in Charismatic-Evangelical Urban Practice: Towards a Practical Charismatic-Evangelical Urban Social Ethic', unpublished DProf thesis, University of Chester, https://chesterrep.openrepository.com/handle/10034/311004 (accessed 09.08.2024).

Wier, Andy, 2015, *Creative Tension in Urban Mission: Reflections on Missional Practice and Theory*, Cambridge: Grove.

9

Is Church Planting a Craft? Training Lessons from Medieval Guilds[1]

CHRISTIAN SELVARATNAM

Training church planters

Who and what are church planters, and what is the most effective way to train them?

The answer to these linked questions is key to the effective identification, training and deployment of people who start new churches; and is of critical importance to institutions responsible for the formation of ministers-in-training. This chapter explores how historic apprenticeship models might inform the methods of training for the next generation of church planters.

For 50 years a modern church planting movement has been growing in England. Now, most denominations and church networks have bold goals for revitalizing churches and starting new Christian communities.[2] However, little real consideration has been directed towards the development of effective training methods tailored specifically for church planters. I suggest the pedagogical apprenticeship methods of the English and European medieval craft guilds – now, of course, mostly lost in practice – offer helpful inspiration and a possible framework to answer these questions.

Apprenticeship is ancient. It has been a cornerstone of education since the dawn of settled human societies.[3] This method of training was essential in the past for turning a novice into a master,[4] focusing on the acquisition of craft skills and the cultivation of the learner's personal creativity and unique style. This teaching and learning approach significantly differs from the didactic classroom training models that are prevalent in today's formal education systems and that underlie the training models for Christian ministry in the Western world.

For over 600 years, leading into the start of the British Industrial Revolution, the training of most English youths and young adults was in the hands of the medieval craft guilds.[5] The guilds employed a tailored apprenticeship system that blended hands-on training with community learning, self-directed learning, evidence-based education progression and the creative development of an individual's craft abilities. In the guilds' workshops, explicit, tacit and embedded knowledge was transferred from one generation to the next, facilitated by skilled training masters who provided personal mentorship to apprentices. Drawing parallels between historical craft guilds and contemporary training efforts highlights the need for effective integration of knowledge and skills.

The availability of training resources for Christian ministry is at an all-time high, with a plethora of high-quality instructional materials readily accessible. However, despite this abundance, genuinely effective training for prospective church planters that integrates theory with practical application remains scarce and relatively undeveloped. To date, many church planters have been left to learn on the job during their first steps in church planting or have resorted to self-education through books and conferences, with only a minority receiving direct mentoring from experienced practitioners. This resonates with Paul's observation to the Corinthians about having numerous instructors yet few spiritual mentors (1 Cor. 4.15).

I will approach the question of training church planters in three parts (explored in greater depth in Selvaratnam, 2022). First, I examine the medieval craft guild model of training as both a case study and an analogical framework for training church planters. When examining the craft guilds, I am considering how their structure and foundational principles could inform and influence contemporary training methodologies for church planters. Following this, I provide a brief survey of some dimensions of apprenticeship training inspired by the guilds but articulated in modern terms and understanding. Finally, I explore an idea that could significantly reshape our understanding of training for church planters: the concept of the artisan, which also finds inspiration from the guilds.[6]

Guild training models

For approximately 700 years, until the British Industrial Revolution in the late eighteenth century, occupational guilds stood as the predominant model for apprentice-style training in England.[7] These guilds played a pivotal role in shaping the development of youths and young adults by imparting skills, instilling ethical values, fostering community engagement and elucidating the intricacies of their chosen professions. Under the guidance of a master-worker, apprentices underwent comprehensive training that encompassed both practical skills and moral principles.[8] It's noteworthy that these master-workers had themselves undergone similar training within the guild system.

The journey from apprentice to master

Guilds facilitated the transmission of vocational expertise through the apprentice system, leading to widespread guild membership among urban craftworkers during the Middle Ages. At the core of the guild structure was the workshop: a self-contained business unit usually housed within the master's residence. A typical guild hierarchy consisted of masters, who had attained full membership status within the guild; journeymen, who embarked on self-guided internships away from their master's workshop for a period of three years; and apprentices, who were recruited by a master and entered into working agreements that included basic training, provisions and lodging (Ryan, 2000, p. 31).

Apprenticeship formed the foundational pillar of the craft guild structure. Typically initiated during their early teenage years, apprentices underwent a rigorous training period lasting between five and nine years under the guidance of their master. Upon joining a workshop, apprentices immersed themselves in learning craft skills and acquiring the specialized, often closely guarded knowledge pertinent to their trade.

On-the-job learning and mastery

Upon completion of their apprenticeships, individuals progressed to the status of journeymen. The term 'journeyman' derives from the French word *journée*, meaning 'day', signifying a skilled worker capable of earning a daily wage for their labour. The journeyman stage represented the second phase of training, characterized by a three-year period of self-directed learning. During this time, journeymen were prohibited from returning to their master's workshop. Instead, they embarked on what was colloquially known as 'wandering' or 'tramping years', travelling and working for various masters for short periods to broaden their skillset. Following the completion of their journeyman years, they could seek recognition as masters within the guild, granting them the authority to establish their own workshops and mentor apprentices.

Training within guilds primarily followed an on-the-job model, wherein learning and work intersected seamlessly (Wallis, 2008). Most of the instruction occurred through observation, imitation and hands-on practice, with apprentices actively participating in productive work while simultaneously honing their skills. Thus, apprentices' training unfolded concurrently with their practical engagement in labour.

Craftsmanship and progression

A fascinating aspect of training within craft guilds is the distinct evidence-based learning progression inherent in the model. Advancement to the next stage of learning and status within the guild hinges upon the production of tangible evidence of one's skills and mastery, not on the completion of a course or a specific length of training. For both apprentices and journeymen, this evidence takes the form of 'pieces' that are carefully assessed by their superiors.[9]

For apprentices, validation comes in the form of one or more pieces that demonstrate their proficiency in specific craft skills and techniques. Similarly, for journeymen, the culmination of their training is typically represented by a single piece, known as a 'masterpiece', which integrally demonstrates their foundational training and what they have learnt from other masters during their travels.[10]

Upon completing their apprenticeship, workers would present their crafted pieces, which served as tangible evidence of competency in their craft trade. These pieces, crafted entirely by the apprentice, typically showcased proficiency in all the techniques inherent on their trade. Successful submission of these pieces led to the apprentice receiving 'papers', akin to a modern-day diploma, and ascending to the status of journeymen.

In certain guilds, journeymen were afforded only one opportunity to submit a masterpiece. Acceptance granted them entry into the ranks of the guild's masters, allowing them to establish workshops, mentor apprentices and fully participate in the guild's activities. Conversely, failure to gain acceptance precluded them from ever attaining master status within that particular guild.

The requirement for pieces and masterpieces extended across a wide array of craft guilds, encompassing even trades not typically associated with artisanal craftwork. For instance, goldsmiths, weavers, apothecaries, carpenters and rope makers alike were expected to present evidence of their skills. Even barbers in fifteenth-century Reims seeking mastery had to demonstrate proficiency in various tasks, including wet shaving, beard trimming, lancet preparation for bloodletting and an understanding of anatomical considerations.[11] Similarly, painters, sculptors and glaziers were tasked with producing painted panels, small statues or stained-glass panels respectively, as dictated by their masters; these pieces often depicted religious themes such as the Virgin Mary, Christ on the cross or local saints.

The guilds offer invaluable insights into structuring effective training for church planters. The immersive on-the-job training provided within the workshop,[12] equivalent to a local church as a place of ministry and learning; the pivotal role of the master, an experienced church leader, in the training process; the breadth of practical experience gained during the journeyman years; and the emphasis on creativity all align well with the current opportunities and training requirements of Christian pioneers and entrepreneurs. Perhaps these pre-industrial models can yet serve as inspiration for enhancing the training of church planters today.

Contemporary apprenticeship training

Building upon the historical context of guilds outlined in the preceding section, this next section aims to develop our understanding of craft training by examining the dynamics of apprenticeship training in the contemporary era. I will explore key elements observed in modern apprenticeship, which draw parallels and continuity with traditional guild practice. Specifically, this will focus on a form of apprenticeship referred to as 'guided apprenticeship learning', one characterized by hands-on learning under the guidance of experts through active participation in authentic workplace tasks.

By considering these components, I aim to flesh out some of the core aspects of guild-apprenticeship training and begin to imagine how these principles might be applied to training church planters in today's context.

Situated learning

The social anthropologist Jean Lave and the educational theorist Étienne Charles Wenger, who jointly developed the concept, propose that 'situated learning' epitomizes apprenticeship, with learning occurring within the context, culture and social milieu (see Lave and Wenger, 1991). Situated learning thus explains how human cognition evolves within social settings, utilizing cultural tools for learning, retention and comprehension. Lave and Wenger contend that learning is inherently 'situated', because it evolves through participation in communities of practice (defined below), where newcomers engage in legitimate peripheral participation,[13] gradually assimilating into the community and its norms.

In this theory, learning and action are inseparable from the context, as knowledge isn't abstract but contextualized and specific, reflecting the culture of practice. So apprenticeship-style learning thrives in communities where novices gradually acquire skills and knowledge through interaction with seasoned practitioners, emphasizing social engagement in skill and idea acquisition.

According to Stephen Billett, cognitive activities in apprenticeships encompass three crucial facets: propositional knowledge, which includes facts and ideas; procedural knowledge, covering methods and skills; and personal and social attributes, reflecting values. These elements collectively form the foundation of an individual's knowledge, which is crucial for addressing the significance and rationale behind workplace tasks (Billett, 1994).

From the perspective of the instructor, the situated learning apprenticeship model of instruction involves four phases: modelling, coaching, scaffolding and fading (Collins et al., 1989, pp. 456–7; also Billett, 1994). Modelling entails novices observing experts, constructing conceptual frameworks for task completion. Verbalizing internal thought processes aids learners in acquiring procedural and cognitive knowledge. Coaching involves experts observing learners, providing guidance, feedback and repeated demonstrations to develop skills. Exposure to various experts offers apprentices multiple models of expertise, fostering an understanding of diverse approaches to task execution. Scaffolding describes support tailored to learners' needs, including task assistance, reminders and cooperative problem-solving.[14] Effective scaffolding necessitates gauging learners' skill levels and task difficulty.[15] Fading involves gradually withdrawing support until learners can function autonomously, transitioning to passive support upon request.

Communities of practice

Lave and Wenger coined the term 'community of practice' in their research on apprenticeship during the late 1980s and early 1990s (Wenger et al., 2022). They describe it as learning extending beyond the traditional student–master dynamic, emphasizing ongoing interactions among practitioners with shared concerns, problems or passions, leading to deepened knowledge and expertise. Their research reveals that apprenticeship learning occurs best in communities of practice, which are groups of individuals united by a shared interest in a craft, fostering continual learning through regular interaction, leading to the development of shared practices.

Communities of practice vary in size and format, meeting either in person or online. They have existed throughout human history, spanning various spheres of life, with individuals often belonging to multiple communities of practice, ranging from core to peripheral involvement.

Lave and Wenger differentiate communities of practice from other groups based on three key elements. First, they possess a defined domain of interest that shapes the community's identity and membership. Second, they are intentional communities engaging in joint activities, mutual assistance and knowledge sharing, fostering innovation and problem-solving. Third, members share a common competence or practice, contributing to a collective repository of experience and knowledge.

Novices transition into a community of practice by engaging in peripheral activities, gradually integrating into the community and acquiring skills, knowledge and cultural practices through social learning processes. Wenger highlights the benefits of these groups, such as reduced intensity and risk, as well as aspects of legitimacy, including usefulness and sponsorship. The experience of apprentices in these groups offers insights into the apprentice–expert relationship, emphasizing learning through social engagement rather than formal instruction.

Mimetic learning

Mimetic learning, defined as learning through imitation or mimicry, is regarded as one of the fundamental processes of human learning, tracing back to the earliest forms of societal collaboration. This concept finds manifestation in various facets of human interaction. For instance, children instinctively emulate the actions and behaviours of their parents, thus acquiring knowledge through mimesis. René Girard (1978, pp. 7, 26, 307) asserts that *all* human behaviour is fundamentally rooted in mimesis. Billett echoes Girard's suggestion, acknowledging the ubiquity of mimetic learning; however, he observes that its significance may not be readily apparent in modern, highly structured societies, where traditional educational systems often overshadow its influence (2014, p. 2).

Despite the prevalence of observational and imitative learning within our culture, the didactic model of teaching still remains dominant. Classroom learning models are often accepted without question as the most natural and effective educational approach, yet this view tends to ignore the learning styles prevalent in modern craftwork. Christoph Wulf offers a valuable insight, building on Girard's theory to highlight the embodied aspect of mimetic learning. He argues that it involves multisensory experiences, not just intellectual ones. (2014, p. 123; 2008, p. 56). Wulf suggests that cultural learning is largely mimetic, creating a deep link between individuals, their surroundings and other members of society. Essentially, mimetic learning cultivates practical knowledge, which is vital for social, artistic and practical pursuits.

Tacit knowledge

Propositional knowledge encompasses factual, theoretical, logical and explicit information, which can be readily recorded and acquired from written sources.[16] In contrast, tacit knowledge, a concept coined by Michael Polanyi, comprises information that proves challenging to convey through writing or verbal expression. According to John Seely Brown and Paul Duguid, tacit knowledge encompasses intuitive understanding and practical expertise, commonly referred to as 'know-how' (1998, p. 91). Polanyi aptly captures this notion by stating, 'we can know more than we can tell', emphasizing the ineffable nature of tacit knowledge (Polanyi, 1966, p. 4).

The elusive quality of tacit knowledge leads many to consider it the most valuable form of knowledge. Jerry Wellman asserts: 'Although tacit knowledge is the most difficult to recognize and handle, it is often the tacit knowledge that leads to significant breakthroughs and is of more value to the organization' (2009, p. 21). As tacit knowledge is inherently embedded within interpersonal relationships, Stephan R. Epstein and Maarten Roy Prak suggest it thrives most effectively within communities of practice, such as craft guilds (2008, p. 7).

Re-imagining church planting as a craft

I suggest that church planters are akin to artisans and should be trained as such.

Creativity, of course, plays a significant role in the activity of church planting. It is well understood that churches are contextual bodies: a unique blend of community, mission and ecclesiology in a local congregation. In best practice, a church plant must seamlessly integrate into its context; it cannot simply replicate the church from which it originates. Understanding the local narrative serves as a crucial precursor to contextualization, a process that demands and is enriched by creativity and the artistic spirit, which is dynamic, adaptable and malleable. Through artistry and creativity, we affirm that every church plant is uniquely endowed by God and called to a specific context, serving as a continuation of the narrative unfolding there. If we hold true to this principle – that no two churches are, or should be, identical – then those entrusted with launching contextual communities inhabit the realm of incarnation. Much like prophets, artists and other creatives, they skilfully craft something new from existing elements.

Learning from jazz improvisation

Perhaps a good illustration is jazz improvisation. Picture yourself attending a jazz performance where the musician delivers a new song, one never played before, and yet the music seamlessly aligns with the setting, the audience and the moment. This is an example of creativity at its best. Now consider the performer's training. Despite never being taught the specific song, they have acquired the necessary skills to deliver it. They would have had to learn the basics of playing their instrument, perhaps practising scales and learning to read music. Next, they would have honed their craft by interpreting and performing other musicians' compositions, receiving feedback on their interpretations. At some point a crucial transition occurs when they shift from imitation to innovation, from copying to creating and composing; over time, they evolve from merely reproducing existing works to crafting their own. And one day they play a new song, consistent with all good music, but fitted contextually to a moment in time and space.

How might church planters connect improvisation with tradition and context, bridging the gap between heritage and innovation? Does the metaphor of jazz improvisation aid our understanding of the role of creativity in church planting, including how planters might engage with legacy practices and navigate the existing and emerging narrative of the context? Picking up on this analogy, Bruce Ellis Benson notes that 'In jazz, knowing the past is what makes the future possible', and goes on to explain that 'learning to be a *Christian* improviser, one must know the entire context: Scripture and the ways in which Scripture has been interpreted in the past', a practice he refers to as joining a '*community* of improvisers' (Benson, 2013, p. 42; emphasis original). Similarly he adds: 'when I play a tune, I am never simply improvising on that tune alone. I am improvising on the tradition formed by the improvisations upon that tune' (Benson, 2013, p. 92). Perhaps, then, rather than rejecting heritage, through creativity the Christian improviser is enabled to build faithfully on Christian inheritance using creative skills. By applying creativity and improvisation to tradition, church planters harmonize the inheritance of the past with the potential for innovation in the present and future of their faith communities.

With this in mind, allow me to propose some aspects of creativity that could be crucial to consider when training church planters.

Unpacking creativity

First, it's important to recognize that everyone possesses creativity. While common notions of creativity often revolve around activities like art, music or dance, it extends far beyond these realms. Creativity manifests in everyday actions such as asking open-ended questions, embracing alternative approaches, exercising imagination and collaborating with diverse individuals. It transcends the confines of traditional artistic expression by encompassing any endeavour where originality and innovation are at play. Creativity isn't solely confined to creating tangible works of art or delivering performances on a stage; it's intrinsic to human existence and applicable to all facets of life. As beings created in the image of God, we inherently possess creative potential, reflecting and expressing divine intention through our own imaginative endeavours. In this sense, creativity serves as a profound reflection of God's character and nature, allowing us to mirror divine creative essence as image-bearers.

Furthermore, creativity serves as a powerful form of empowerment. For instance, it might involve recognizing and nurturing the potential of emerging leaders, providing them with the encouragement and freedom to devise solutions in their own unique ways. Oftentimes, constraints, scarcity and challenges spark innovative thinking, prompting individuals to devise creative solutions to pressing problems. Working with new people or challenging circumstances inherently involves a willingness to take risks, a crucial attribute relevant to training for church planting. Genuine creativity cannot flourish without a readiness to embrace uncertainty and venture into uncharted territories. Adopting a creative approach to tasks involves recognizing the potential for mistakes and being willing to adjust strategies in response to fresh insights and evolving situations. Flexibility is crucial, given that creative efforts naturally require experimentation and the ability to adapt.

As suggested by the jazz illustration, nurturing and unleashing creativity can be viewed through two distinct stages. The first involves investing in foundational skills and abilities, typically achieved through stimulating experiences and repetitive skill-building tasks. However, it's important to recognize that there exists a critical juncture at the end of initial training where creativity may be stifled if individuals are solely engaged in rote repetition without room for generating ideas and experimenting.

The second stage is characterized by imaginative exploration of challenges. Since creativity often flourishes in an environment of trust and play, it's beneficial to adopt a youthful or playful mindset. Playfulness fosters imaginative and adaptable approaches to overcoming obstacles. Children exemplify this effortlessly; they are unconcerned with grades or evaluations, wholly focused on developing their passions without regard for external judgement.

Creativity is essential to Christian training

Creativity is more than attractive window-dressing of the Christian faith; rather, it emanates from deeply ingrained convictions regarding the essence of Christian life and the divine purpose. It embodies a vision that eschews rigid programmatic approaches, favouring instead a dynamic engagement with the unpredictable movements of God's Spirit. Such an approach ensures that training relationships remain open to divine freedom and the unexpected workings of the Holy Spirit, thereby distinguishing genuine discipleship from the mere replication of religious practices. I suggest that only by integrating apprenticeship with the liberating force of creativity and artistry can we cultivate a church planting training ethos that authentically responds to the creative essence of the gospel.

In contemporary training methods, heavily influenced by industrial and post-industrial organizational paradigms, there is often a lack of emphasis on recognizing the importance of creativity and artistry as important skills for Christian ministry. This oversight is noteworthy because mastering these skills can enable genuine innovation while preserving a robust connection to historical wisdom. The industrial view of work, which often reduces workers to mere components within a mechanistic system, highlights the prevailing focus on theory and scholarship. Consequently, many current training models, especially in the Western context, tend to adopt a highly structured, uniform methodology.[17]

Could a craft-based apprenticeship model, drawing inspiration from artisan training and the organic metaphors of the New Testament, signal potential shifts in training paradigms and enhance existing methods more effectively? Such an approach would nurture church planters as distinct creators, acknowledging the uniqueness of each context and developing the skills to organically foster church growth, rather than adhering to a rigid training regimen.

Before drawing final conclusions, I suggest three practical approaches to re-imagining church planting as a craft.

First, accomplished church planters should play a leading role in selecting, training and shaping the ministerial development of new church planters, particularly in the initial phases of their training. Considering the importance of a strong personal and professional fit in the master–apprentice relationship, perhaps akin to the bond between a parent and child, might it be preferable for veteran planters to have the autonomy to choose their apprentices?[18] And would it be wise to ensure that these 'experts' are invited to contribute to strategic discussions on church planting within their networks?

Next, early training for church planters should ideally take place within the context of a newly established church or one actively engaged in planting efforts.[19] This hands-on approach, where apprentices participate in ministry activities under close guidance, not only allows them to observe experienced ministers but also to be observed and evaluated in their ministerial engagements. This method extends beyond the mixed-mode training offered by some training institutions, suggesting that the church environment should be the focal point and foundation of the learning experience for prospective church planters. Contrary to, for example, the current two-phase training model in the Church of England, which starts in theological colleges and is followed by local church engagement, this proposal advocates for beginning with practical church involvement as the first stage.[20]

Third, to effectively start Christian communities in a post-Christendom world, planters must be encouraged to think creatively and innovatively, tailoring new churches to their specific contexts. This creativity, reminiscent of pre-industrial work values, is crucial for establishing contextual and authentic church expressions. Thus, fostering creativity should be a key component of every church planter's training. The craft guild model of apprenticeship, with its emphasis on contextual creativity, offers a versatile framework ideally suited for training pioneering church planters in character development, practical skills and innovative approaches to ministry. At the heart of this model is empowering creative mentorship by a church planting master – an expert who not only practices church planting but also personally guides the next generation.

Conclusion

When contemplating the future of church planting, it's essential to blend the lessons of history with the practical demands of our time. In changing times, the church needs to evolve its training methods to better equip ministers and pioneers for the challenges ahead. This involves not just looking back to the mentorship models of the past but also integrating them with contemporary strategies that emphasize real-world experience and community engagement.

The aim is to create a more grounded yet forward-looking approach to nurturing church planters, one that fosters stronger partnerships between theological institutions and local churches to ensure that training is both academically sound and deeply embedded in the practical realities of creative ministry. By doing so, we can prepare church planters who are not only theologically informed but also adept at navigating the complexities of modern society, ready to establish vibrant, relevant and contextual communities of faith.

This vision calls for a commitment to continuous learning, innovation and adaptability among church leaders, encouraging them to be proactive in addressing the evolving spiritual needs of their communities. Thus planters will be equipped not only with the tools of ministry but with the heart of a poet and the soul of an artist, echoing sentiments reminiscent of my favourite quotation related to church planting, which is from Irenaeus of Lyons: 'The church is planted like Paradise in this world' (Irenaeus, 5.20.2). By adopting this approach, the 'church in renewal' can continue to serve as a beacon of hope and transformation in an ever-evolving world, enabling the ancient gospel message to resonate anew in the hearts of today's people.

To achieve this, we must embrace a new culture of mentorship and apprenticing where experienced planters guide novices, not in a prescriptive manner but in a relational, creative, immersive journey of discovery and growth. This mentorship will be a crucible for innovation, where the wisdom of the mentor and the fresh insights of the apprentice blend to create new pathways for the gospel in our world.

As we look forward to the next season of ministry, let us envision not just a growing church but one that is thriving, pulsating with the creativity and energy of an expanding community in love with Jesus. This is the future we are called to forge, one where church planting is a craft and divine art, co-created with the Creator, offering hope and light to a world in need of God.

Notes

1 Some of the material in this chapter was first published in Selvaratnam, 2022.

2 For example, in 2021 the Church of England adopted a goal to start 10,000 new Christian communities in the next decade (Church of England, 2021).

3 Stephen Billett suggests the first evidence for apprenticeship is the Neolithic Agricultural Revolution, over 10,000 years ago (Billett, 2016, p. 618).

4 In this chapter, I have opted to retain the terms 'master' and 'journeyman' due to their historical significance within guild structures; however, my use of these terms is inclusive, referring to practitioners and trainers of both genders. I am also mindful of the contemporary discussions surrounding issues of privilege and power that the term 'master' might evoke.

5 The key scholarly commentators on medieval guilds are Anthony Black, Walter Cahn, Stephan R. Epstein, Robert Ignatius Letellier, George Unwin, Sheilagh Ogilvie, Geoffrey Gowlland, Eamon Duffy, Steven R. Smith, Patrick Wallis and Sylvia L. Thrupp. Their extensive study of the primary data is invaluable to understanding the guilds.

6 In this chapter, I do not specifically address formal theological training, which I believe is vital for genuine and long-lasting Christian ministry; instead, readers are encouraged to reflect on how the concepts explored here complement its well-understood benefits.

7 Other countries, including Japan, Ireland and North America, have historical apprenticeship systems. However, I have chosen not to reference these due to the distinct nature of their methodologies, which could lead to confusion if intermingled with the examples I discuss.

8 For a comprehensive introduction and analysis of English Medieval Craft Guilds, see Ogilvie, 2018.

9 As an illustration, in some parts of the global church community it is common practice for ministry candidates to demonstrate their initial learning by establishing one or more house churches. This requirement might include tasks such as evangelizing, fostering leadership skills in others and effectively managing the transition of leadership roles.

10 In literature this is described using various terms including *magnum opus* (Latin for great work), *chef-d'œuvre élevé* (French for high masterpiece), 'masterpiece' or 'masterwork'. See Cahn, 1979.

11 For examples of guild 'pieces' in different trades see Boileau, [1879] 2012.

12 In the contemporary era, there are other forms of on-the-job training besides those modelled on the guilds, such as mentorship programmes, job shadowing, job rotation, internships, industry visits, attendance at competitions, cross-training opportunities and action learning, which involves guided problem-solving in the workplace.

13 The term 'legitimate peripheral participation' describes the process by which newcomers gradually move towards more complex, central roles in a community of practice, through active participation and interaction with more experienced members. See Lave and Wenger, 1991, p. 29.

14 The concept of scaffolding in education was introduced by Jerome Bruner in 1976. The idea is explained more fully in Cairney, 1995, p. 36 and Wood et al., 2006, pp. 90, 98.

15 Scaffolding requires that instructors accurately assess the 'Zone of Proximal Development' (ZPD) for their trainees. The ZPD signifies the gap between what learners can accomplish independently and what they can achieve with the support and encouragement of a skilled supervisor. It involves presenting challenges that encourage growth without leading to overwhelm, while also ensuring that tasks are sufficiently demanding to maintain the learners' motivation. For more about ZPD, see Wood et al., 1976.

16 For a good introduction to this idea, see Polanyi, 1997, p. 96.

17 Over the past two decades, the emergence of mixed-mode training schemes has started to shift the foundational approach to ministerial training. However, despite these developments, Western training and formation programmes for ministers-in-training predominantly remain centred on academic and classroom-based methodologies.

18 Although we should be careful with a selection process operating in this way as it could unintentionally favour bias. Yet it might be possible to let experienced trainers choose their trainees if this approach is part of a larger system designed to prevent favouritism and discrimination; ensuring each qualified candidate is matched with a compatible mentor, to enhance training effectiveness through stronger mentor–trainee relationships.

19 Anecdotal evidence indicates that churches engaging in church planting often see a notable boost in leadership development. While the complete reasons for this remain unclear, it's evident that the potency of the training experience gained in such churches adds significant value. This is over and above the specific learning opportunities directly related to church planting.

20 The practical phase of training (the 'curacy stage') could become the initial step, preceding formal theological training, which currently serves as the first stage. Alternatively, a new foundational phase based in a local church setting could be introduced as an integral component of the early training and selection process.

References

Benson, Bruce Ellis, 2013, *Liturgy as a Way of Life: Embodying the Arts in Christian Worship*, Grand Rapids, MI: Baker Academic.
Billett, Stephen, 1994, 'Situating Learning in the Workplace – Having Another Look at Apprenticeships', *Industrial and Commercial Training* 26(11), pp. 9–16, doi:10.1108/00197859410073745.
——, 2014, *Mimetic Learning at Work: Learning in the Circumstances of Practice*, New York: Springer.
——, 2016, 'Apprenticeship as a Mode of Learning and Model of Education', *Education + Training* 58(6), pp. 613–28, doi:10.1108/ ET-01-2016-0001.
Boileau, Étienne, 2012 [1879], *Les métiers et corporations de Paris: XIIIe siècle. Le livre des métiers (Book of Trades) d'Étienne Boileau (1879)*, Hachette Livre-BNF.
Brown, John Seely and Paul Duguid, 1998, 'Organizing Knowledge', *California Management Review* 40(3), pp. 90–111.
Cahn, Walter, 1979, *Masterpieces: Chapters on the History of An Idea*, Princeton, NJ: Princeton University Press.
Cairney, Trevor H., 1995, *Pathways to Literacy*, London: Continuum International.
Church of England, 2021, *Vision and Strategy*, from https://www.churchofengland.org/about/vision-and-strategy (accessed 23.03.2024).
Collins, Allan, John Seely Brown and Susan E. Newman, 1989, 'Cognitive Apprenticeship: Teaching the Crafts of Reading, Writing, and Mathematics', in *Knowing, Learning, and Instruction: Essays in Honor of Robert Glaser*, ed. Lauren B. Resnick, Hillsdale, NJ: Lawrence Erlbaum Associates, pp. 453–94.
Epstein, Stephan R. and Maarten Roy Prak (eds), 2008, *Guilds, Innovation, and the European Economy, 1400–1800*, Cambridge: Cambridge University Press.

Girard, René et al., 1978, *Things Hidden Since the Foundation of the World*, trans. Stephen Bann and Michael Leigh Metteer, London: Bloomsbury Academic.

Irenaeus of Lyon, *Against Heresies* (c. 180), in Stefan Paas, 2016, *Church Planting in the Secular West: Learning from the European Experience*, Grand Rapids, MI: Eerdmans, p. 13.

Lave, Jean and Etienne Wenger, 1991, *Situated Learning: Legitimate Peripheral Participation*, Cambridge: Cambridge University Press.

Ogilvie, Sheilagh, 2018, *The European Guilds: An Economic Analysis*, Princeton, NJ: Princeton University Press.

Polanyi, Michael, 1966, *The Tacit Dimension*, New York: Doubleday.

——, 1997, *Personal Knowledge: Towards a Post-Critical Philosophy*, London: Routledge.

Ryan, J. G., 2000, 'Early Irish Crafts and Apprenticeships: An Historical Background', in *Prometheus's Fire: A History of Scientific and Technological Education in Ireland*, ed. Norman McMillan, Carlow, Ireland: Tyndall Publications, pp. 25–50.

Selvaratnam, Christian, 2022, *The Craft of Church Planting: Exploring the Lost Wisdom of Apprenticeship*, London: SCM Press.

Wallis, Patrick, 2008, 'Apprenticeship and Training in Premodern England', *The Journal of Economic History* 68(3), pp. 832–61, doi:10.1017/S002205070800065X.

Wellman, Jerry, 2009, 'Introduction', in *Organizational Learning: How Companies and Institutions Manage and Apply Knowledge*, Reston, VA: AIAA.

Wenger, Etienne, Richard McDermott and William M. Snyder, 2002, *Cultivating Communities of Practice: A Guide to Managing Knowledge*, Brighton, MA: Harvard Business School Press.

Wood, David, Jerome Bruner and G. Ross, 1976, 'The Role of Tutoring in Problem Solving', *Journal of Child Psychology and Psychiatry* 17(2), pp. 89–100, doi:10.1111/j.1469-7610.1976.tb00381.x.

Wulf, Christoph, 2008, 'Mimetic Learning', *Designs for Learning* 1(1), doi:10.16993/DFL.

——, 2014, 'Mimésis et Apprentissage Culturel', *Le Télémaque* 45(1), pp. 123–36, doi:10.3917/tele.045.0123, 123.

10

Venturing Upstream: Community Organizing as a Resource for Church Planting in a Post-Christian Culture

AYO AUDU AND CATHERINE BUTT

Introduction

As Archbishop Desmond Tutu urged, there comes a point when we need to stop just pulling people out of the river. We need to go upstream and find out why they are falling in.

When few in our communities have any connection with the gospel story, Community Organizing provides a powerful means of building trust, gaining reputational credibility and creating space to explore questions of meaning, purpose, vocation and faith. This chapter considers how the methodology and tools of Community Organizing might offer a rich resource for exploring where the Spirit is at work in and among people, and discerning how we might participate in this work. It asks whether new worshipping communities might emerge out of a shared desire to integrate an awareness of God and God's work with a yearning to address injustice.

We argue that with the three primary aims of strengthening the local organization, developing leaders and making change for the common good, Community Organizing can offer a sustainable framework for church planting, congregational growth, and leadership in the midst of a rapidly changing culture and a volatile economic and political landscape.

Catherine's story

My parents, like many of their generation, have a firm Christian heritage. My mum is C of E and my dad is a Methodist. When, in 1981, they moved with their young family into a brand-new house in a brand-new town in the north-east of England, they tried to go to church. They tried to go to their parish church, which was just up the hill and round the corner. I say 'tried' because it turned out not be as easy as just turning up and joining in.

I was probably four years old. One Sunday my mum took me to church. I think my dad had already decided there wasn't much there for him. Mum persisted a little longer. It was expected that I would join in with 'Sunday school' – which, as I remember it, consisted of a woman reading me a story from an old picture book in a tiny, cold vestry with one of those heaters with electric bars that had negligible impact on the temperature of the room. Four-year-old me didn't fancy that very much, so I made this clear in the only way a four-year-old knows how. It was tantrum time! My mum scooped me up under her arm and whisked me out of church. The big, heavy, wooden door slammed behind us, and we never went back. This is one of my very earliest memories.

Recently I asked my mum whether my memory resembled reality, as she had experienced it. Was that really the last time we tried church? Was it really that dramatic?

'Yes,' she said, 'that's about right. There was nothing there for us. People made us feel like we had moved into a house that had spoiled their view. They made us feel like we didn't belong there.'

Whether or not my or my mum's recollections are historically accurate, it's clear that, despite their best efforts, my parents were not served well by their local church as they tried to settle into that growing community.

You are probably reading this wee chapter of this book because you never want anything like this to happen to anyone, ever. Perhaps you are involved in the work of trying to make church and faith and 'God' more accessible to people who are searching for something they can't quite put their finger on. I imagine that, like me, you are also frustrated that the church seems to so often shoot itself in the foot when, on the one hand, we say, 'All are welcome!' and on the other, people who attempt to make a way in are met with strange looks and words that make them feel like they've entered a parallel universe where they will never find a home.

It's hard not to think 'what might have been' for my parents had they been offered a warm welcome, kind words and open arms at a time when they were coping with young children, elderly parents, recent bereavements and all the usual demands of working as secondary school teachers in the public sector. And it's hard not to blame the people who claimed their own seats in church and the vicar who clearly had no idea what it was like to manage small children. (On one of the occasions my mum had attempted church, he apparently made a comment in his sermon wondering how a parent could lose their child when they were out and about. My mum had just that week survived losing my toddler sister at the supermarket.)

As someone who has known the benefits and blessings of being part of different church fellowships since I first made my way back as a teenager, I do wonder 'what might have been' for those who try to go to church and are not met with a welcome that encourages them to stay. We're not even talking about people who are so far off that they would never darken the door of a church. These are people who are, for one reason or another, at one moment or another, ready to come in.

Reflecting theologically on my childhood memory and my current practice, what it comes down to is this: I refuse to believe that my parents' salvation (however we define that) has been jeopardized by the fact that the church was utterly abysmal at extending them decent hospitality all those years ago. We could debate theories of atonement and salvation, and the role our personal choice and subsequent discipleship might play; but the fundamental question is this: Who is ultimately responsible for someone's (eternal) life? Surely only God. I think we know this, in theory. But how far does our practice truly match up?

What are we, as church planters, as theologians, as practitioners, to make of this? My story is not unique. How are we to respond in what we all seem fairly satisfied to call our 'post-Christian' culture, when it is less and less likely that anyone will make that sort of effort to *come to* church? How are we to fruitfully integrate our response to this kind of story – which is probably a mix of anger, frustration, horror and shame – into our contemporary practice and into a life-giving soteriology that will inspire us over the long term?

My contention, arising out of my own context and the opportunity we have had over recent years to explore and experiment in this area, is that the methodology and tools of Community Organizing, which is a particular way of working for social change in the interests of the common good, offer us a way of doing just this. If this is new, good places to start are Citizens UK (www.citizensuk.org) or The Centre for Theology and Community (www.theology-centre.org).

First, Community Organizing offers us the space to confidently own the fire that motivates us in the work we do. Community Organizing encourages us to articulate our *self-interest* – the things we see and experience in 'the world as it is' that cause us pain, sorrow and anger. This is a powerful vocational motivation. Things should not be the way they are, and we want to make a difference. People should not turn up to church and be in any doubt that they have a place there. Regardless of age, experience, background, motivation or means, the unconditional love and welcome of God should be as apparent as it is possible for it to be. This is why I do what I do.

Community Organizing acknowledges and plainly articulates that 'the world as it is' is full of injustices, on a structural and a more personal scale. Wherever two or three are gathered, there follows organizational dysfunction, relational conflict and almost inevitably some measure of inequality. We might call this 'the consequence of the Fall', or as Francis Spufford puts it, 'The human propensity to fuck things up' (Spufford, 2013, p. 27).

And in the context of the themes of this book, we've certainly managed this with the church, haven't we? It's a mess – or at the very least it's not what it could be; there isn't space for everyone; people don't hear the gospel in ways they can recognize and respond to; there's a paucity to our spiritual awareness and practices. Not to mention the more structural or systemic failings and the many shortcomings with regard to safeguarding that have recently come to light. However, we also see the beauty and the holiness and the potential. We badly want things to be different and are moved to offer ourselves to make a difference. What do we actually want to change, and why? In identifying our self-interest, we are encouraged to discern, name and articulate the things that grieve us and that we dream can be different.

Second, as well as acknowledging the world as it is, Community Organizing also gives space for a vision of 'the world as it should be' – a vision, in Christian terms, of the kingdom of God, where human beings are able to thrive in their own vocations and in relationship with each other and with their Creator.

How do we edge further towards this 'world as it should be'? Community Organizing seeks to build and harness *relational power*. It is in genuine connection with one another that we build momentum for change – change for the common good, not just in my own personal interests. This is change that emerges from listening and responding to one another as equals. We might say that we are preferring one another's needs to our own.

Community Organizing offers a critique and an alternative to the mode of power often employed – either explicitly or implicitly – in the practice of church planting. Too often church planting is characterized by an assumption that a particular formula will have a particular effect – and sometimes it does, but we have to ask 'With what genuine long term benefit?' and 'At what cost?' Ben Aldous reflects powerfully on these questions (Aldous, 2022, p. x). Relational power, after the pattern of Christ, comes from 'emptying ourselves of all but love' – too often we have been puffed up and full of all sorts of other rubbish instead. My colleague and friend Ayo reflects in more depth on this below from his own perspective.

Third, in a culture and a church where burnout and poor mental health are a threat to our corporate well-being and the mission of the church, Community Organizing offers *an intentional cycle of action and contemplation that helps to sustain us over the long term.* It is understood that lasting fruit takes a long time to grow, that real change is hard won and needs protecting once achieved, and that we need one another in order to survive and thrive.

Church planters love results, and inevitably we get caught up in monitoring progress in qualitative ways. Partly, we are longing and looking for encouraging signs, but often we are dependent on funders who need to see a return on their investment and who are gagging for missional ideas and packages that are demonstrably replicable. At worst we fall into the trap of competition and comparison. We must resist the lie that busy-ness, activity and a full programme are what nourishes real spiritual transformation, and the fallacy that replicability means we can guarantee 'success'.

Community Organizing encourages regular *disorganizing to reorganize*, recognizing that what worked last time won't necessarily work this time. We are challenged to intentionally dismantle what we have come to rely on to keep us going. This can be a healthy and stimulating approach that helps keep us fresh and accountable.

I am convinced that God's work of salvation – of 'reconciling the world to himself' – will not be compromised by the shortcomings of a church that often seems incapable of offering a welcome to those who are searching for a place to call home. God is bigger than this. God is already and always active in the world in ways that we are sometimes reluctant to recognize and acknowledge. In today's post-Christian culture, we are in need of a wide and expansive soteriology; a humble, curious pneumatology, and an ecclesiology that allows for innovative responses to the lived experience of those we serve. The practice of Community Organizing can help us towards these.

Ayo's story

Community Organizing methodology offers us a chance not only to appeal to a post-Christian context; it also speaks to the colonial legacy now attributed to missional initiatives. The planting of churches in places such as Nigeria, where I grew up, continues to be viewed through the prism of colonial enterprise. The role of missionaries in the colonization of Africa following the Berlin Conference of 1884 has been articulated exhaustively elsewhere. Harvey Kwiyani hints at this collusion when he argues that 'mission and colonialism were viewed as two sides of the same coin – and that coin was the domination of the nations' (Kwiyani, 2020, p. 46). Even when there were no explicit links with the colonial enterprise, the outworking of missionary endeavour was implicitly colonial

(Kwiyani, 2020, p. 46; Donovan, 2019, p. 6). This is why the language of church planting has a morally problematic underbelly for me.

Can it be argued that the same missionary impulse now finds expression in the 'worship first' model of church planting? A 'form of spiritual gentrification' where:

> people who are not a part of a community or social context move there and set up shop in 'Jesus' name', driven by a belief that they are starting from scratch, with nothing, and are called to establish spiritual communities for the sake of people with whom they have not built relationship. (Crosby, 2021)

Alicia Crosby queries what outcomes are envisaged when 'people with means and privilege enter into a space and exert their will over that of the people who are longtime residents'.

This trend is portentous. It indicates a theology of planting that is yet to repent of a desire to take over and dominate. I find myself agreeing with Ben Aldous when he argues that this model of planting 'brings a tyranny of change that does not bode well for the future Church' (Aldous, 2022, p. 53). This state of play informs identification by Aldous et al. of the major problem with pioneer ministry as 'too often see[ing] new places as areas of potential discovery and colonisation, not as places where God is already at work among the indigenous people' (Aldous et al., 2022, p. 9). Crosby asserts that 'time and time again people with racial and economic privilege exercise the hubris to start something outside of the places that they've called home just because they want to and they can' (Crosby, 2021). I wonder then if a corrective to this might be an approach that seeks to identify that which pre-exists our arrival, honours and dignifies what has already gone ahead before considering the feasibility of catalysing divine activity.

That identification can take place within the *1:1 relational meeting*, which is the core tool of Community Organizing. Space is offered for the other to be heard and for the Holy Spirit's prevenient activity to be recognized and named, allowing it to come into focus and be celebrated. Practitioners no longer arrive in a context with a set mission to make converts and plant churches. Instead, they hear the residents, then seek to respond in love. After all, as Donovan notes, 'Evangelization is the process of bringing the gospel to people where they are, not where you would like them to be' (Donovan, 2019, p. xiii). There is a lot in contemporary literature about the importance of listening. What is seldom discussed is how this should be done. What follows is an attempt at proffering the 1:1 relational meeting as a tool for listening well.

Unlike when the language of catalysis is borrowed from chemical processes, the practitioner's listening posture ought to open them up to being changed by the Holy Spirit. This is seen in the relinquishing of any preconceived ideas of what their mission is in that context. It presupposes equity in the power dynamic. It establishes relational power, as Catherine has described above, and the power imbalance inherent within the 'worship first' model can be redressed.

What does this deep listening require? It requires setting aside our priorities in order to hear the other. It requires a recognition of our power and privilege. It requires humility. It requires a de-skilling. It requires kenosis. We are only able to do this as we are imbued by the Holy Spirit with love for the other. That love enables us to offer the other the dignity of being heard. The dignity of being noticed. The dignity of being valued. We seek to join in only when we have discerned the Holy Spirit already at work. When Vincent Donovan is asked by a Masai tribe whether his 'tribe' has found the Most High God, he responds, 'No ... I have come a long, long distance to invite you to search for him with me' (Donovan, 2019, p. ix). Donovan was willing to set aside his theology in order that a theology that reflected the context could emerge. Chris Lane suggests that the humility shown by Donovan has echoes of St Aidan's seventh-century mission to the tribes of northern England; that is, not imposing the gospel from a position of power, but offering it with openness and a willingness to listen and learn (Lane, Foreword in Donovan, 2019, p. viii).

There must be an acceptance that there is no compulsion for the practitioner to join in. They only do so in response to the Holy Spirit, the other and a humble assessment of their own ability with the Holy Spirit to further the work that is already ongoing. This posture is radically different from the colonial era missionary endeavours that proceeded on the basis of the 'European belief in their own superiority and that their domination of the world was God-ordained' (Kwiyani, 2020, p. 47). This is hardly surprising given that the Edinburgh Missionary Conference of 1910 ushered in the so-called 'Christian Century' by concluding that Africa 'had nothing to offer religiously' (Sanneh, 2003, p. 18).

If, as Stephen Bevans argues, 'all theology is contextual' (2018, p. 30), what scope is there for church planting to make space for a faithful homegrown theology that reflects its context? It is no wonder Christianity in Africa only grew numerically once the colonizers had left (Donovan, 2019, p. 5). This was due to the emergence of a theology that reflected the local context. The expansion and spread of Christianity was virtually limited to those societies whose people had preserved the indigenous name for God. Should it come as a surprise, then, that across Africa 'the apparent congruity between Christianity and the indigenous name for

God finds a parallel in the fact of Christian expansion occurring *after* rather than during colonialism' (Sanneh, 2003, p. 18; emphasis original)?

Continuing to apply models of church planting weighed down by problematic historical baggage is akin to what St James derides as looking in the mirror and immediately forgetting what one looks like (James 1.23–24). We need an honest reappraisal of our inherited church planting practice and theology, particularly on an institutional level.

A renewed posture of curiosity and humility and a willingness to hold contextual antecedents with dignity may help us along the path towards planting sustainable churches that in turn birth other churches. In committing ourselves to intentional relational conversations, may we listen to what the Holy Spirit is already saying and attend to our own posture of power. Here might we find ourselves on holy ground, laying down our own agendas in readiness to be re-formed, by Christ and by our context.

Catherine and Ayo: concluding remarks

We were born within eight months of one another, in the same academic year, but 3,000 miles apart and separated by many cultural differences. Our families look very different, and our paths through the respective education systems in western Nigeria and northern England bear minimal resemblance to one another. We have both navigated an 'interesting' mix of privilege and prejudice during our lives so far. Our journeys of faith have taken different turns but, intriguingly, have both been shaped by Pentecostalism and the charismatic movement, the evangelical roots of the churches where we found faith, an affection for and commitment to the Anglican church (along with intermittent episodes of intense frustration!) and the exploration of more contemplative spirituality. We look back with gratitude when we remember the manner in which God graciously allowed our paths to cross, and are humbled by what we have learnt together along the way, and in particular how we have been shaped by each other.

A key aspect of our recent learning has been our exploration, with others, of Community Organizing as a rich resource for mission. It has, for us, become part of our spiritual discipline and a foundational practical framework for ministry. The 'why' of our mission, which we must not lose sight of (Paas, 2021, p. 146), might be summarized thus: we invest in our community – through careful listening to their experience of the world as it is, building relational power through intentional 1:1 conversations, and taking action for the common good – in order that we might experience liberation from bondage and greater fullness of life.

There is wonderful potential for us to be transformed, together, more into the likeness of Christ. In short, we long to participate in the work of God who is 'reconciling all things to himself in Christ'.

Community Organizing offers a resource for mission that is humble yet confident, courageous yet compassionate, unashamedly focused on taking action for social change yet sustained by intentional contemplation and evaluation. It will be perfectly clear that we don't have a fully coherent answer to the question 'What are you doing?' However, we are excited to learn all we can as we do our best to discern the Spirit's movement around, between and within us. We consider it a great privilege to participate in even a small way and to share our reflections here.

To follow up:
www.stfrideswides.org
ayo@stfrideswides.org
vicar@stfrideswides.org

References

Aldous, B., 2022, *The God Who Walks Slowly: Reflections on Mission with Kosuke Koyama*, London: SCM Press.
Aldous, B., L. Larner, A. Schleifenbaum and R. Sidhu, 2022 'Problems with "Pioneering" Mission: Reflections on the Term "Pioneer" from Germany, South Africa and the UK', *Ecclesial Futures* 3.1, pp. 5–22.
Bevans, S. B., 2018, *Essays in Contextual Theology*, Leiden: Brill.
Crosby, A. T., 2021, 'But What is Church Planting, if not Spiritual Gentrification Persevering?', https://www.aliciatcrosby.com/blog/2021/3/4/but-what-is-church-planting-if-not-spiritual-gentrification-persevering (accessed 03.03.2023).
Donovan, V. J., 2019, *Christianity Rediscovered: An Epistle from the Masai*, London: SCM Press.
Kwiyani, H., 2020, *Multicultural Kingdom: Ethnic Diversity, Mission and the Church*, London: SCM Press.
Paas, S., 2021, 'Missional Christian Communities in Conditions of Marginality: On Finding a "Missional Existence" in the Post-Christian West', *Mission Studies* 38.1, pp. 142–60.
Sanneh, L., 2003, *Whose Religion is Christianity? The Gospel beyond the West*, Grand Rapids, MI: Eerdmans.
Spufford, F., 2013, *Unapologetic: Why, Despite Everything, Christianity Can Still Make Surprising Emotional Sense*, London: Faber & Faber.

Reflections on Part Two

One of the central issues arising from the chapters of Part Two is the formation of those men and women being trained to lead in new church contexts. All four chapters pick up on the need for training to focus specifically and contextually on the needs of the community and the giftings and backgrounds of its leaders. For instance, as Wier stresses, pioneering is a distinctive role that needs to be recognized as such, rather than resorting to the dismissive, 'Aren't all church leaders pioneering in their own way, anyway?' As Selvaratnam highlights, the ministry of planting cannot be easily taught in the confines of a theological college or classroom. If starting new churches is important for the future of the church, then these reflections must be heard.

However, a guiding theme that often shapes the discernment (or recruitment) of new church leaders in major denominations in the West is 'deployability'. Candidates must be able to understand the breadth of their traditions and be prepared to exercise leadership in less than ideal circumstances. For instance, it is increasingly the norm in the Church of England that full-time stipendiary clergy are responsible for multiple parishes, many of which are too small to financially support a full-time priest. And this reality must also inform the ways in which we train and admit new ordinands for training. There is a certain amount of common sense to this notion: there is no use in pouring years of resources into a practitioner who is only useful to one context and place, or else their ministry will cease when their time in that context finishes.

However, in talking about national deployability, a culture of decline can easily slip into the narrative around training and discernment; ministers need to be able to confront the 'realities' of ministry in the coming decades and have first-hand experience of working in declining contexts. But as Ayokunle's chapter so forcefully highlights, this view of 'deployability' seems only to extend narrowly to the confines of the Western institutional church. In taking a broader, global perspective on the church, this narrative of decline is put in a much broader context, according to which institutional decline is a small part of the life of the church. And so we might ask: How far does deployability reach? Only to the insular demands of an institution? Are we training people for decline-management in an institutional church? Or more broadly, for the ministry and mission of God, as so powerfully depicted in Part One?

Moreover, as well as raising questions about the scope of the concept of deployability, these chapters also highlight a tension between the broader needs of an institution and the wider church, and the specific needs of contexts and communities. Can the kind of skills Audu and Butt find rooted in Community Organizing be taught in a general way? Or are they specifically tied to concrete communities and places? Surely, as Selvaratnam argues, there are some transferable skills acquired in learning the 'craft' of church planting; a practitioner who has several years of experience in engaging with communities in the north-east of England will have learnt tools and techniques that might equip them to serve in deprived areas of Scotland, even if there is a significant amount of cultural, contextual learning to do. But how generally can these tools and techniques be taught and learnt?

Almost every major denomination and tradition operating within the United Kingdom has some strategy around starting new churches (or 'new things', to borrow a phrase from Foulger's (2024) research). And so these questions around training, discernment and deployment are not likely to become less significant at any point. Nor are they confined only to the question of how to train clergy, ministers or senior leaders. As Wier's chapter shows, there is a need to understand distinctive roles within the church, their place in contributing to *new things*, and to provide relevant resources to empower people in these roles. It will not do just to double-down on clergy training. In his recent challenge to the funding of new youth ministry initiatives in the Church of England, Pete Ward urges the Church of England to ensure that the money they are investing is not wasted because of a failure to address systemic issues around training and culture:

> As various dedicated courses and schemes have closed down, youth ministry training risks becoming too generic, without enough connection between those who are innovating on the ground and those who are being trained. Practitioners need to support, and learn from, each other. The Church has also failed to offer the kind of terms and conditions of employment that can sustain a career. Low pay (and the sense that clergy will always carry more status in the organisation) eroded the confidence of those we had trained and, after one or two jobs, most moved on. (Ward, 2024).

Ward's point is surely true of ministry training more generally. If the epitome of church leadership is seen as the 'deployable' minister who can manage decline well, then the issues raised in the chapters of this part of the book will not be resolved. No amount of funding will solve the issue, either. The questions raised challenge the culture, mode and method of training across church traditions.

References

Foulger, Will, 2024, *New Things: A Theological Investigation into the Work of Starting New Churches across 11 Dioceses in the Church of England*, https://www.cranmerhall.com/wp-content/uploads/2024/03/New-Things-Final-1.pdf (accessed 22.03.2024).

Ward, Pete, 2024, 'The Magic Money Tree for Work with Children and Young People: Good News?', https://viamedia.news/2024/01/09/the-magic-money-tree-for-work-with-children-and-young-people-good-news (accessed 22.03.2024).

PART THREE

Context: Learning from New Churches

11

Small, Simple, Slow: Missional Community as Faithful Ecclesial Expression in the Context of Late Modernity

PAUL BRADBURY

Introduction

In 2008 I was the grateful recipient of an invitation from the Diocese of Salisbury to start a new expression of church in Poole, Dorset that would be orientated to those with little or no experience of time-honoured church.[1] A year later we started a small expression of church called Reconnect, which we described as a 'missional community'. That community spent its first year developing what we call a 'Way of Life', a set of statements that expressed our aspiration as to how we as a community might live out the challenge of the gospel together. We also established an evolving 'rhythm of prayer', resources for prayer based on a mixture of the daily office and points of gathering for the community to come together in prayer. These two elements, a way of life and rhythm of prayer, are the foundation that continues to support our life together (see https://www.reconnect-poole.org.uk).

Fifteen years ago the term 'missional community' was not new. In the late 1990s and early 2000s, St Thomas' Crookes in Sheffield, under the leadership of Mike Breen, had explored the development of 'mid-sized missional communities' alongside the large congregational gatherings. At around the same time, Phil Potter at St Mark's, Haydock had encouraged a more missional mindset for the small groups in the church through the adoption of a 'cell church' model. He then introduced a mid-sized missional community structure that encouraged the formation of new communities with a particular missional call to a place or network of people (Hopkins and Breen, 2008). The spread of these ideas and practices, through the likes of 3DM (https://www.3dmovements.com/) and

The Order of Mission (TOM, https://www.missionorder.org/), has since seen this emphasis on smaller, more locally contextualized communities of people as the locus for ecclesial life and mission gain traction in the UK and further afield. Similar communities have emerged from within the 24/7 Prayer movement (Freeman and Greig, 2007) and the alternative worship movement.[2]

Despite these various streams of the development of missional community, the missional ecclesiology expressed by these small communities has struggled to gain credence. The publication of popular books by the likes of Alan Scott and Francis Chan, both well-known leaders of large, gathered expressions of church, now advocating the dispersed and contextual dimension of the church's mission, has hinted at a mainstream change in emphasis (Chan, 2018; Scott, 2018). Nevertheless, in its concern to renew the growth and financial sustainability of the church (General Synod, 2017), the Church of England has directed large sums of money through the Strategic Development Fund towards the planting of new congregations. The instincts of many Church of England dioceses, who apply within a competitive bidding process for these funds, has been to continue with the congregation as the main unit and agent in the formation of new ecclesial communities.[3]

Despite this, new networks of small missional communities continue to emerge. By the time the pandemic hit, Reconnect had multiplied into four missional communities in different neighbourhoods of Poole. I had passed on the leadership of Reconnect to concentrate on developing its parent charity, Poole Missional Communities, as a nurturing space for local missional communities and as an advocate for the mixed ecology of church (https://www.poolemc.org.uk). I began to connect with others across the UK working in similar ways to us and discovered a whole host of networks of missional communities, of various denominations. Perhaps these networks grew in the pandemic, or perhaps the pandemic created the environment whereby these networks found their voice. Either way they came to my attention in a way that suggested something was happening that the church needed to take notice of.

Over the course of six months, I interviewed seven leaders involved in this movement.[4] This chapter brings the results of these interviews into conversation with my own experience of the missional community movement and with current discourses in missional ecclesiology. I aim to explore the distinctiveness and relevance of missional communities, in particular in relation to the Church of England and its expressed intention to reverse its observed decline and its ambition to start a substantial number of new communities of faith in the coming decade (Cottrell, 2021).

Travelling lighter

We need to travel more lightly. And I think God has a new future for us. And it's a future which is described better by the relational, doing life together, God at the heart of it, God present, [us] being led by the Spirit.

For many early adopters of missional communities these forms were part of a restructuring of existing churches to better orientate their members for mission in their own contexts. The hope was that a single church organization could hold in tension four sizes of gathering, which would better enable the church to inhabit dimensions of gathered worship, pastoral care, discipleship and mission.[5] While many large churches have attempted this restructuring around mid-sized communities, few seem to have made a complete transition in a sustainable way. The network of missional communities I researched placed an emphasis on the local missional community. The gathering of these communities into a more congregational space was of less importance.

This observation tallies with a significant shift that is taking place in the disposition of many in our churches away from Sunday-by-Sunday congregational worship and towards the embracing of a more dispersed identity of the church. People are reframing their understanding and association with the church in new ways. And one of the key drivers for that reframing is a desire to be able to focus more intentionally on witness along the grain of their own lives. Steve Aisthorpe's research into 'church leavers' revealed that 'among Christians who are not engaged with a church congregation, for some, their concern to be effective in that mission was instrumental in deciding to move out, or remain out, of congregational life' (Aisthorpe, 2016).[6] One third of those Aisthorpe surveyed agreed with the statement 'Not being involved in a traditional church congregation frees me to pursue what I believe is my Christian calling' (p. 117). This shift was also articulated among those I interviewed:

This post-Christendom, post-congregation thing, is much bigger than we might dare to imagine. Everyone's hammering away at running Sunday, and that needs to keep happening, but most of our resources go into that and most time and effort, but we found a load of people sensing, feeling and being nowhere or being in a liminal space.

Likewise, another leader said that the principles that informed the missional community network forming under his leadership *'were the same as "church"'* but that *'they're more beautiful and deeper when they are free'*.

Might the distinctiveness of small missional communities for many be in terms of the reframing of the dimensions of Christian communal life in ways that are less demanding of people's time and energy? Might their distinctiveness therefore be in the degree to which they enable people to fulfil their perceived calling as witnesses to Christ within the capacity and context of their own lives?

Being with

You don't plant churches, you just live your life, and then you realize one day that you've got a church.

One of the clear intentions for the life of Reconnect when we started was to place the responsibility for witness on our life as a community. We sought to avoid mission projects that looked for resources of time and energy from within the community. Rather we placed an emphasis on the patient business of living well as a Christian community, developing a pattern of prayer and our Way of Life. We also looked to enable a more inductive approach to any kind of organized mission, inviting people to self-organize around activity they might already be engaged in and already enjoy doing. Out of this approach emerged a series of groups and small projects that helped build relationships and community around activities as diverse as brewing, felt-making, gardening and journalling. A similar posture of mission is articulated by those I interviewed, a posture that might be summarized as a commitment to a mutual 'being with',[7] a commitment to life together in mutual and open conversation with the lives of those the community lives among.

This missional disposition signals a distinctive shift away from mission as activity and towards mission as the fruit of communal being. Consequently it's not '*running an event that we can tick a box and say, we've done some mission*'. Rather it's more like '*We'll model a Christian community and grow in character and do life well.*' Likewise, in the context of a village that has experienced significant brokenness, division and unforgiveness, the missional community seeks to become '*a community of others that refuses to split and disagree*'. The concept of a '*mission field*', which can be seen as having an externalizing effect on a shared context, is displaced by a sense of mission being the fruit of living well as communities of Christ. The community's mission field is '*just kind of wherever I am*' – '*Every day is a personal life being lived in such a way that it shines. And so in a way we're less aware of who our mission field is.*'

Might the distinctiveness of missional communities also lie in their missiological disposition whereby mission is what happens when the community commits itself to live well together as Christian disciples in the midst of the lives of those whose context it shares?

Five values of missional community

From the 15 years of my own experience of leading and being part of a network of missional communities, and thickened by these interviews with other network leaders, I developed a list of the five values that distil the essence of missional community. These values articulate my own sense of how the shift towards a lighter and more mutually present expression of Christian community is embodied. These values will not necessarily be the way in which the communities associated with those I interviewed express their own sense of identity and practice. However, along with a commitment to prayer and a 'Rule' or 'Way of Life', whether that is written down in some form or not, these values provide an articulation of what these communities hold in common in their approach to their communal life:

- **Small** – Christian community that is small enough to enable us to be 'one another',[8] to adapt quickly to the changing world around it, to be participative and foster belonging.
- **Slow** – Christian community that resists the accelerating pace of modern life with events and programmes that must always be better and more popular than the last, that doesn't exhaust people, that moves on average at a human pace, the pace of love, and the pace that allows for the voice of God to be heard.
- **Simple** – Christian community that is earthed in people's lives: the kitchen table, the back garden, the café and the street; that holds lightly to the heavy burdens of buildings and staff teams and is therefore simple enough for relationships to remain the priority.
- **Sent** – Christian community that is consciously in the world in the name of the One who sends: local and deeply attentive to its context, not imposing its own agenda, not just meeting a perceived need on its own terms, but joining in with the story of a place to help make authentic connections between the life of a community and the good news of the gospel.
- **Serving** – Christian community that serves the missionary Spirit of God and therefore serves its local community and serves the desire that people have for fullness of life and for loving relationships with one another, with creation and with God through Jesus Christ.

I have sought therefore to sketch out in words the nature of the small missional communities that are currently proliferating, their values and their practices. Space restricts me to a very short sketch as a summary of the life of these communities. A fuller description would be welcome. However, I hope what has preceded has given enough for us to explore some other key questions. What significance do these communities have for the mission of the church in our secular age? How relevant are these missional communities for church planting? To what extent might these communities offer an important option for the church as it seeks to engage with new contexts and contexts now significantly disconnected from the life of the church?

Refounding for mission

A great deal of attention has been paid to an analysis of the cultural change we are going through in terms of the decline in religious affiliation and the consequent decline in attendance and commitment to the mainstream denominations of the church in the West. This is an important area of study but it tends to turn the complexity of what is taking place into a binary of those who continue to attend church and those who don't. We are trying to read the signs of the time, but only through the lens of our own anxiety about the decline of the church.[9] Reflecting on the description of missional communities given earlier, I want to suggest that missional communities are a sign of a refounding of the church in the light of two fundamental crises in the context of late modernity that affect the church along with the whole of Western society – crises in our habitation of first, time and second, place.

Andrew Root argues that the crisis we face as a church is not primarily one of decline, but one of time. The logic of modernity, he argues, is the logic of acceleration.[10] Time no longer has any connection with the sacred. Modernity has transformed time from an inherent condition within God's creation, indeed a creature of God's creation, to a commodity, a resource, that can be used, spent, wasted. In spiritual terms we have become a people 'who think we have to fit God in rather than fit in with what God is doing' (Swinton, 2016, p. 30). The result is acceleration, the drive to do more and more with less and less time. For organizations, one of the consequences of this acceleration is an idolization of innovation as the means by which they can 'stay ahead'. This desperate need for innovation is, Root argues, just one of the consequences of a more fundamental existential dependence on growth in order to keep an organization viable. Our future as a church becomes dependent upon growth in a way that affects how we understand and practise our life as a church. It becomes our hermeneutic, the lens through which we approach the practice of church life (Root, 2021 and 2022).

Furthermore, our human experience in the midst of this world of acceleration becomes one of 'alienation'. That is, an experience of exhaustion, disaffection and a disconnection from the kinds of deep, relational and meaningful experiences that give us a sense of the fullness of life. As Root describes, we are 'moving so fast for the sake of the good of the new, which stabilizes our identities and institutions, that the world becomes dull and lifeless. Trying to keep up, we become too tired to actually live' (Root, 2021, p. 182). This experience extends to our experience of church in terms of frenetic activity, innovation and endless demands on people's time and resources. So what Root suggests might be termed *la fatigue d'être église* (Root, 2021, p. 37) is an extension of the cultural malaise affecting the Western world in late modernity.

For the church there are no easy answers to the challenge of acceleration and alienation. We find ourselves in a double-bind, caught between being the kind of organization that connects with a culture that sees busyness and growth as a kind of higher good and yet one that competes for the time and energy of those who come to church. The church becomes just one player in a society that is in essence a marketplace for people's time and attention. A dilemma exists too between engaging with the culture of the society we are in and yet also offering a prophetic challenge to many elements of it. In this respect, a single church congregation may not be able to offer both engagement and challenge in the same organization. Larger, busy churches, for example, may do well in demonstrating relevance within the busy culture of late modernity but struggle to also provide a sustained, meaningful expression of deep community in which the slower work of relational discipleship and spiritual growth takes place.[11] However, might a mixed ecology of churches that includes those deliberately offering a prophetic communal expression of life in the rhythms of sacred time at least be able to hold that dilemma open? Might such a deliberate mixed ecology provide varied paths of discipleship and spiritual growth for people grappling with the need to live as Christians in late modernity?

The second crisis element lies in the habitation of place. Part of the consequence of acceleration, and the experience of alienation that accompanies it, is an alienation with regard to place. Geographers make the distinction between space and place. Where space is a more neutral concept that encapsulates the physical, measurable nature of somewhere, place connects more deeply with history, story and with the contingencies that have shaped a location. Modernity has favoured space over place.

The drive for growth and efficiency has downplayed the local and the particular in favour of large business models that iron out difference. Thus, for example, high streets look the same from one end of the country to the other.[12] This 'McDonaldization' of society[13] likewise has its parallels in the church, with pragmatic approaches to church growth focusing attention on what 'works' in society in general, and less on the particularities of place (Drane, 2000).

Small missional communities present one example of an expression of church that looks to take place seriously, over and above space. The incarnational theology that informs the disposition of 'being with' in the particularity of place is foundational to these communities. Further, they represent the expression of a missional ecclesiology that rejects a kind of instrumentalization of space, and the resources contained within it, in service of the church. The corollary of the alienation of place by modernity is a rendering of the complexities of place into flat cartographies of potential resource that can be exploited for modernity's ends. In ecclesiological terms this influence of modernity alienates churches from their context, and externalizes contexts into demographies of resource described in terms such as, for example, 'target audience'. The practice of missional community seeks to inhabit a 'cartography of love'[14] for a place. This will involve deep listening to a context, its people and its history. And it will involve bringing this listening into conversation with a deep attention to Scripture and to the voice of the Holy Spirit at work in a place. This amounts to a conscious disposition for the church in society, the adoption of a much humbler and more participative relationship towards that particular part of the world that God has called us to. It signals a recognition that the church can no longer adopt any kind of hegemonical position within society in terms of what makes a good place. The evolving work of creating places that make for an experience of the fullness of life is one of partnership, in which the church enters into conversation and creative partnership with others. Such a disposition harbours an openness to the potential that 'the LORD is in this place, and I was not aware of it' (Gen. 28.16, NIV).

Missional communities and church planting

What then might small missional communities have to offer in terms of church planting? How can they help the church evolve in its call to be a witnessing communal presence within the complexity of late-modern society? To begin to answer these two connected questions you have to ask: What is church planting in late-modern Britain actually for? There is a suspicion that the current attention paid to church planting within the Church of England may well have more to do with a concern to restore the institution than to renew its witness. Stefan Paas has argued that much church planting in Western Europe is motivated by nostalgic visions towards restoring the kind of institutional strength that was the experience of Christendom, or by visions of denominational expansion (Paas, 2016). Within the secular context of the West,[15] however, the argument for these visions is increasingly unfounded.

Yet what the instrumentalizing of church planting as a method reveals is an untethering of missional ecclesiology from its roots in the church's divine vocation. Church planting is what happens when the church responds faithfully to its call to express the command of Christ to 'be my witnesses in Jerusalem, and in all Judea and Samaria, and to the ends of the earth' (Acts 1.8, NIV). In that sense, as Paas argues, 'the Church does not exist to change the world or expand constantly … "doxology" is the purpose of the Church' (Paas, 2019, pp. 222–3). The church is not the end for which church planting is the means. Doxology, expressed in faithful lives of discipleship with others in loving attention and service to the world, is the end within which the creation of new Christian communities may well be a means.

In the embodiment of that doxological life the church has always morphed and changed in its forms and practices in ways that reveal an ongoing creative conversation between Scripture, tradition and context. When we reflect on the form and practice of the church in history and across cultures, we see a bewildering diversity of ways of being church, many wildly different from our own.[16] The forms we call church are more accurately 'emergent phenomena' (Duerksen and Dyrness, 2019, p. 26) arising from this ongoing practical exploration at the interface between Scripture, tradition and context.

So my question is: To what extent might small missional community be a faithful form of church that God is calling into being by his Spirit in the context of late modernity?[17] To which one response might be 'It's too early to tell!' Nevertheless, what I observe are communities of faithful disciples responding to that apostolic call of the Spirit to form Christian community in new contexts, often at the edges of society where the church is absent. They are doing so in ways that, in their commitment to the incarnational imperative of 'being with' those in their community in a Christlike disposition of solidarity, dialogue and partnership, mean their method (if it can be called a method) is rooted in relationality and being. And they are doing so in ways that seem to be offering a practical-prophetic response to the experience of alienation in terms of place and time that is the predicament of the late-modern West.

For these reasons I do believe we may be witnessing a renaissance of the kind of prophetic-apostolic communities of prayer and practice that have been a dominant feature of the church in other eras but which have been something of a Cinderella within particularly the Protestant church since the Reformation. Such expressions of church have historically existed in creative conversation with more institutional forms of church (Winter, 1974).[18] Indeed, it is from these small, agile missional communities that renewal has flowed into the institutional church in times of social upheaval and crisis. Those in positions of responsibility with institutions must therefore ask how to create the space and resource for these communities to continue to multiply and flourish within a mixed ecology of church.

Notes

1 The use of the term 'time-honoured church' attempts to avoid creating false binaries in how the modern church is often described. Terms such as 'traditional' or 'inherited' can often be used in contrast to 'new' or 'fresh' forms of church. This implies little or no engagement with tradition on the part of newer churches and can be construed as a critique of older churches. 'Time-honoured church' is a term that seeks to bring tradition, and by implication newer churches, within the perspective of a longer view of history.

2 See Cray et al., 2010. Another strand of this movement might be discerned among groups exploring Christian communal life in the light of the climate crisis, drawing inspiration from a powerful phrase from the Catholic philosopher Alasdair MacIntyre: 'What matters at this stage is the construction of local forms of community within which civility and the intellectual and moral life can be sustained through the dark ages which are already upon us ... We are waiting not for Godot, but for another – doubtless very different – Benedict' (MacIntyre, 1981, p. 305). See for example Oldfield, 2023.

3 An independent analysis of SDF-funded projects between 2014 and 2021 shows that over half of the funds were awarded to resource church projects. These projects amounted to nearly 40% of all projects funded. See Chote et al., 2022, pp. 31–2.

4 These leaders were associated with Anglican, Baptist and Independent denominations. Quotes from the interviews are presented in italics in the following discussion.

5 Joseph Myers' book *The Search to Belong* was particularly influential in this regard (Myers, 2003). Myers argued that there are four levels of social connection that were needed to enable human flourishing: intimate space, personal space, social space and public space. Prayer partnerships/triplets, house groups and congregational worship were seen to fit three of these four spaces. Mid-sized missional communities were designed to fulfil the function of social space, a dimension that was perceived to be lacking in church structures as they were currently organized.

6 Aisthorpe's research was among those who are no longer affiliated to a congregation. In that sense they had 'left church'. However, his research showed that

far from having lost their faith these people were motivated by a desire to better live out their faith beyond the demands and responsibilities of a congregation.

7 This phrase is associated with the missional theology of Sam Wells. See for example Wells, 2018.

8 John V. Taylor argues for the significance of the term 'one another', used frequently in the New Testament when describing the early church. Taylor asks what kind of structure fosters the kind of participative life in the Spirit that these pictures evoke and which guard against the tendency towards intuitionalism and control. Taylor argues that the answer lies in the testimony of the early church, which displays a consistent participative quality throughout the New Testament. This can be seen in the word *allelon*, 'one another', which punctuates the New Testament 'like a peal of bells' (Taylor, 1972, p. 126). Taylor goes on to argue that 'the ideal shape of the church is such as will provide this "one-another-ness" with the least possible withdrawal of Christians from their corporateness with their fellow men in the world' (p. 148). That size and shape is therefore likely to be small: small enough to allow for 'one-another-ing' within and protecting against the alienating effect that large structuring inevitably brings. Taylor therefore argues for the renewal of the 'little congregations' as a shape and size of church that is better able to embody the participative spirit of the early churches' witness of *allelon*.

9 Thus the language of churched, dechurched, unchurched, which remains a common lens for scoping out the landscape for missional ecclesiology.

10 Root draws extensively in his argument from the German philosopher Hartmut Rosa; see for example, Rosa, 2014.

11 In this respect Root notes the dilemma many, in particular larger congregational churches, face between relevance and 'resonance'. Resonance is the word Root uses to describe the kind of deep relational experience of fullness of life in contrast to the alienation created by the experience of acceleration (Root, 2021, ch. 14).

12 See Will Foulger, 2023, in particular chapter 1 for an excellent discussion of the differences between place and space. It could be said however, post-pandemic, that in the arena of local retail, place is making a comeback as local high streets adapt to the embeddedness of internet shopping and look to offer distinctive, local and particular shops in their locality.

13 A term coined by George Ritzer (Ritzer, 2015, cited in Foulger, 2023, p. 35).

14 A term I offered in a longer reflection on pioneer ministry and contextual listening. See Bradbury, 2016, chapter 5.

15 The phrase 'secular context' does not, in my use of it, simply mean a diminishing of religion in public life or of religious affiliation, but a re-expression of religious practice primarily through authentic individual expression and spiritual quest. In this sense I am following Charles Taylor's assessment of the secularization of the West. See Taylor, 2007.

16 Duerksen and Dyrness, 2019, explore how the contingencies of political and cultural context have shaped the church through the history of the West and argue that our assumptions about the normative status of the congregation as the basic form of church emerges more from its historical and colonial history than from any theological priority.

17 Another related and important question is: To what extent might our normative view of certain forms and models of church blind us to the validity of new forms of church emerging in new contexts?

18 See also Lings, n.d.

References

Aisthorpe, Steve, 2016, *The Invisible Church*, Edinburgh: St Andrew Press.
Bradbury, Paul, 2016, *Stepping Into Grace*, Abingdon: BRF.
Chan, Francis, 2018, *Letters to the Church*, Brighton: David Cook.
Chote, Robert, Sarah Clark, Stephen Smith and Busola Sodeinde, 2022, *Independent Review of Lowest Income Communities funding and Strategic Development Funding*, London: Church of England Archbishops' Council, https://www.churchofengland.org/sites/default/files/2022-03/irls-final-report-2.pdf (accessed 10.8.2024).
Cottrell, Stephen, 2021, *Simpler, Humbler, Bolder: A Church for the Whole Nation which is Christ Centred and Shaped by the Five Marks of Mission*, London: Church of England General Synod, GS2023, https://www.churchofengland.org/sites/default/files/2021-06/gs-2223-vision-and-strategy.pdf (accessed 10.08.2024).
Cray, Graham, Ian Mobsby and Aaron Kennedy, 2010, *New Monasticism as Fresh Expressions of Church*, Norwich: Canterbury Press.
Drane, John, 2000, *The McDonaldization of the Church*, London: Darton, Longman & Todd.
Duerksen, Darren T. and William A. Dyrness, 2019, *Seeking Church: Emerging Witnesses to the Kingdom*, Downers Grove, IL: IVP.
Foulger, W., 2023, *Present in Every Place? The Church of England's New Churches, and the Future of the Parish*, London: SCM Press.
Freeman, Andy and Pete Greig, 2007, *Punk Monk: New Monasticism and the Ancient Art of Breathing*, Grand Rapids, MI: Baker Books.
General Synod, 2017, *GS 1978 Report of the Task Force on Resourcing the Future of the Church of England*, London: Church of England General Synod, https://www.churchofengland.org/sites/default/files/2017-11/gs%201978%20-%20resourcing%20the%20future%20task%20group%20report.pdf (accessed 10.8.2024).
Hopkins, Bob and Mike Breen, 2008, *Clusters: Creative Mid-sized Missional Communities*, Anglican Church Planting Initiative.
Lings, George, n.d., 'Why Modality and Sodality Thinking is Vital to Understand the Church', Church Army, http://churcharmy.org/wp-content/uploads/2021/04/george-lings---why-modality-and-sodality.pdf?x71717 (accessed 10.8.2024).
MacIntyre, Alasdair, 1981, *After Virtue*, London: Bloomsbury.
Myers, Joseph R., 2003, *The Search to Belong*, Grand Rapids, MI: Zondervan.
Oldfield, Elizabeth, 2023, 'The Kind of People We Need at the End of the World', *Ekstasis*, available at https://ekstasismagazine.substack.com/p/the-kind-of-people-we-need-at-the (accessed 10.08.2024).
Paas, Stefan, 2016, *Church Planting in the Secular West*, Grand Rapids, MI: Eerdmans.
——, 2019, *Pilgrims and Priests: Christian Mission in a Post-Christian Society*, London: SCM Press.
Ritzer, George, 2015, *The McDonaldization of Society*, 8th edn, London: Sage.
Root, Andrew, 2021, *The Congregation in a Secular Age*, Grand Rapids, MI: Baker Books.
——, 2022, *Churches and the Crisis of Decline*, Grand Rapids, MI: Baker Books.
Rosa, Hartmut, 2014, *Alienation and Acceleration: Towards a Critical Theory of Late-modern Temporality*, Malmö, Sweden: NSU Press.

Scott, Alan, 2018, *Scattered Servants*, Colorado Springs, CO: David Cook.
Swinton, John, 2016, *Becoming Friends of Time*, London: SCM Press.
Taylor, Charles, 2007, *A Secular Age*, Cambridge, MA: Harvard University Press.
Taylor, John V., 1972, *The Go-Between God*, London: SCM Press.
Wells, Sam, 2018, *Incarnational Mission*, Norwich: Canterbury Press.
Winter, Ralph D., 1974, 'The Two Structures of God's Redemptive Mission', *Missiology* 2.1, pp. 121–13.

12

Co-creating Churches Playfully

TINA HODGETT

Introduction

Playfulness is becoming a more common theme in church conversations and missional practice; it seems that a tide of playfulness is coming in over a more austere shore. Although I wouldn't have had the language for it at the time, I believe looking back I was called to engage in the mission of God playfully. I began to play first by leading Sunday worship and then started to wonder how to engage with people outside the church in playful ways. During my pioneer curacy, members of the congregation and I experimented with new ways to connect with people beyond church walls, and as a team vicar I created playful forms of church, as well as leading the largely traditional congregation in creative and embodied expressions of faith in the public space.

Later as leader of the Pioneer Project in the Diocese of Bath and Wells I observed the practice of other pioneers called to birth new worshipping communities proceeding with an instinctual playfulness in their local context. They were aware of other methodologies in church planting but were drawn instead to what I am calling a playful approach. I was intrigued to know if they saw what they did as play and decided to interview them to find out.

In this chapter I describe the very small research project I carried out with seven full-time paid pioneers (lay and ordained) employed by the Diocese of Bath and Wells (six of them under the terms of the Pioneer Project financed through the Church of England's Strategic Development Fund). I discuss definitions of play, and then make an attempt to articulate what the elements of playful church planting practice might be. I draw on research from education, neuroscience, systems thinking and psychology to try to illuminate where this approach has resonances with other fields of thought and practice. I finish by suggesting possible ancestors and relatives of play and playfulness in the Christian tradition.

Where am I in the research data?

I was one of three co-designers of the Bath and Wells Pioneer Project and the main architect of the concept framework, which aimed at culture change catalysed through pioneering. As Project Leader 2018–21, I was responsible for writing role descriptions. These reflected my own emerging understanding of pioneer practice and theory, although the advertising parish and deanery significantly shaped the final versions and the word 'play' didn't appear in any of them. I helped shortlist and interview the candidates. The final decision on the pioneer appointment rested with the local incumbent, but it can be seen that my involvement in the recruitment process will have had an influence on who chose to apply and to a lesser extent who was ultimately appointed. In considering how common a playful approach is, therefore, it is likely that this sample of pioneers more closely reflects my own theology and practice than a group chosen under other circumstances.

The research took place in February and March 2023, 18 months after I left the project. Since I was no longer in an oversight role I hoped it would be possible for the pioneers to speak freely to me about their practice.

In drawing descriptions out of the data, I have held the interview responses in tension with my own experience and been aware of viewpoints that chime with my own hypotheses and those that are different. I have presented both, but the eighth voice in this account is mine, shaping the results inevitably with a certain amount of subjectivity.

The interviewees

In total, seven of the nine SDF pioneers were invited to contribute to the research, which consisted of structured online 1:1 interviews. Six accepted. Two were not invited because I had not observed them engaging in what I would call playful practice. One pioneer declined the invitation to participate; they did not relate to the subject of the inquiry. I then included one other full-time paid pioneer whose playful practice I knew well. The data therefore includes the responses of seven individuals in total. It is informed by what I know of their context and the churches that have arisen during their time in post.

Five of the respondents to my interview questions agreed they used the word 'play' to describe what they do. One preferred the idea of re-imagining and another of experimenting. Both of these named fun as an associated important concept.

Most of the project pioneers were called to challenging contexts. Their five-year term included the whole of the pandemic and one of the pioneers resigned in September 2021. Each of them has been highly conscientious: they were and are deeply connected in their communities, have had impact in other ways than establishing church and carry significant responsibility in their local contexts.

Reporting the results

Given the size of the data sample in this research I have employed various strategies to avoid identifying the respondents. I have shared quotes without assigning them to any particular interviewee, give minimal background information, and used the pronoun 'they' throughout to refer to single individuals, both male and female.

Mark-making

From the responses of the pioneers I attempt to draw the outlines of a playful approach to church planting as it emerges from attentive listening to the results of the interviews, the commonalities between them and the unique aspects that act as keys to understanding and interpretation. One of the pioneers describes her pioneer practice as partly 'mark-making', and I try here to sketch some first marks on a page about this playful practice to give it language and visibility. It is a tentative enterprise for a number of reasons: each pioneer proceeded in a unique way according to their own personality, experience and context; the small sample size makes any firm conclusions unlikely; and there is an inherent resistance of playfulness to definition. It is worth noting that this form of playful church planting has areas of overlap with what has been called elsewhere 'innovator-type pioneering' (Bradbury and Hodgett, 2018).

Defining play

Brian Sutton-Smith begins *The Ambiguity of Play* with the words: 'We all play occasionally and we all know what playing feels like. But when it comes to making theoretical statements about what play is, we fall into silliness' (Sutton-Smith, 2001, p. 1). In her book on playing in (adult) theological education, Courtney T. Goto asserts that it eludes definition 'because one cannot easily encapsulate the essence of playing' (Goto,

2016, p. 14). She goes on to explain that 'Playing is mostly grasped by way of experience, and experiencing is pre-conceptual – what is formed before words come to mind.' In other words, it is possible the pioneers are engaging playfully with their environment, and only afterwards – in some cases at least – are able to articulate what they are doing and why. As this was the first time they had been asked about their practice in terms of play, they were feeling for appropriate language. Goto recommends describing and characterizing 'playing' rather than defining it (Goto, 2016, p. 15).

Despite these reservations about defining play, I offer here some common definitions from academics at Sheffield University. Richard Phillips, Chair in Human Geography, suggests play is primarily a spirit that encourages us to experiment, explore and follow our curiosity. According to a senior lecturer in early years education it is 'playing with reality – figuring out the boundaries of the social world, but also at times transforming them, pushing them, creating new boundaries'. The professor of the Department of Education gives the key ingredients of play as self-directed activity, intrinsically motivating, about the means and not the ends, using the imagination to act 'as if' (*Definitions of Play* video).

Outlining a playful practice

In the interviews with the pioneers discussing their practice, theology and understanding of play, a number of common themes emerged.

A posture of openness

Interviewees described a posture of openness to God and others. This incorporated the possibility in any moment of the discernment of the next step forward in their ministry through the people and circumstances around them. It was variously characterized as living a dot-to-dot kind of life in which the pioneer was the line that joined the dots; 'knowing you have to take lots and lots of small steps to get to a bigger place'; as discovery, with a space being opened up in which God would create the content; as a non-linear journey; as a process of gradual revelation. There was an embrace of uncertainty, unknowing, and a turning away from planning in favour of allowing things to emerge: 'I describe what I'm doing as playful or playing because there's an unknown-ness about it – I'm thinking in a playful way that's kind of open-ended.'

Playfulness is thus characterized as a kind of treasure hunt, a being in the flow of the unfolding narrative of God in a given place and time. It seems to include what Bill Sharpe calls 'future consciousness', which he defines as 'an awareness of the future potential of the present moment' in which there are infinite possibilities (Sharpe, 2013, p. 27). One pioneer described it like this: 'It's like stepping into the wilderness where there are no boundaries on what you see ... there's lots of space for discovery ... and you want to discover what's possible in this situation.'

In the language of Willie James Jennings in his commentary on Acts, these pioneers can be seen to be giving themselves up to what he calls divine desire; to be open to 'yield to the Spirit in the present moment' (Jennings, 2017, p. 11), to be led in a direction a more planned approach might not allow.

Improvisation

Part of the practice of playfulness involves working with what is already there. This may mean that the character, interests, background and gifts of the pioneer (and perhaps their team) shape the nature of the ministry in partnership with other factors in the environment. It is a highly contextual approach and an asset-based one, a response to God's question to Moses in Exodus 4.2, 'What is that in your hand?': 'I'm playing with what's around me and what God's asking me to do ... and in that playing there's so much freedom and expression ...' The word used by another pioneer for this was 'improvisation':

> The direction of travel is quite responsive so the next step of playful stuff is looking at what's already happened and building from it ... lots of 'What if' kind of questions ... What if we did this ... and what if we didn't ...?

One pioneer told the story of reframing their whole approach to growing a new community after they set up a recreational space for their personal well-being and found that neighbours, colleagues and people from their wider network started to give (unasked) fairly random materials to develop it. The pioneer began to recognize that God was playing with him in the space: through prayerful conversation God would reveal what each donation was for, and so God and this child of God improvised an environment for a gathering place together in a playful way.

Dreams, the imagination, flow and the unconscious

Some of the pioneers had received pictures or visions that shaped their understanding of what they had been sent to do. Obviously they didn't know if or how those dreams or their desires and ambitions would come into being but the dream provided a compass point to set a course and orientate themselves by. They embraced the gift of imagination to visualize an unrealized future and take action towards it. Gerald Arbuckle calls people who practise in this way 'dreamers who do' (Arbuckle, 1997, p. 109).

Some spoke of pioneering as 'doodling in the margins', an acknowledgement of God's involvement on a non-rational, subconscious level: 'being with God and being with the people not really knowing what you're doing but when you step back there's something there'. According to positive psychology, there is a state of flow involved in true play. Flow is characterized by the complete absorption in what one does, and a resulting transformation in one's sense of time (Nakamura and Csikszentmihályi, 2001). One or two pioneers hinted at this experience in their practice: 'You're immersed moment by moment at that point in time rather than knowing that you have to get to a certain place by 4 p.m. when playtime's over.'

Experimentation, risk-taking and failure

Pioneers are often identified by their willingness to take risks. These pioneers were open to experimenting. One said: 'Pioneering feels like throwing jelly to the wall ... because you never know the impact of what you're doing ... if anything's going to stick literally.' Gathering people in a challenging context required innovation and the willingness to try out new ideas, along with the willingness to fail. Play was considered a natural way to learn: 'We learn through play ... it's a safe place to fail ... not everything we plant grows ... we have to have the energy and resilience to pick it back up again and replant differently. We can do that lightly with play.' One person claimed that with an experimental approach there was no such thing as failure: 'You either learn or you succeed ... and pioneering's always about playing with ideas.' To hold this posture you have to let go of outcomes.

Letting go of outcomes

This was a dominant theme in the conversations. Most contributors referred to it:

> I'm giving up my understanding, my logic and my knowledge of what I'm doing and allowing God to meet me in that space where I'm not responsible for whatever the outcome is going to be ... [I'm] just interacting with God through play in the moment and the outcome manifests through that.

> There's a sense the journey is the precious treasure rather than a final outcome ... when you're in true play there's no outcome you're aiming for.

> In the structures in which we work outcomes are pre-determined ... so the struggle is to reinterpret what outcomes are ... and obedience is an outcome in itself ...

A pioneer who created a garden project says:

> It's that thing about intentionally planting a church ... or being with people and seeing if church grows ... if the garden becomes church then that's fine ... the intention is to see what God's doing with people in the garden and see where that leads us.

Beau Lotto describes the difficulties human beings encounter in dealing with uncertainty. Solutions to emerging challenges are hard to find when our evolutionary wiring predetermines we stay safe to preserve life; our instinct to self-protection militates against risk-taking. He suggests that the solution that evolution itself has given to uncertainty is play, because in play uncertainty is celebrated (Lotto, 2017, pp. 285–6). He states that play 'does not have a post hoc nature'; in other words, play is its own reward. He calls science 'play with intention' (p. 287).

Lotto further explains that play complexifies our systems, creating possibilities of unpredictable results out of which flows greater inspiration. The playful pioneers hold a deep conviction that new ways of being church are both possible and desirable. They commit to a kind of scientific practice that enables discoveries of new ways of being church to emerge through the joint agency of God, the people who enter the relational space, and the pioneers and their teams who create that space. They intuitively seek to fulfil the definition of missiology given by Ivan Illich as:

the science about the Word of God as the Church in her becoming ... the Church as surprise and puzzle ... the Church when her historical appearance is so new that she has to strain to recognize her past in the mirror of her present; the Church where she is pregnant of new revelations for a people in which she dawns. (Illich, 1970, p. 87)

Positive and negative affect

Playful pioneers report high levels of positive emotion associated with their work: words like 'excitement', 'freedom', 'joy', 'wonder', 'fun' and 'happiness' pepper their conversation. They also acknowledge that it comes at a price. Lotto qualifies his celebration of play by stating paradoxically that it is hard work (Lotto, 2017, p. 286), and pioneers equally report stresses, challenges and frustrations that occur through their methodology, with one declaring that the 'fun helps me endure more'.

Creating agenda-free space

Closely linked to the letting go of outcomes is a letting go of agendas. As Rooms (2015) has shown, it can be disingenuous to suggest that any intentional missional act is 'agenda-free', and it would be worth exploring further how pioneers understand this term. It seems to be associated with a number of other values: prioritizing the building of authentic relationships above everything else; being with and for people; creating space for people to be part of a community in which all have an equal right to belong, regardless of faith stance; and the letting go of power: 'I think play straightaway puts everyone on the same level. You can't be in charge of play. Rather than be a leader of a new church, be a facilitator of play.' Pioneers were welcoming of partnership with other individuals and organizations of all kinds. They wanted to downplay their personal agency in favour of allowing the agency of the Holy Spirit and community members to shape the space. One person describes this clearly:

> We have a garden with families ... You just don't know who's going to turn up ... but when they do there's no agenda: you can sit with children ... in the mud kitchen, you can plant some seeds, or sit by the fire with [name]. If you want to measure something, we just created a space to play ... There's no expectation of people when they walk in, there's no one leading it particularly, and beautiful conversations happen with one another, starting new friendships.

The same person described in some detail the challenge of holding a playful stance in their spirit and practice, having to resist the internalized voices pressing them to begin some kind of structured worship service in the style they had previously seen as default, but sure they were in the flow of the divine purpose holding space for play: 'Every time I try and go back to default I lose my peace.'

Foolishness, vulnerability, childlikeness

A number of pioneers consciously adopted postures that made them appear foolish or vulnerable. One described their work as 'like playing hopscotch and the stone's gone too far and you stand on a leg and lose balance and have to hop'. They minister in what is sometimes a transitory community and expressed the fragility of their work and the disappointments it repeatedly caused:

> In this context they say they'd like to be with you and help and they don't come … or you invest time to grow great relationships with people and they move out of the estate. You think you're making great spiritual progress with people and they say: 'I've been inspired by your faith and I've started my own witching journey' or they come to faith and go to another church across town.

The person who gave the description above of pioneering as 'doodling in the margins' was partly making reference to being in places 'at the edges' of the church's normal reach. The pioneers are often motivated by a 'devotion to peoples undesired and unknown' (Jennings, 2017, p. 9), a desire to widen the circle of inclusivity. As Jennings observes, the disciples in the earliest days of the church are always being pressed to go to those with whom they would prefer never to share space. Often the 'undesired people' need an invitation to join in. A childlike approach reduces intimidation, lowers barriers and is open to those who have been unable to connect elsewhere: 'I think it's almost something about not being taken too seriously … it's like people say: What're you doing? There's a curiosity about play.'

Often the pioneers are engaging in some kind of embodied creative activity in the public space, such as art, gardening, craft or community service that is visible to all and people are invited into, as children join in with play in a playground.

One pioneer recounted an experience of a rehearsal for a service of Vespers for people exploring faith, noting how mistakes were made in rehearsal and laughed about. They attested that the mistakes and laughter became the source of deep connection when the worship took place shortly after. Some of the pioneers were aware of how foolish they appeared and yet felt the rightness of being childlike for the sake of the gospel. Some have found it difficult to speak about play in other church circles because of its possible implications of frivolity or immaturity, fearing to be misunderstood:

> Play can be a burden ... our understanding of play ... when no one understands what you're doing and you can't articulate it because you don't even understand what it is ... It's freeing but it's lonely ... When [other people in my church circles] hear 'play' they think you're not taking [mission] seriously.

Certainly play is seen as something only appropriate to the life of children (Sutton-Smith, 2001, p. 7). It is often seen as demeaning for adults, and I write this chapter with some trepidation lest I portray gifted and devoted colleagues in a way that means their work is belittled or trivialized. One pioneer admitted they only use the 'play' word with other pioneers:

> I have conversations with God all the time [about play] cos I'm totally sold on the idea that for the kingdom to come we need to play, but I think that very word comes with misunderstanding ... So to talk about it in other contexts of more traditional understandings it diminishes the seriousness of play.

Certainly Jesus' warning to his disciples that they need to become as little children if they want to enter the kingdom of heaven (Matt. 18.3) is rarely interpreted as a requirement to be playful, despite the fact that play is the unifying characteristic of a healthy childhood across epochs and cultures. Playful forms of church have emerged, usually for children or intergenerational groups, but the idea of playfulness as a way of being for all or specifically as a mode of mission occupies very little space in the life of the church or in academic literature.

Holding a creative tension between 'work' and 'play'

There is obviously a tension in being employed to work within the structures of the church to grow a new Christian community and approach it in a playful way such that you are reliant on God's agency and timing, on the circumstances of the context and the community. Pioneers described the tensions of working within an organization that struggles to understand the postures, hypotheses and theologies informing their practice. Asked how they held this tension of proceeding playfully in an employed role, one contributor explained the paradox like this:

> [Play] is a method ... How that expectation [to work] is to be met is through play ... It's one of the means of exploring God that's offered as a method within the larger framework of my paid post but the way I'm fulfilling my requirement to work is play.

Outcomes

It is not my intention here to evaluate playfulness as a methodology, but I can state that seven new worshipping communities have emerged so far through the ministry of the pioneers in the study. Churches have arisen, most of them in outdoor spaces, most playful, often intergenerational. One of these is among a specific demographic group who were never in view at the start of the project. One is a community regularly gathering more than twice as many worshippers than the local parish church and families have been baptized in a context where it is known to be hard to reach new people. A third is a network of five different communities with people flowing among and between them like a circulatory system; some of these offer worship services, others not.

A playful tradition?

What I have here described as a playful approach has connections with earlier Christian traditions. First the Celtic, in its love of meeting with God in the everyday, in creation and creative activity; second the monastic, with its attention to the moment and rhythm of action and contemplation; third the mystic, especially where it is guided by visions and spiritual intimations and seems beyond articulation; and fourth Eastern Orthodox, with its understanding of the Christ-figure as holy fool. In Eastern Orthodoxy, playfulness was seen as useful 'in challenging the hegemony of even good [spiritual] categories' (Valantasis, 2005, p. 167). The Episcopal priest Richard Valantasis applies the quality of playfulness to discipleship rather than mission, but I believe it can be equally powerful in enabling church planters to discover alternative pathways towards growing new communities of followers of Jesus.

The pioneers in the study rooted their concept of play variously in the personhood of God as playful Creator; in the life, practices and parables of Jesus; in the idea of prayer as 'thinking with the heart'; in the teachings of Paul in 1 Corinthians 9 on 'becoming all things to all people' and the consequent need for contextualization between Scripture, culture and tradition. Their hypotheses underlying playful church planting would be worth further study.

Conclusion

I have sought to describe here a practice of co-creating churches playfully with God in the local context, based on the outcomes of interviews on play in pioneering with seven practitioners. From the data it can be seen that the aims of this playful approach are to make room for possibilities that might otherwise be excluded; to widen the circle of invitees by lowering the barriers to joining in; to enable a dynamic interplay between God the Holy Spirit, community members and the pioneer in shaping what is formed; to work with the resources that exist; to leave the outcomes to God; and to allow contextually specific new forms of church to develop and grow through their own distinctive re-imagining, fun and play. It is a study of possibility for the church, offering potential ways forward into an adjacent but not yet glimpsed or realized future.

References

Arbuckle, Gerald A., 1997, *Refounding the Church: Dissent for Leadership*, London: Geoffrey Chapman.
Bradbury, Paul and Tina Hodgett, 2018, 'Pioneering Mission is … a spectrum', *Anvil* 34.1, pp. 30–4.
Definitions of Play [video], University of Sheffield, https://digitalmedia.sheffield.ac.uk/playlist/dedicated/73342701/1_czbfkcb4/1_fb7kxzta (accessed 10.8.2024).
Goto, Courtney, 2016, *The Grace of Playing: Pedagogies for Leaning into God's New Creation*, Broadstairs: Pickwick Publications
Illich, Ivan, 1970, *The Church, Change, and Development*, Freiburg: Herder & Herder.
Jenkins, Timothy, 2008, *An Experiment in Providence: How Faith Engages with the World*, London: SPCK.
Jennings, Willie James, 2017, *Acts: A Theological Commentary on the Bible*, Louisville, KY: Westminster John Knox Press.
Lotto, Beau, 2017, *Deviate: The Science of Seeing Differently*, London: Weidenfeld & Nicholson.
Nakamura, Jeanne and Mihaly Csikszentmihályi, 2001, 'Flow Theory and Research', in C. R. Synder and S. J. Lopez (eds), *The Oxford Handbook of Positive Psychology*, Oxford: Oxford University Press, ch. 18.

Rooms, Nigel, 2015, 'Missional Gift-Giving: A Practical Theology Investigation into what Happens when Churches Give Away "Free" Gifts for the Sake of Mission', *Practical Theology* 8.2, pp. 99–111.
Sharpe, Bill, 2013, *Three Horizons: The Patterning of Hope*, Charmouth: Triarchy Press.
Sutton-Smith, Brian, 2001, *The Ambiguity of Play*, Cambridge, MA: Harvard University Press.
Valantasis, Richard, 2005, *Centuries of Holiness: Ancient Spirituality Refracted for a Postmodern Age*, London: Continuum.

13

A Tale of Two Churches

STEPHEN SQUIRRELL

Introduction

This chapter explores two church revitalization projects and attempts to reflect theologically on how their engagements with parish and the sacraments have aided their mission. Revitalization in both of these cases refers to the strengthening of an existing congregation by the addition of new members and the provision of new leadership.

Our first church, St Peter's, was in a three-church partnership and was struggling numerically and financially.[1] Three years ago a team of members and trainee clergy moved from a nearby resource church. Since then, the church has grown in size, from under 30 to more than 100 on a Sunday, shored up the finances and embarked on renovating parts of the premises that had been unused for decades. St Peter's is in the charismatic evangelical tradition.

Holy Trinity is located less than a 10-minute drive from St Peter's. The previous incumbent at Holy Trinity faithfully served the parish for 30 years, but by the end of his tenure the congregation filled only the choir stalls. As at St Peter's, the Bishop wanted to revitalize this church and approached a resource church to ask for assistance. Two years ago the former curate at the sending church became the priest at Holy Trinity and brought with him a handful of people. Since the revitalization began, the church has grown from 15 to 55 at weekly Mass and the giving has increased six-fold. Holy Trinity is in the Anglo-Catholic tradition.

Both revitalization projects have seen increased attendance, increased giving and increased interaction with the parish through community engagement. Both were supported by resource churches. In the case of St Peter's, this resource church is a BMO church with a large ministry to young professionals.[2] In the case of Holy Trinity, the resource church was a neighbouring Anglo-Catholic parish. The churches are geographically close and both are red-brick buildings from the same era and in the same style. Both have notably personable and skilled clergy. As well as the similarities, however, there are significant differences between the two projects. St Peter's built a team of 30+ people to move from the resource church. These included several experienced lay leaders. The priest at Holy Trinity told me that he was amazed that roughly seven people joined him from the sending church, as – he wondered – 'Who would want to leave their parish church?' This alludes to some fundamental differences in the projects, which I will draw out according to two themes: parish and sacraments.

In exploring the stories of both revitalization projects through the lens of parish and the sacraments we will see the unique charisms of both traditions and the ways mission and church regeneration cannot be seen to belong to any one tradition alone.

Church revitalization

Before considering the story of the churches in more depth we need to consider revitalization within the Church of England. Revitalization projects are a key part of the mixed ecology of mission and ministry that is currently being encouraged. Archbishop Stephen Cottrell (2021) speaks of the need for 'parishes revitalized for mission'. The emphasis on a mixed ecology of ministry sometimes entails a strained dialogue between church planting movements and groups such as Save the Parish.[3] Revitalization – when done well – might offer the chance to see growth and health in existing parish structures, breathing new life into the parish system. And in this sense, the parish revitalization might serve a useful purpose in mediating between sometimes opposing camps.

I have suggested that both revitalizations have been *successful*. This is a notoriously controversial word in church contexts and one that is very difficult to define. One possible – though inadequate – definition is that success equals growth. The phrase 'healthy things grow' encapsulates this sentiment and is widely used in church planting circles. Archbishop Cottrell's phrase 'revitalized for mission', however, takes us beyond simply numerical growth and centres effective mission at the heart of what revitalization is for. Mission in this context is the ultimate goal, which will probably include but not be confined to growth. This mission, I suggest, is the living out of the gospel through proclamation and demonstration. That is to say, at the heart of revitalization work with a future is the mission to live out, communicate and demonstrate the love of Christ.

Mission is part of the heritage of both charismatic evangelical and Anglo-Catholic traditions. From the revivalism of Charles Finney, to the evangelism of John Stott in London, to the renewal and restorationist movements in the 1970s/80s, and the contemporary influence of Alpha and the Church Revitalisation Trust, evangelicalism has centred on the call to a mission that draws people to a personal relationship with Christ. The catholic tradition in the Church of England also has a tradition of mission. Whether one considers the slum priests focused on mission to poor urban communities, the missional drive of the Oxford Movement, the current activism of the Centre for Theology and Community or the preaching, campaigning and ministry of Bishop Philip North, mission is integral to authentic catholic witness – just as it is to evangelical witness.

Mission involves both proclamation and demonstration and these forms of mission have been successfully undertaken by both churches.

St Peter's – in their own words

In a 2021 interview with a church planting organization, the leader and churchwarden at St Peter's described the journey up that point:

> Even though the church looked a bit run down when we arrived, there was a core community of about 20 people who had been faithfully praying. This core team welcomed us in unbelievable ways ... It felt like we came home and like we stepped into a place that had been prayed over and consecrated for many years. Even though it looked like things were decaying, like the building or the garden, it felt like there was still incredible life and that we are seeing the outworking of this community's prayers in what's now happening. It reminds me of the Easter story – new life comes out of the tomb.

The team saw themselves as stepping into an ongoing story that had been started before their arrival. This differs from some models of church planting – in which the new community pioneers from scratch. The staff and leaders at St Peter's have made great efforts to honour the heritage of the church before their arrival. As a revitalization rather than strictly a church plant, the new team have situated themselves in the story of an existing community.

The churchwarden comments on this tension between the old and the new. He acknowledges:

> The long-standing members had to adjust to having a leadership team and no longer making day-to-day decisions. Things happen a bit faster in bigger congregations – sometimes we need to move forward more

quickly so we had to learn to let go and trust the leadership team to make the best decisions for the church.

Attendance at St Peter's grew significantly during the pandemic and is now 100–150 on a Sunday. There are more than 40 children in weekly attendance and there is regular engagement with the community through dance clubs, parent and toddler provision and lots of community outreach. The garden mentioned above has been refurbished, the organ room converted into space for children's activities and offices, the roof fixed, and the old mission hall, which had lain derelict for decades, has become a space for art and community work, and will become a co-working space to serve the needs of the area.

Holy Trinity – in their own words

The story of revitalization at Holy Trinity is described as centring 'around the Eucharist'. Moreover, 'The regular pattern of worship and prayer in the church is the source from which everything else in the life of this parish church flows. Our service to and witness in the local community is rooted in our worship together.'

They list as their highlights of the journey so far: starting 'a new weekly baby and toddler group, which is now regularly attracting 25–30 families each week' and has led to 'baptisms'. They have also renewed 'use … of the Church Hall' and enlivened 'the musical life of the church. Last summer, [they] started a series of Saturday lunchtime concerts, working with local musicians, with admission by donation in addition to hosting local orchestras and choirs.'

The activities listed serve the local needs and demographics and are well attended. They add that:

> Regular cake sales and a café on Saturday mornings have proved other ways through which we can get the church doors open and welcome new faces. We recognize that people enter our church for all sorts of different reasons and with different needs. We want to make crossing that threshold as easy as possible. Whether you're a regular church goer or not, all are welcome here. We've also rebuilt our social media platforms so you can keep up to date with our news.

That phrase 'Whether you're a regular church goer or not, all are welcome here' is something we will explore in depth in our analysis of parish.

They continue: 'We take regular food collections to either the local

Soup Kitchen or Foodbank' and conclude that 'We were delighted to welcome nearly 500 people through our doors across our Christmas services this year.' The priest also highlights the reinstating of the midweek Mass, which draws a wider attendance than Sunday, and maintains the eucharistic heart of the church's witness. The emphasis on eucharistic worship, music and social action is fully in keeping with the Anglo-Catholic tradition.

How then do these two projects overlap and diverge as we consider the role of parish and the sacraments in their mission?

Parish

The parish is a much-discussed element of Anglican ecclesiology today and this conversation is often so siloed that traditions talk past one another. The charisms of evangelical and catholic Anglicanism can generate very fruitful engagement with parish – leading to successful revitalization – in their own unique and different ways.

For St Peter's, there is a sense in which the parish is a given location for mission and service. At Prayer and Worship evenings, the parish is regularly prayed for, and needs within the parish named before God. This understanding of mission is akin to missionaries who would travel to a new place in order to spread the gospel. Indeed, Alison Milbank (2020) notes that among her university students in the Vineyard network of churches, there was a draw to the Church of England because of the defined nature of the mission field. At Holy Trinity, the engagement with parish is somewhat different. The sign that stands outside the church whenever it is open reads 'Come and See – Your Parish Church is Open'. Rather than inviting the outsider to an Alpha Course or an evangelistic service, Holy Trinity asserts that the church is already at the centre of the common life of the parish. And whether the resident attends or not, the church is in some sense 'theirs'. Of course, the approaches to parish are not binary, and indeed both churches employ elements of both approaches. St Peter's and Holy Trinity understand their responsibility to the parish – and the centre of their social engagement and community service is based on very local needs, such as foodbanks, charities, night shelters and more.

In the case of St Peter's, the evangelistic engagement with the parish served to build the core team who revitalized the church three years ago. Coming from a large BMO with an emphasis on local mission and evangelism, they built a team of 30-plus skilled lay leaders who were energized about the new project, and happy to move church to support the revitalization. In this way, parish boundaries were not a straitjacket but were engaged flexibly in order to serve the ultimate goal. The leader at St Peter's lives just outside of the technical parish boundary but has lived, worked and invested in the area for decades before ordination. A flexible arrangement with the technicality of parish boundaries has not blunted the local focus but has enabled innovation for local mission.

The three years of mission since St Peter's began revitalization have demonstrated sustained engagement with the local area. This has included community audits in which local needs were surveyed and then directly responded to. No one could accuse this theology of being disengaged from its locality, yet a flexible approach to place on the part of its core team – located across a large urban area – arguably facilitated this local focus. The engagement with parish at St Peter's has deepened over time, perhaps enhanced by the less restrictive approach to parish in the launch phase, which enabled the building of a strong core team.

The revitalization of Holy Trinity began with a much smaller core team than at St Peter's, in part because the team joined from a neighbouring parish church, while the team at St Peter's came from a larger BMO church. But what has continued to emerge at St Peter's is a remarkable sense of the local. Will Foulger (2018) says: 'The first principle [of Anglican vocation] may be called "paying close attention". It is, he [Jenkins, 2006, p. 7] states, "less one's job to bring God into a place than to discern him in it".' From the ministry to local parents, to the lunchtime concerts, to the cake sales, to the links with the local schools, to the sustainable and plastic-free food vendor that parks outside the church on a Saturday, the mission and character of Holy Trinity is local.

This was demonstrated in the response to the recent death of a much-loved local headteacher. Though not officially linked to the school, the priest at Holy Trinity has developed close links with the school community. In the week following the tragic death, the church opened for parents, children and staff to come and reflect. They came to light candles and to take time, in a local holy space, which in some sense belonged to them. The sermon the following Sunday, and then again on Ash Wednesday, mourned the loss, so keenly felt in the community and in the congregation. The church served as a space for the congregation to hold the school community in prayer. This demonstrates a profound integration of church and locality.

Alison Milbank (2023) suggests that successful parishes will need to make a 'virtue of vulnerability'. She gives the example of a church with a large grass border and no resources to manage this 'in house'. They shared their need with the community, who came to their aid, and now maintain the garden. At St Peter's, through the donation of local labour to renew the garden, plant trees and rejuvenate the land, this vulnerability and collaboration with the community is in evidence. In her directive to make a virtue of vulnerability, Milbank is not simply suggesting a pragmatic solution to meeting church needs; rather she is suggesting a posture of humility within the community. The parish church of the future, she suggests, will not dispense all the answers from a great height, but live in solidarity with the community around it.

The Archdeacon in his recent report on Holy Trinity commends 'the small but faithful and resilient congregation ... who have opened their hearts and the doors of their church to the opportunities of being refreshed and renewed'.

I argue that both the evangelical and catholic approaches to Parish can aid the health of parish revitalization. But how do the respective theologies of the sacraments aid their mission?

Sacraments

St Peter's, even when there were fewer than 50 in regular attendance, was led by three ordinands, with a priest-in-charge resident at the sending BMO church. This meant that the Eucharist was celebrated roughly every six weeks – a frequency not uncommon in this tradition. Less frequent celebration of the Eucharist in this setting meant there was a lower requirement for ordained leadership, which enabled the three then-ordinands to take on more responsibility early in their ministry.

This flexibility has served the church's growth, by enabling lay leaders to carry more responsibility. For St Peter's, the Eucharist is the *real presence* but it is also a meal of hospitality and of welcome. At the conclusion of a recent preaching series on the Eucharist, the church members ate large chunks of bread and drank grape juice together to symbolize the unity of the body and the welcome at the Table. This understanding of the Eucharist as primarily hospitality is evident in the Maundy Thursday celebrations in which church members open their home for supper parties, to invite the stranger in and build community. This differs from the gathered worship on Maundy Thursday at Holy Trinity, with the stripping of the altar and night vigil. Sacramental worship in this context has been contextualized to address contemporary needs of welcome, hospitality, food and embrace.

While this has enabled growth at St Peter's and is in keeping with the tradition of charismatic evangelicalism, it must be emphasized that the catholic style of sacramental worship at Holy Trinity has not hindered growth at all – and quite the reverse.

In the beauty of the worship at Holy Trinity, centred on the weekly Eucharist, the members encounter something transcendent. One of the first acts in the Holy Trinity revitalization was to restore the midweek Thursday Eucharist, which is now regularly attended by people outside the Sunday congregation. Not only does opening the church doors attract visitors, it represents the undergirding of prayer and sacramental witness that has been vital to the success at Holy Trinity. Bishop Philip North (2022) has commented on the sense of holiness in the tent at the annual Walsingham youth pilgrimage as young people made use of confession. This atmosphere of repentance is similar to the reported public and private confession prominent in the 2023 Asbury outpouring. The beauty of holiness, and personal and collective piety, are fully accessed across the theological and ecclesiological spectrum. And the sacramental theology of both St Peter's and Holy Trinity has much to commend towards its mission. The rootedness of the church in its local history is demonstrated in the worship at Holy Trinity. Each week the servers process in carrying a locally discovered cross dating back more than 500 years. The following of the liturgical calendar, with locally understood seasons such as Lent and Advent, offers parishioners opportunities to participate in worship that mirrors their own lives – punctuated by anticipation and sorrow and loss – in a vast sea of ordinary time.[4] The church calendar, as used at Holy Trinity, is demonstrably missional.

This was most evident on harvest Sunday in 2022, where the congregation were encouraged to bring as much food as they could spare to church, beyond the usual foodbank donations. During the preparation of the Table for the Eucharist, the children processed to the altar, carrying the food brought by the congregation, which was then blessed and dropped off at the local foodbank following the service. Eucharistic worship here is intertwined with all-age ministry and locally focused community action.

There is something profoundly missional about the eucharistic worship at Holy Trinity. For Alexander Schmemann (1973), the Eucharist is the 'Mount Tabor' from which the church is sent each week into the world. In the weekly Eucharist, ordinary elements become more than themselves. And so the ordinariness of the lives in the pews is dignified. At Holy Trinity the weekly Eucharist is preceded by sharing the peace; reconciliation, love and mission are enacted within the congregation and beyond the walls of the church.

For Louis Bouyer, the Eucharist proclaims the Gospel and 'aims ... at a restoration of the real' (Olsen III, 2014). In the harvest Eucharist at Holy Trinity, the congregation were restored to the reality of local life – the cost-of-living crisis, the role of all-ages in worship and service and the generosity of God that engenders personal response. I argue that this engagement with reality, facilitated by Anglo-Catholic sacramental theology, is profoundly missionally attractive. As well as infant baptisms coming from the parent and baby groups, Holy Trinity has baptized adults since the revitalization began. Moreover, in spite of the smaller attendance at Holy Trinity there are up to 15 children among the 50 present most weeks. The traditional Anglo-Catholic and eucharistic worship at Holy Trinity has not hindered the project but rather added to it.

I have argued so far that revitalization for mission belongs properly to all traditions – evangelical and catholic. But if we are to see continued success in these projects and more arising, what needs to be done?

Here are some tentative recommendations:

1. **Active Funding** The revitalization at Holy Trinity has been done, to quote the priest, on a 'shoestring'. The growth in vitality and numbers is remarkable, and yet they operate with a fraction of the budget and staffing of larger charismatic evangelical churches. There are numerous factors at play here, including the prominence of giving within the church. But those outside established networks of large churches are less likely to access funding that would serve the mission. This is linked to my second recommendation.
2. **Equal access to grants** Alison Milbank (2023) has called for 'national resources and information on which parishes could draw for grant application, which is professional work'. Currently churches with larger staff teams are more able to access grant funding because of the in-house expertise in bid writing. The smaller staff teams at some churches makes this impossible.
3. **Cross-tradition learning** If we see the various traditions as having unique missional charisms, then we must facilitate learning across the traditions. In the examples we have considered, St Peter's could learn from Holy Trinity about use of the church calendar for mission, while Holy Trinity could learn about raising lay leaders and volunteers. This sort of shared learning would be invaluable, not only as pragmatic help but as a way of respecting the unique gifts each tradition brings.

Conclusion

This chapter has been the exploration of two revitalization projects and an attempt to think theologically about their successes. It is not possible to make sweeping recommendations or generalizations based on such a small case study. Nevertheless, we have seen in two concrete examples how the parish revitalization model might both 1) facilitate growth and 2) honour the parish system with all its missional strengths. Moreover, parish revitalization is something that can occur with notable success in evangelical and catholic settings. The charisms of both traditions facilitate new life in a beautiful and generative way and should be listened to across the theological spectrum for the building up of the body of Christ in the Church of England.

Notes

1 Both churches have been given pseudonyms.

2 BMO refers to Bishop's Mission Orders. More information is available here: https://www.churchofengland.org/resources/parish-reorganisation-and-closed-church-buildings/bishops-mission-orders.

3 'Save the Parish' began in 2021 with the stated aim of encouraging 'the redirection of a greater proportion of the Church's money and resources to the Parish system' (https://www.savetheparish.com/).

4 Trinity Church, an Anglican Church plant in Washington, USA, has made the ancient church calendar integral to its contemporary mission. The prevalence of ordinary time reminds us that 'ordinariness too is holy ground beneath our feet'. Moreover, it locates the use of the church calendar in the call to participate in the life of Christ: 'This is why the historic church adopted the liturgical calendar over the centuries. Not to impose legalistic days throughout the year, but to re-order our year according not to the academic calendar, or the harvest calendar alone, but to the life of Christ into whose life we are invited now as participants' (Trinity Washington, n.d.).

References

Cottrell, Stephen, 2021, *Vision and Strategy Address – General Synod November 2021*, https://www.archbishopofyork.org/speaking-and-writing/sermons/vision-and-strategy-address-general-synod-november-2021 (accessed 18.02.2024).

Foulger, William J., 2018, *Present in Every Place: The Church of England and the Parish Principle*, DthM diss., Durham University, http://etheses.dur.ac.uk/12856/1/WJF (accessed 18.02.2024).

Jenkins, Timothy, *An Experiment in Providence: How Faith Engages with the World*, London: SPCK, 2006.

Milbank, Alison, 2020, 'Parish Value in the Modern Marketplace', *The Once and Future Parish Conference*, Zoom conference, 5 December.

———, 2023, *The Once and Future Parish*, London, SCM Press.

North, Philip, 2022, *Catholic Evangelism* [podcast], 18 March, https://podtail.com/en/podcast/holy-c-of-e/ (accessed 18.02.2024).

Olsen III, Cyrus P., 2014, 'Myth and Culture in Louis Bouyer', *Gregorianum* 95.4, pp. 775–99.

Schmemann, Alexander, 1973, *For the Life of the World*, New York: St Vladimir's Seminary Press.

Trinity Washington, 'The Church Calendar, Trinity Church Wenatchee', https://www.trinitywenatchee.org/church-calendar (accessed 18.02.2024).

14

Anglo-Catholic Church Planting: It Does Happen!

JOHN WALLACE

Introduction

This chapter is derived from my doctoral research into church planting being undertaken by Anglo-Catholic churches. I also compared this with what Victorian Anglo-Catholics had done. They were very mission-minded and were responsible for building a large number of new churches, especially in expanding urban areas. I will also briefly mention two men, one ordained and the other a layman, who can be seen as examples of the drive to build churches in order to spread the gospel, particularly to the working classes. For my research, I visited three very different churches over a period of 18 months before the first Covid lockdown, and these visits inform this chapter.

It concludes with thoughts for the future. Unlike many church plants that come from evangelical churches, there are no formal networks for Anglo-Catholic church planters, and those involved often feel quite isolated. It is suggested that a network be set up to support those who run such church plants, both for the support of church planters but also for the sharing of ideas and good practice.

My interest came about as a result of the experience of the church that I attend and where I had been churchwarden previously as well as being a member of the PCC since 1984. It is situated in a town 40 miles north-west of London that is now very much a commuter town with a number of large housing developments. The church is liberal catholic by tradition and is part of a large team benefice, the largest benefice in the diocese and the parish itself is also one of the largest parishes in the diocese with a population in excess of 28,000.

We became concerned that there was little obvious Christian presence in what was, at that time, the newest estate. The parish church was some distance away; so after considerable discussion both within the parish, the wider team and with the Diocesan Director of Mission, it was agreed to appoint a pioneer priest to live and work in those estates, and he established what eventually became a weekly worshipping community in the local school.

Seeing this significant missional activity, I asked myself whether other churches of the same tradition were doing similar things in their parishes. This formed the basis of my research into Anglo-Catholic church planting.

I looked at what Anglo-Catholics had done historically and then the more recent fresh expressions material, especially *Mission-shaped Church*. Steven Croft commends it to the whole church and does not see any reason why Anglo-Catholics should not be involved in church planting. Perhaps this statement was at the time a little naïve. However, it urged Anglo-Catholics to become involved, although there is anecdotal evidence of a lack of practical and financial support for Anglo-Catholic parishes. This theme came out very clearly in my research when one priest strikingly said that while Anglo-Catholic church planting is encouraged, in practice Anglo-Catholic churches are in competition with the larger and better resourced evangelical churches. The process of writing bids for specific funding is a complex technical skill and many Anglo-Catholic parishes feel at a disadvantage in this respect. They either lack those who have such skills or cannot afford to engage a costly bid writer. This is an issue that needs addressing to make a level playing field. Access to mission funding should not be limited to those churches that have people with the skills to write bids or the means to employ such a person.

By quite a random process, I eventually identified three church plants. There is no network that would easily help to identify Anglo-Catholic plants, unlike that organized through HTB for its plants, so I had to rely on information from a web of contacts and 'contacts of contacts'! Having identified these churches, two in London and one in the East Midlands, I contacted their priests with my proposal. All of them were happy with what I wanted to do. I then had face-to-face meetings with them. Fortunately, I was able to complete all my research before the Covid lockdown and closure of churches.

My research activity had to be realistic, given my range of other commitments, so I aimed to attend each church monthly over a period of 18 months. I felt that this would give enough information for me to provide a thick description of each church. At my first attendance, each priest introduced me and explained what I was doing. This was very helpful and it enabled members of each congregation to be involved in some way. It meant that a number of people would ask me on a regular basis about my research, which I found to be very supportive.

Of the two churches in London, the one in west London was very much like the one where I worship, relaxed liberal catholic. The other in north London was very traditional, under the alternative episcopal oversight of the Bishop of Fulham. The Roman Rite was used in its services, as had been the norm in the planting church for a considerable number of years. The third church, in the East Midlands, was very new and met monthly in the church Junior School hall.

Each of the churches had different origins. The west London church arose from an initiative by the Area Bishop to keep open a church that was in a very poor state. It was attached to a thriving Anglo-Catholic parish as a last-ditch attempt. Fortunately, a newly arrived priest could see some potential in it and with some members of the congregation started to work to make the church active again.

The north London church was established at the extreme southern end of the parish, in a building owned by the church but which had been let for secular use for many years. It opened over seven years ago and holds its service at 5 p.m. This enables the parish priest to lead the worship as well as giving an alternative time for potential worshippers. It has now a very well-established congregation.

The East Midlands church was much newer and grew out of a school assembly. The original parish church, which gave its name to the school, was closed in 2010 and so there was a lack of an obvious church presence in the area. The parish was also dissolved and integrated into a large Anglo-Catholic parish. The school took the initiative to ask the diocese to do something about this lack of obvious Christian presence. A priest was appointed as a pioneer. He was housed by the diocese and the Anglo-Catholic parish paid his expenses, as well as having him available to assist with worship. A Bishop's Mission Order was later put in place, but there seemed to be little other support. At the time that I was about to finish my research visits, it was announced that the sponsoring church was withdrawing financial support. The plant was then put under the wing of a large evangelical church with a history of church planting, albeit following a different model, to ensure its survival. The founding priest later resigned.

At the end of my research, I had final interviews with the three clergy, which I recorded. These conversations confirmed six themes that I had provisionally identified and which also correlated with what I had found earlier in the literature. These are the themes; they are not ranked and each church prioritized them to fit its own situation.

Community

Each church had its own view of what community actually meant in its context. The different demographics of the parishes also affected this. The incarnational ministry of priests in their parishes was a key tenet of Victorian Anglo-Catholicism, where many priests, even those from different social backgrounds, lived in very deprived parishes. This is still the case today, as in many parishes, especially in inner cities, the priest is the only professional who is living there. In many parishes there seems to be a tension between ministry to the regular worshippers, where the vicar is often seen as their chaplain, and ministry to the wider parish. Some churchgoers resent this as they believe that they are paying, via the Diocesan Parish Share Scheme, for *their* vicar, whose energy should therefore be directed towards 'the regulars'. This view is at odds with the formal Church of England position that 'the cure of souls' shared by the bishop and the parish priest relates to all who live in the geographical parish. This is affirmed at every installation or licensing service. I am seeing this tension lived out in my own parish as, at the time of writing, we are in vacancy and developing a parish profile to attract the 'right' priest.

Worship

Each church had a somewhat different approach and emphasis to worship but all of them saw it as of great importance. This shows the Anglo-Catholic emphasis on regular worship and especially the celebration of the Eucharist (although the East Midlands church had not yet reached that stage of development). For various logistical reasons relating to the venue where worship takes place, it may be necessary to adjust the ceremonial to fit. An example of this is where the altar is placed on a narrow platform, too narrow for the priest to walk or stand in front of it.

Leadership

This theme was identified both by each of the priests but also, importantly, by their congregations. As I talked to people over coffee, they often commented on the way in which Father X was leading the church; they depended on clear leadership and drive to fulfil their mission. That is not the same as the anecdotal view of Anglo-Catholic parishes, where the mantra 'Father says so' is used to explain everything that is done in the parish at the behest of the vicar. It is also different from 'management'. A church leader should inspire people to follow and contribute to their vision for the mission of the parish.

Vision

Part of the role of the church leadership is to carry forward the vision that has been identified. The vision can come either from internal prayer, discussion and thought in the PCC or the wider congregation, or be the outworking of an external (usually diocesan) vision. A cursory glance at the vacancy advertisements in the *Church Times* shows how most dioceses prioritize their visions. 'Where there is no vision, the people perish' (Prov. 29.18, KJV). So vision is essential for mission. But vision needs to have substance, and not just be a strap-line on a church's noticeboard or diocesan advertisement. It needs to be owned by the whole church community.

Growth

By definition, a church plant should grow; after all, planting is a horticultural metaphor, as one of the clergy pointed out to me. Each of the churches wanted to grow numerically within the physical limitations of their premises as well as spiritually in the knowledge and love of God. Growth also was important for all of them as a way of increasing contact with their wider communities – not just regular churchgoers. This is so important, as it prevents a congregation from becoming a comfortable and exclusive 'holy huddle' rather than being 'a city built on a hill', which 'cannot be hidden' (Matt. 5.14). Growth can arise from a number of different activities, but the personal witness of individual Christians is often the most successful. Remember the way Philip unconditionally invited Nathaniel with the words: 'Come and see' (John 1.46).

Sustainability

This theme is very much an unspoken one. Members of congregations, as I have found from experience over many years, do not even consider this issue until the priest announces that they are leaving. This usually comes as a shock to them. As a result, sustainability is often not on the local church's agenda. There is also the myth, and in some dioceses the reality, that vacancies are extended for financial reasons. Clergy vacancies leave a void for every congregation, very much like a bereavement, but in a church plant, where there is often little supporting infrastructure or few lay leaders, a gap of any length of time in leadership can be fatal for the plant. Those responsible for filling vacancies need to be aware if this.

It is worth considering at this point some of the history behind Anglo-Catholic church planting, especially when one recalls the number of Anglo-Catholic churches that were built in Victorian times, particularly but not exclusively in our large cities. You can see them still, even when they have been turned into carpet stores or car exhaust centres! The Oxford Movement, with its emphasis on the renewal of the church, gave an impetus for mission. To exemplify something of this I want to introduce Fr Richard Temple West and Mr Richard Foster, two lesser-known but significant figures for church growth.

West was born in 1827 into an aristocratic family. He was ordained in 1853 and served in a number of parishes. In 1848 he became curate at All Saints, Margaret Street, then as now a leading centre of Anglo-Catholic worship. There was concern over the lack of a similar place of worship in west London; he undertook, with the blessing of his incumbent, Fr Upton Richards, to look for a site to build a church. He found one, alongside the Grand Union Canal west of Paddington station, in a very deprived area. He erected a 'tin tabernacle' for worship and set about building St Mary Magdalene, which became a well-attended and thriving church.

West's ministry was not confined to worship, as he saw that the gospel had social implications, and so the educational and social needs of his parishioners were important to him, since at that time there was little other public provision. He therefore involved himself in ways of meeting these needs. He ministered there until his death in 1892.

Richard Foster was born in 1822, into a family with connections with the importing of goods from South America. At the age of 13, his father gave him a choice: either prepare academically for ordination training or go into the family business that was managed by his uncles. He chose the latter, as he hated Latin and Greek, at that time an essential part of ordination training. He was a regular worshipper but saw that the church was not meeting the needs of the growing population of London, especially in the area in which he lived, which was vastly expanding in population. He therefore became a firm supporter of church expansion, and as his wealth increased so did his financial contributions to church building as well as to other charities. His biographer records that between 1858 and his death in 1910, he gave away about £380,000, sometimes in small but often repeated amounts. As an example, he paid completely for the building of St Barnabas, Walthamstow and the foundation stone reads:

> This church of St. Barnabas Walthamstow is to be built at the cost of Richard Foster a merchant of London as a thanksgiving to Almighty God for numberless mercies during a long life. This stone was laid by the aforesaid Richard Foster on 4th September 1902, being the day on which he completed his 80th year.

If one examines closely the attitudes of these two men, it can be seen that the six themes which I identified from my research were replicated in their approach to the mission and witness of the church. These themes from West and Foster are as relevant and identifiable today as they were 150 years ago. They were devoted to worship, offered in a way that they saw fitting to God. They were involved in the wider community, particularly in supporting those in need. They had vision for the growth of the church and showed inspiring leadership. The only area missing is sustainability, as I do not think this would have been an issue for them in the nineteenth century, since they believed that what they were establishing would continue unchanged into the future.

So what is the way forward for Anglo-Catholic church planters? Most importantly, there needs to be some structured way of linking them for support, encouragement and the sharing of ideas, similar to the network around Holy Trinity, Brompton, right across the Anglo-Catholic spectrum from traditionalist to liberal. There is plenty of opportunity but leadership and some sort of structure are missing. What is being developed by the Archbishop of York's Mission Enabler, working with the Bishop of Beverley, to reinvigorate rural traditionalist Anglo-Catholic churches in the Northern Province, is a model to be commended.

Reflections on Part Three

In our Introduction to this book, we acknowledged the perceived polarity between pioneering and planting, noting Moynagh's two models (worship first/serve first), and expressed a desire to resist the temptation to endorse a one-size-fits-all ecclesiology. The four chapters in this part of the book exemplify not only this mixed reality of the church's life, but also the riches that can be found in attending to the church's diversity. We read, in Bradbury's chapter, of the power of the small intentional missional community and the ways such groups can adopt this posture of 'being with' in profound ways within their communities. In Hodgett's powerful reflections on playfulness, we hear of the creative and innovative ways pioneers have engaged with context, creating communities in which there is freedom, life and openness to the work of the Holy Spirit. In Squirrell's chapter we see the stark contrast between evangelical and catholic approaches to church planting in the Anglican tradition and the ways working within structures and traditions can breathe new life and fresh missional vision into the church through revitalization. And in Wallace's chapter we see the ways those within the Anglo-Catholic tradition have found ways to think creatively and with fresh vision about mission, both historically and in the contemporary church. In the combination of these four contributors, we have seen concretely the importance of affirming and hearing from the diversity of voices in the conversation.

Yet we must also acknowledge that this pioneer/plant tension is only one of many tensions that exist within the practice of starting new church communities. As Foulger's research has highlighted, planting in the Anglo-Catholic tradition is almost non-existent. In a recent report covering 11 dioceses in the Church of England, Foulger found only five cases of Anglo-Catholic 'new things', in a sample size of 900 (Foulger, 2024, p. 29). As we have seen in both Wallace's and Squirrell's chapters, the starting of new Anglo-Catholic communities has an important contribution to bring to the conversation. It is also surely the case that there are examples of pioneering Anglo-Catholic communities (such as some of the examples in Croft, Mobsby and Spellers, 2010). And so it is also reasonable to think that the catholic/evangelical tension doesn't map neatly on to the pioneer/plant tension. But these voices are largely absent from the wider conversation on the theology of planting, or else they exist primarily as critics of the conversation (see Davison and Milbank, 2014, for example).

Perhaps one reason for a lack of diversity in churchmanship and tradition is primarily a translation problem. As Stefan Paas observes:

> For many Christians, Roman Catholics in particular, 'church planting' (*plantatio ecclesiae*) designates the classic activity of the first foundation of the Christian church in the so-called mission fields. Any other Christian community formation, subsequent to this first planting, may be an additional structure or an extension of the church, but it is not church *planting*. (Paas, 2016, p. 3, emphasis original)

More generally, there is not a consensus around what counts as starting a new 'church' and what is simply a missional activity of an existing church. The move towards 'mixed ecology' after the publication of *Mission-shaped Church* (as many contributors to this book have highlighted) has led to a diversity of ecclesiologies and a lack of consensus around what counts as starting a new church. Foulger's (2024) report on 11 dioceses in the Church of England found no common definition used by any one diocese. But importantly, this is not to say mission is not happening in the Anglo-Catholic tradition, nor that new things are not being started. Consider the recent launch of Choir Church in Blackburn Diocese, an initiative to teach choral anthems to school children and engage their families in worship (Church of England, n.d.). In a different context, we might look at the Crask Inn, a rural pub owned by the Scottish Episcopal Church in the remote Scottish Highlands, in which eucharistic worship is held regularly, alongside the running of a functioning pub at the heart of the community (Scottish Episcopal Church, n.d.). Neither of these contexts embrace the language of 'church planting' or 'pioneering'. Yet both are engaging in missional activities not discernibly different from the kinds of practice described in the four chapters of Part Three. Perhaps neither of these cases would have been picked up in a report like Foulger's, given the lack of shared language around starting new things. But this isn't to say new church communities are not being formed.

If we are serious about avoiding false binaries and perpetuating monochrome perspectives, then more work is needed to attend closely to the use of language and to examine its theological implications. Should we strive for a common language around starting new churches? Is this even possible? These are some of the questions we believe will need to be attended to if we are to engage in the rich and fruitful reflection on contexts of many kinds, shapes and sizes.

References

Church of England, 'Choir Church', https://www.churchofengland.org/media/press-releases/choir-churches-be-funded-part-projects-spread-christian-faith (accessed 23.03.2024).

Croft, Steven, Ian Mobsby and Stephanie Spellers (eds), 2010, *Ancient Faith, Future Mission: Fresh Expressions in the Sacramental Traditions*, London: Church House Publishing.

Davison, Andrew and Alison Milbank, 2014, *For the Parish: A Critique of Fresh Expressions*, London: SCM Press.

Foulger, Will, 2024, *New Things: A Theological Investigation into the Work of Starting New churches across 11 Dioceses in the Church of England*, https://www.cranmerhall.com/wp-content/uploads/2024/03/New-Things-Final-1.pdf (accessed 22.03.2024).

Paas, Stefan, 2016, *Church Planting in the Secular West: Learning from the European Experience*, Grand Rapids, MI: Eerdmans.

Scottish Episcopal Church, 'Crask Inn', https://www.scotland.anglican.org/church/the-crask-inn-lairg/ (accessed 23.03.2024).

PART FOUR

Ecclesiology: A Theology of New Churches

15

Growth in the Gaps and Cracks: A Reflection on Polity, Tradition and Praxis in Planting and Pioneering

ALI WILLIAMS

Introduction

'Good Teacher, what must I do to inherit eternal life?' (Mark 10.17) asks the rich young ruler in Mark's Gospel. This man's preoccupation with 'doing', through structures, observances and actions, entirely aligned with his socio-religious praxis, where what is done constitutes and maintains belonging and righteousness. By his own admission he had been perfect under the law, keeping every commandment even from his youth. But 'Jesus, looking at him, loved him', and responded, 'You lack one thing' (Mark 10.21). This one thing turns out to be everything.

In the same way, the church is preoccupied with structures, observances and actions. Our organized polity and our desire for knowing over being too often leaves planting and pioneering as an auxiliary praxis limited to the margins, while the church proper continues in the mainstream organizational centre. Pioneering is relegated in its activity to the gaps and the cracks that occur in context, where the parish system has lost its vocation to people, of time and place. However, with the advent of various strategies to resource planting within the central church, we risk perpetuating the inherent problems that led to this crisis, as the church focuses on upholding and resourcing the continuation of our current practice. What future does Jesus offer the rich young ruler as the 'author and disrupter' of faith? (Hodgett, 2023). I believe this reformation moment in the church is reorientating us to look outward once again, calling for the radical reordering of our intentions and instincts, reshaping our praxis and forms.

The twentieth century saw a paradigmatic shift in our understanding of mission, where 'mission is not the enterprise that transforms reality, but something that is itself being transformed' (Bosch, 1991, p. xv). The Church of England itself has recognized this from *Mission-shaped Church* (Cracknell, Male and Olsworth-Peter, 2019) to the 'Growing Faith' report (Clinton, Genders and Male, 2019) aiming to reorientate our praxis, purpose and intention. However, justified criticism continues to question how such paradigm change will be resourced, structured and aligned, or better still, integrated within our current polity.

I will argue that in summary our understanding is moving beyond mission as an event or separate action of the church into the foundational identity of the church. Moving perhaps, as the rich young ruler is challenged to, from a superficial adoption of epistemological assent and fuller acceptance of an ontological expression of who we are. The very nature of epistemology is sought and expressed within a context. It is as much fixed to time and place as we are, and therefore impermanent, and subject to reformation or even malformation depending on our wider experience and understanding. This shift releases us from the primary aim of soteriology as an outcome or event, or the often prideful impartation of faith in missions to the rest of humanity. It reorientates us from a maintenance model to a pioneering mode. Last, it confronts in us times when we have sought to use it as an expansion of our ecclesial category or influence.

Ontologically, mission is not primarily an activity of the church, but an attribute of God in which the church participates (Bosch, 1991, p. 372). Our prophetic proclamation of the constants of the gospel, today more than ever, needs to be done with a deep conviction of the importance of context (Bevans and Schroeder, 2004, p. 361). As Paas asserts, even the aspect of our personhood that we consider to be immortal, our soul, prays in an accent, in a language, of a culture, of time and place within the broad history of the world (Paas, 2019, p. 197). Our soterial identity can never be disembodied from our lived experience. Salvation 'becomes concrete ... in and through community' (Paas, p. 204). Our ontology, epistemology, methodology and praxis are intimately layered and complex in their interdependence, as well as in their affective influence. Such reductive fixation on form, method or model is in peril of perpetuating a preoccupation with our internal factors, which is precisely what such systems and church growth enterprises wish to address.

I have come to recognize this reductive fixation on structures, knowledge and form over the last 20 years in my lay and ordained work within pioneering and planting ministries. From cathedral to pit village, chaplaincy to missional community, this superficial adoption of epistemological and ontological principles is expressed across the cavernous gulf of tradition and denomination, to a greater or lesser degree. As Ruth Padilla DeBorst summarizes, the fundamental challenge confronting the church post-Christendom is that we have wrongly confused the 'the kingdom of God with the institutional church, the gospel with culture' (2016, p. 91). So it is that I wish to frame the following discussion in my experience of raising a missional community to establish new worshipping community and church. Our vision and premise was to build a house for the Lord that was entirely imbedded in the everyday life of those in the local area. This allowed us to frame the conversation in the sense of a paradigm shift in our posture and understanding of the church's vocation and intention. The work we undertook required different instincts (Foulger, 2023, p. 10). For context, I was sent to a rural, former mining-village church in the north-east to raise a missional community, who would discern a new church expression and community hub. The village had previously suffered the closure of several churches in the last 15 years. The community is in the bottom 3% in Church Urban Fund deprivation indices, as a category D village. The church had enough funding to cover the rent of a community building. We planted from one village into another village, next-door-but-one, in the neighbouring parish. We were outside the support and resourcing of church network, or parish system, without a Bishop's Mission Order or equivalent alternative structure. We had a tiny amount of seed funding (amounting to £8,000 for three years) from Diocesan Strategic Development Fund underspend, and no money to recruit paid staff. Yet we 'had it in [our hearts] to build a house for the Name of the LORD' (cf. 1 Chron. 22.7, NIV), a house that was totally imbedded in the context, primarily among the unchurched and dechurched of the local area. We sought vision, prayed, dreamed, sought vision, gathered a team, sought vision, and raised leaders, all of whom were in their 70s and 80s, and we sat in the ambiguity of planting in the grey areas and liminal spaces of polity. It is the story of the revitalization of one church, who discovered an intentionality to place and people, while the established church within the same parish remained resistant.

The resistant parish congregation was predominantly female, who had mostly attended with their grandmothers and had been dispatched to afternoon Sunday school in their younger years. They often then drifted away until they were retired or widowed, when they returned to church, expecting to find it as it had been some 50 years earlier. In the majority of cases, their expectations were met. Concern for proper praxis and its formative nature is inculcated in parishioners. Their intentionality to their context and understanding of mission was explicit: their understanding of mission was: 'It is that the church structure, style and location are already appropriately in place. All that is required is that those outside the church accommodate themselves to what already exists' (Morisy, 2003, p. 13). The jealous older sibling to any new prodigal, they were ambivalent at best and aggressively against at worst. In their view, the church exists to serve its members, and its decline is not a sign of increased irrelevance, but more a condemning marker of a cultural atheism in which they remain an exilic outpost of better times past. Most staggeringly, the women of this resistant and hostile congregation were entirely devoted to their community, yet their worshipping life could not be more distinct from their community relationships. The background anxiety was, of course, fear that what they share might change if others joined; that it would be incumbent on them to adapt.

Concern for form in what our worship looks like, and our reasoning for inhabiting it in our preferred form, is a preoccupation that predates the inauguration of this particular church and was a consistent theme within the early church. As differing people inhabited shared places and spaces they asked similar questions of right and proper praxis. Today it is as much a concern to Reformed charismatic evangelicals as it is to Anglo-Catholics. The primacy we give to the sphere of tradition – explicit and implicit forms and praxis in gathered worship – are worth considering. I do not believe it is helpful to force a false dichotomy between 'assimilate' or 'replicate' models and 'fresh expression' or 'emerging' forms of worship within a community. My criticism is that we have prioritized epistemology over ontology, too readily reducing communities of faith to what we do and how we do it. Our method and epistemology fused inseparably and were given supremacy, all the while ontology was relegated to the busyness of doing. In so doing, our church expression becomes rigid and primarily concerned with proper practice, the function of practice in establishing and reforming ecclesial culture, and how this informs the self-narratives of Christian members.

I believe we all require established form in worship to some degree, whether we favour formal liturgical rhythms or have devised alternative liturgies for inhabiting our worship; a rhythm, familiarity, sometimes spontaneity. The form's purpose is to facilitate encounter with the living God and gather into an ecclesial fellowship those who are present, that the newness of God may break upon us afresh to generation and to generation and to generation. However, fellowship constituted on form implies the same error in understanding that lies behind the paradigmatic shift in our understanding of mission as something we 'do to', so that others join us by assimilating and learning to 'do what we do'. There is little room within this model for the generous mutuality of a community founded deeply within the individual expression of context. Our universal belonging is so easily reduced where we become less founded in salvation wrought by Christ, and more in likeminded adoption of style, theological position and other such secondaries. Robust defenders of these cultural liturgies, such as Nicholas Healy (2003) and James Smith, argue that in developing a philosophical anthropology and in examining 'what Christians do' (Smith, 2009, p. 11), we reveal what we believe and who we are. For them, culturally operant practice is the conduit of an epistemological telos within the universal church. Such knowledge is then birthed through habit (or *habitus*) rather than belief (Smith, 2013, pp. 80–3). It is true that much of our doctrine within the Church of England is inhabited through the repetition of our liturgy or through our teaching and preaching. However, I would push against the notion that 'right practice' always inculcates true belief, whether through 'structured' or 'loosely structured' practices (Healy, 2003, pp. 294–5). Intention and motivation are of utmost import. Being able to perform or mimic a practice simply reveals that you have been enculturated into embodying that particular practice. It does not mean that the motivation is true, nor that the purpose or function of the practice has been understood. A believing member of a congregation can participate in an act of loosely structured *or* structured sacramental worship, giving attention to its proper performance, and yet fail to understand its meaning or purpose. After all, a 'practice' is any 'sustained, co-operative pattern of human activity' (Healy, 2003, p. 289).

As such, we can be as much 'malformed' as 'formed' by unquestioning encultured practice. Although the behaviour may contribute to a sense of belonging and cultural assimilation, the consequence in instances such as these has no pedagogical or discipleship value (Healy, 2003, p. 294).

Complicity in the performance of these practices undoubtedly creates ecclesial identities and a sense of being incorporated (as we integrate patterns and forms into our expression we are in turn embodied, lit. *in corpore*), re-membered into the ecclesial body. Faith expressions are systematized within culture; therefore, their very establishment is subject to the influence of cultural normalcy at the time of reception (Healy, 2003, p. 294).

As such, reliance on systematic inherited forms without reflexive change and compromise fails to enable widespread inculturation of the gospel, and does not prompt the reform and renewal of the church. Furthermore, such emphasis reduces the expression of each part to conformity, where what is 'signified' by worshipping practice – God – is replaced by the primacy of the 'signifier' (Beaudoin, 2016, p. 8).

'Transformation occurs from a person's inner life, or from the inside-out' (Barrett, 2013, p. 1). Relying on the ability of liturgy to transform from the outside-in adopts a posture of dominance and 'cultural mastery' (Alvesson, 2013, p. 121) imposed from above, denying the mutuality of influence that we each have in common communion in community. We cannot 'do inculturation' by analysing the culture to be evangelized and reinterpret the Christian message in its light. Such a process could only result in a superficial adaptation of the gospel 'from above'. Inculturation is essentially a community process 'from below' (Archbishops' Council, 2004, p. 91).

Culture is complex, formed through the 'simultaneously predictable and unpredictable patterning of the independent actions of many people, whereby all are influencing while simultaneously being influenced' (Flinn, 2019, p. 35). As such, suggesting unilateral acceptance of any single 'idealized' vision only diminishes the mutual and contingent nature of humanity's interrelating and the ongoing participation of God within all his creation. Reducing such multiplicity to a set script perpetuates a self-fulfilling prophecy whereby God is experienced as present in the routine instances of praxis.

The evidence of an overreliance on 'habit-forming praxis' is laid bare throughout our missional statistics. With the closure of several churches in the space of 15 years, when congregations found their church no longer viable the majority of believers did not go elsewhere, to a new worshipping community, nor did they choose to form a new ecclesial community in the village outside of their previously held denominational traditions; they simply stopped going. Their faithfulness was to a place and a time and a routine, and their discipleship fixed to a particular expression in a particular place. Their praxis did not, in and of itself, sustain anything other than their membership for as long as that expression was available to them.

Hazardous reliance on prescriptive definitions of proper structured practices wrongly invests in the reproduction of form, in such a way that Christianity is reduced to the perceived level of 'Christianicity' (Beaudoin, 2016, p. 16), where 'continuation of Christianity' is only viable if it 'lives continually in practice' (p. 8). Where this happens, our focus becomes entirely on internal factors of worship, which are there to serve those who come to worship (Roxburgh, 2010, p. 128). Such preoccupation is entirely contrary to the *missio Dei*.

For me, this is the nub of the matter. Christians were never a church of enclave, we are always a church of *missio*. Within the Church of England, within our liturgical praxis we gather together in worship and praise, in the presence of the one whom we worship. We gather in Scripture, immersed in the story of the people of God, finding ourselves within it. We often gather around the table, and then we are sent – to gather back in turn, making disciples who make disciples who make disciples. Although attending to our internal factors in our gathering may give us a sense of moving on in depth, when internal factors are given primacy the majority of new congregational attendees tend to join from other churches. The energy for perfecting our internal workings outweighs the missional imperative to make new believers, and the outcome conforms to all the pitfalls of attractional growth, from which neither the emerged traditional church nor the traditional replication church plant models are immune.

Currently, our polity serves to uphold and resource the continuation of our practice, which ought to prompt robust and critical reflection on what dictates the release and deployment of central financial resources, the creation of new training pathways, models of community engagement, pathways of discipleship, methodologies for transitional change and cultural renewal. In as much as the rich young ruler was seeking a framework, action or knowledge, I truly believe that our polity, and our sense of tribalism and tradition, through network or denominational expression, have led to an overreliance on an epistemological framework and basis of faith for belonging and missional engagement. These do not take enough into consideration the diverse complexity of culture and context or allow themselves to be shaped by their environment.

Relating this to my experience in the north-east, the gift of being minimally resourced was that we had very few outcomes prescribed. We entered, as a team, into a two-year discernment of contextual identities, cultural rhythm, story and opportunity. We grew into the context as God gave us a heart for the people of that place, while we sought him for their flourishing. We did not have a posture that was fixed by the outcomes layered into set forms. We grew into our context and we grew in symbiotic mutuality and relationship together. If we had outcomes in mind, they were more in line with resourcing models, in direct proportionality to our funding, financing and resourcing structures. Much of what emerged in that growing together, from grassroots faith, would have been subjugated under a strategy in a top-down, prescriptive model.

In praxis, giving primacy to ontology and context requires us to tend to different instincts. Rather than assuming we know what it is a community needs, we should instead ask:

1. What are your hope and dreams for this place? What is their vision of a hopeful future?
2. What do you want us to do? A member of the community said to me: 'People come here and "do" to as long as the funding lasts. Then they leave us.' The principles of incarnation do not model 'doing to' but dwelling with, even as Emmanuel is 'God with us', and became God in us and through us, through the death and resurrection of Jesus Christ. It is modelled on service, love of neighbour and seeking justice.

3. What do you want to give? This last is the most fundamental principle, which created slipstreams of relationship and collaboration; not based in power and influence and a dependency of one party on the other but on choice, release and growth, within both parties. Reciprocity cannot flow in one direction, rather it is a co-created wellspring that is shared between God and each party.

We were co-creators of all that we did. Our worship space was curated from community. We asked people to bring objects that spoke of God's character or their experience of God. Over time we were gifted myriad expressions of love and grace: in an hourglass from a woman living with terminal cancer, a bicycle reflector, sea glass that has been smoothed and shaped by the relentless pressure of the waves against sand. We had crosses brought from closed churches, holding hearts, children's drawings, artists' mannequins shaped into postures and groups; acorns, rainbow money boxes, a Davy lamp from the days of the coal pits – all manner of objects that signified God's shared story with his people. Generous, bold and courageous, it was playful and a bit messy and utterly, breathtakingly beautiful, and a living testimony that grew and moved with the people who joined us, along with the cultural calendar and the church's seasons. Nothing was started without community members to lead, and we looked for calling and heart above capability. It was slower and messier, but enabled people to grow and begin to stand outside the false limits they had been constrained in, both in community and within worship. Both liturgical and creative: Zumba grew into Praise-ercise, the community nativity service ended with Carol-oke, the café was a 24/7 prayer space where bread was broken over the tables of community gathering. We discovered our shared story and rewove the fabric of community together, as people gathered and realized their own shared experience. Newbigin wrote: 'the only hermeneutic of the gospel, is the community of men and women who believe it and live by it' (Newbigin, 1989, p. 32).

The image I reach for to capture this zeitgeist/reformation moment in the church's history is pictured in Figure 1.

It feels to me like our predominant method has been to raise beautiful, tender vines in glass jars or terrariums; beautiful, self-contained little ecosystems of faith community, governed by internal factors, preferences and styles. But the gospel was never intended for glass jars. It was always planted in the ground, grown in the context and reality of everyday life. Our sad heritage has often been to plough up the growth of other expressions in order to establish or further the growth of our own way.

I truly believe that we can no longer promote or uphold these predominantly epistemological, maintenance-heavy frameworks. Perhaps

Figure 1

the call to return to ontology first feels frightening in the face of epistemology. Instead of certitude it offers playful ambiguity. It calls us to move beyond form and network and affiliation to specific traditions, and brings us outside the self-imposed limits of our denominationalism or former formation. It forces us to release our hold on where we have bound 'God too closely to material transactions' (Williams, 2003, p. 3). Instead of learning to behave, it call us to become more fully aware of our belonging, our being-in, and within time and place, reorientating us from religious enterprise to spiritual postures of listening and intention. It requires risk and generosity, but most of all an openness and intentionality to context that is not driven by fear that not doing what we do, the way we have done it, will somehow bring the end of our expression of church. To be honest, the death of our traditions will come less by our ability to reorientate and loosen our grasp on what we share together, and more by how prescriptive we continue to be about what we share. I have rarely known statements as sad as: 'As long as it [the church] sees me out.' Reorientating our identity towards a missional and ontological emphasis enables the church to stop planting for the sake of the church. We have always been called to plant for the sake of the gospel; make disciples, and diverse church communities will follow. However, it is a slower, smaller path. It takes sustained intentionality towards context, networking out and gathering back, in an endless loop, which orbits all the places where people gather to form a truly mixed ecology of people, time and place. It reorientates us from a parish system to a parish vocation. It recognizes that the system does not always best serve or promote the intentionality of the church to its context, in new or pre-existing forms. Its existence in a context does not necessarily promote its intentional connection to place or relationship with its people.

The gaps and the cracks in the ground of our parish system are widening. The church has a choice. It can choose to grow into the liminal spaces in between, and prosper where God is meeting and renewing his creation, or it can continue to plant terrarium models. For 'the church exists by mission, as the fire exists by burning' (Brunner, 1931, p. 11). The only question that remains is whether the church can bear the cost or whether, like the rich young ruler, it will turn away sad.

References

Alvesson, M., 2013, *Understanding Organizational Culture*, 2nd edn, London: Sage.
Archbishops' Council, 2004, *Mission-shaped Church: Church Planting and Fresh Expressions of Church in a Changing Context*, London: Church House Publishing.
Barrett, A., 2013, *Asset-Based Community Development: A Theological Reflection*, https://resources.depaul.edu/abcd-institute/publications/publications-by-topic/Documents/ABCD_Theological_Reflection_2013.pdf (accessed 14.04.2020).
Beaudoin, T., 2016, 'Why does Practice Matter Theologically?', in J. A. Mercer and B. J. Miller-McLemore (eds), *Conundrums in Practical Theology*, Leiden: Brill, pp. 8–32.
Bevans, S. B. and R. P. Schroeder, 2004, *Constants in Context: A Theology of Mission for Today*, Maryknoll, NY: Orbis Books.
Bosch, D. J., 1991, *Transforming Mission: Paradigm Shifts in Theology of Mission*, New York: Orbis Books.
Brunner, E., 1931, *The Word and the World*, London: SCM Press.
Clinton, D., N. Genders and D. Male, 2019, 'Growing Faith: Churches, Schools and Households', GS_2121.pdf (https://www.churchofengland.org/sites/default/files/2019-01/gs-2121.pdf (accessed 16.12.2023).
Cracknell, H., D. Male and E. Olsworth-Peter, 2019, 'Fresh Expressions 15 Years On', https://ccx.org.uk/content/mission-shaped-church-15-review/#a-mission-shaped-church-and-fresh-expressions-15-years-on/1/ (accessed 29.08.2024).
Flinn, K., 2019, *Leadership Development: A Company Approach*, London: Routledge.
Foulger, W., 2023, *Present in Every Place? The Church of England's New Churches, and the Future of the Parish*, London: SCM Press.

Healy, N. M., 2003, 'Practices and the New Ecclesiology: Misplaced Concreteness?', *International Journal of Systematic Theology* 5.3, pp. 287–308.

Hodgett, T., 2023, 'Coming our Fighting for Pioneering' (23 October), 'Coming out fighting for "pioneering"' (29 December) – CMS Pioneer Mission Leadership Training (churchmissionsociety.org).

Morisy, A., 2003, *Beyond the Good Samaritan: Community, Ministry and Mission*, London: Continuum.

Newbigin, L., 1989, *The Gospel in a Pluralist Society*, 3rd edn, London: SPCK.

Paas, S., 2019, *Pilgrims and Priests: Christian Mission in a Post-Christian Society*, London: SCM Press.

Padilla DeBorst, R. P., 2016, 'Integral Transformation', in C. Ott (ed.), *The Mission of the Church: Five Views in Conversation*, Grand Rapids, MI: Baker Academic, pp. 41–69.

Roxburgh, A. J., 2010, *Missional Map-Making: Skills for Leading in Times of Transition*, San Francisco, CA: Jossey-Bass.

Smith, J. K. A., 2009, *Desiring the Kingdom: Worship, Worldview, and Cultural Formation* (Cultural Liturgies Vol. 1), Grand Rapids, MI: Baker Academic.

———, 2013, *Imagining the Kingdom: How Worship Works* (Cultural Liturgies Vol. 2), Grand Rapids, MI: Baker Academic.

Williams, R., 2003, *Anglican Identities*, Plymouth: Cowley Publications.

16

'We're going to plant a church on Friday': Reflections and Learnings on Church Planting

CATHY ROSS

Introduction

The title is a statement that was made to me by a young woman ordinand, excitedly going off on a church placement where this was awaiting her – planting a church on Friday. I have started this chapter with her statement because it alludes to some of the questions and themes that I would like to consider – such as: What is church planting and where does it happen? Who plants the church? What might be the timeframes? What are our motivations? What language do we use?

I would like to reflect on church planting from a missiological perspective, because that is my area of interest and experience over the years. I am not a church planting practitioner. I teach, lead and – most importantly – learn on a programme dedicated to enabling pioneers to be engaged in God's mission by listening to the Spirit and respecting their local context. I have learnt so much from our pioneers, some of whom are involved in church planting, and it is those insights I would like to reflect on here.

In preparing this chapter, I realized that my husband and I have been involved in a church plant in Aotearoa/New Zealand. It was not called that back then but with hindsight I can see that is what you would call it now. We got involved very soon after the new minister and his young family arrived. He was the curate for this mission district church, as it was quaintly called. It was the daughter church in a poorer and mixed neighbourhood of the mother church in the next neighbourhood, where I had attended church as a child. There was a solid Anglican church building and literally a few older women in the church. I was finishing my MA in languages and then training to be a teacher. Steve was finishing his medical studies and working as a junior doctor. We threw ourselves into this and made lifelong friends. We prayed, we hosted a large youth group; later there was a mums and toddlers group, home groups; later still refugees and asylum seekers were welcomed, the curate became a vicar and the mission district became its own parish. This church was one of our main supporters when we served overseas in Rwanda, DR Congo and Uganda with the New Zealand Church Missionary Society (CMS).

Looking back, our approach consisted of prayer, spending time – lots of time, on hospitality, deep friendships, love for the people. It sounds simple and in many ways it was. No one was in a hurry to achieve anything – we were young; we had time. There were tensions with the mother church; the vicar there did not like what we were doing – accused us of being Congregationalist, which none of us ever understood! The church grew, people from the neighbourhood came to know Christ – not in large numbers, but there were new converts and people's lives were changed in various ways: less drinking, less debt, less abuse. Of course, there were disappointments too – broken marriages, unpaid debts, people moving on in what was a transient neighbourhood for some. Around three years ago the church closed. Our last service in that church was my father's funeral in 2018 – even then we could see it was struggling. We were – are – so sad that this thriving community is no more. Well, it is no more in that particular space and place. I could speculate as to why it closed and we could learn some lessons from that – but that is not the learning I would like to draw out from this. I have learnt over the years (one advantage of growing old, although I hope I always remain future-looking!) that things come and go. Not everything lasts for ever. There is a vulnerability at the heart of our faith – the cross stands as a reminder of that. Not everything lasts for ever and that is OK. It might be a hard lesson to learn, especially when we are in the midst of it, but that is reality. God's Spirit blows where the Spirit wills and it is not all up to us. That is so important to remember – God is God and we are not.

Questions

I would like to pose some questions on church planting – in fact I was asking some of these same questions nearly ten years ago when my colleague David Dadswell and I did some commissioned research into church planting and we researched 27 church plants across England (Dadswell and Ross, 2013).

First, what is church planting? One of our findings back then, as is still the case today, is that the language is problematic and not shared. Different people have different understandings of what constitutes a church plant. Some find the language of church planting to be transactional and practised as a one-way process. So what exactly is it? Think about that for a moment: What is it for you? Where you are, in your context? Presumably it is something about growing or developing a church. So what is church? Is it a building? Of course we know church is not just a building; it is God and the people, but it seems that our imaginations are so colonized, we still think of buildings, services, priestly leaders and all that goes along with that. I have seen the reporting forms for church planters from one diocese – they ask about average weekly attendance at services, at home groups, Alpha groups, foodbank attendance, number of school visits and assemblies. This certainly presupposes a particular understanding of and approach to church planting. So what might church look like in your context? Does it have to meet on a Sunday? Does it need to be in a building? Does it need to meet weekly? Do you need a priest as leader? Do you need communion every week? I know I am asking some difficult questions here for those of you who are ordained Anglicans and for whom priesthood is a holy and precious vocation. But I think mission and context forces us to ask such questions. It may mean taking risks and letting go of some of our sacred cows and traditional expectations. The Roman Catholic missiologists Steve Bevans and Roger Schroeder write movingly about this and how difficult it is to divest ourselves of our particular set of lenses and filters – it is a life's work, they claim:

> 'letting go' means 'letting be,' and this always involves a risk for the sake of the gospel. Outsiders need to let go of their certainties regarding the content of the gospel. They need to let go of cherished ideas and practices that have nourished and sustained them in their own journeys toward Christian maturity. They need to let go of the symbols that anchor them in their human and Christian identity and let go of the order that makes them comfortable. (Bevans and Schroeder, 2011, p. 92)

Of course, we may not think of ourselves as 'outsiders'. But normally, we are. Even in my context all those years ago, the next neighbourhood was very different from where we had grown up. Context really is everything.

So what might church look like in your context? John Taylor's writings have really helped us to think about this in CMS. He wrote that the world is 'the church's milieu' (Taylor, 1964). Jonny Baker took this as his starting point for a superb chapter on church in the book we co-wrote on some of Taylor's writings (Baker and Ross, 2020). He claims that we are stuck and implores us to use fresh imagination when it comes to thinking about church. He then develops a range of intriguing metaphors to imagine what church could be – like yeast, a forest, a nursery, a movement, fringe dwellers, lots of little congregations. Taylor himself was a fan of church as small groups that include worship, evangelism, biblical reflection and service; and always, he said, non-Christians must be part of these groups. It is fine that they are small. Small is beautiful. Research by Church Army into fresh expressions in 2016 was entitled *The Day of Small Things* (Lings, 2016) because so many of these new communities were small, 15–55 in number. Small is beautiful. One of CMS's founding principles is 'Start small'. So what might a church plant look like in your context? Become unstuck, imagine some new ways, slay some sacred cows, take risks, imagine a new sort of ecosystem for church in your place and space.

Next question: Where do we plant churches? Where are the contexts we go to for church planting? I realize that some of you may have no choice, as you go where you are sent by the diocese. It is interesting and informative to reflect on where the church plants are happening. When we did our research ten years ago, 23 out of 27 church plants were in middle-class areas. That means only four were not – about 1/7 or 14% were not in middle-class areas. Of course, church planting, as with mission, can happen anywhere and everywhere – the whole world needs to experience the glory of God. But maybe we need some focus and challenge here. CMS has recently adopted a more intentional approach in our work, which is to be at the edges. I know edges and centre are contested language. Where is the centre and the edge and who determines this? And those who are deemed to be at the edges do not necessarily feel themselves to be on the edge – wherever the edge actually is! So it can sound patronizing but bear with me, please. One of the things we say at CMS is: 'Come with us to the edges and discover God at work in ways you might not have expected.' Jesus loved those on the edges or margins of society. He was drawn to them – the women and children, the unclean, the prostitutes, the tax collectors, the unwell. He healed them, removed their burdens of shame, he noticed them and restored their dignity. The African American theologian Willie James Jennings tells us that Jesus attracted crowds and that he often gathered people who preferred not to be together; people from the edges and elsewhere (Jennings, 2020, p. 151). The Peruvian liberation theologian Gustavo Gutiérrez writes powerfully about exercising a preferential option for the poor – not because the poor are better than others or more virtuous but because:

> What the preferential option for the poor reveals is that the calculus of the gospel is not the same as our world's. In present structures, attention is given first to the powerful and the wealthy, with the poor receiving, perhaps, the leftovers. This is far from universal love. But only when we opt preferentially for the poorest and weakest can we even begin to

display universality – anything less is tainted with the exclusive ways of present social structures. (Gutiérrez, 2013, p. 29)

This is an important challenge for us as we ask ourselves: Where do we plant churches?

From a slightly different angle, Taylor was well aware of this and I think would have approved of our strapline, as he wrote: 'If you are concerned with movement and growth in a Church or in a society, look to the fringes. Watch the things that are pushing out on the edge' (Taylor, 1965). The CMS strapline again: 'Come with us to the edges and discover God at work in ways you might not have expected.' So where are the edges for us, are we there and what are we learning that will change us?

Final questions, which I have grouped together, before I move on to some themes and stories: Who plants churches and why? At face value, who plants churches is obvious – we do. Most of you here are church planters – you and a team of friends around you, I hope. But really, is it you? It is God who plants churches. We know this and that is our espoused theology, but I think our operant theology, the theology we live by and practise, might be different from this. Perhaps we need to be reminded of the *missio Dei*. It was Taylor who gave us the now succinct and popular summary of mission as 'seeing what God is doing in a situation and trying to do it with him' (Taylor, 1974). He rooted this in Christology and the Spirit, for Jesus had his eyes opened by the Spirit to recognize God at work in the world: 'Jesus said to them, "Very truly, I tell you, the Son can do nothing on his own, but only what he sees the Father doing; for whatever the Father does, the Son does likewise"' (John 5.19).

When we engage in church planting, do we wait to discern what God is already doing in our context? Are we listening in the neighbourhood? My Kiwi friend and colleague Mark Johnston, formerly at the University of Glasgow, has designed a resource of this name to help us do this. He writes:

> the practical 'listening' involves paying attention to the physical and social dimensions of our neighbourhood, and meeting and listening to stories of neighbours and people we meet. They ask themselves three questions:
> - What's going on in our local neighbourhoods of the community?
> - What's going on that we have not noticed before?
> - What's God beginning to show us as we notice what's going on? (Johnston, 2018)

These may all be helpful ways of beginning to discern the *missio Dei* in your context.

So is it you who is planting the church? Well, yes and no. Is it God? Yes. Is it the locals? Yes. The Roman Catholic missionary Vincent Donovan, in his beloved book *Christianity Rediscovered* (2019), argues that once the gospel has been accepted, it no longer belongs to the missionary – or church planter for our purposes – it belongs to the people. We need to believe and trust that the locals are now under the guidance of the Holy Spirit, who will lead them towards a faithful expression of faith in their own context. Back in 1912, Roland Allen, a USPG missionary to China, wrote a book, now a classic, entitled *Missionary Methods: St Paul's or Ours?* in which he argued that Paul did not plan his missionary journeys but was guided by the Holy Spirit, and that Paul did not stay in one place very long in order to allow the locals to take over so as not to create dependence. He wrote some challenging words:

> Want of faith has made us fear and distrust native independence. We have imagined ourselves to be, and we have acted so as to become, indispensable. In everything we have taught our converts to turn to us, to accept our guidance. We have asked nothing from them but obedience. We have educated our converts to put us in the place of Christ. We believe that it is the Holy Spirit of Christ which inspires and guides us: we cannot believe that the same spirit will guide and inspire them. We believe that the Holy Spirit has taught us and is teaching us true conceptions of morality, doctrine, ritual: we cannot believe that the same Spirit will teach them. (Allen, 1962, p. 144)

We have to allow the locals to take over and run the new faith community in their way, in their place, in their context. How long that will take is a matter of prayer and discernment but perhaps not as long as we think!

One final comment on who is engaged in church planting: when we did our research ten years ago, of the 27 church plants we researched, 26 of them were led by white men. When Will Foulger put out a call for papers for a church growth conference in 2023, he received offers of 15 papers, all from white men. So Will went hunting for diversity – and found some! But it seems that not much has changed.

And why do we plant churches? Because we long to see all things renewed by God, we long to see God's kingdom come, we long to see all things under the Lordship of Christ. It sounds clear and simple, and at our best, that is what we want. However, we do need to keep examining our motives: Why are we doing this? Is it just because there is diocesan funding from the Strategic Development Fund (SDF)? Is it because of diocesan targets? In 2020, Oxford Diocese announced the intention to plant 750 new congregations – an ambitious plan.[1] By 2027 the Diocese of Derby aspires to have 5,000 new disciples, 2,500 new transformation stories, 1,000 new local lay leaders, 500 new community projects/partnerships, 500 new worshipping communities and 50 new ordained vocations.

We need to ensure that our motivation is in tune with the movement of the Holy Spirit, and that takes time, listening, discernment, humility and an ability to flex and change direction – just as Paul had to when he tried to go to Asia and then to preach in Bithynia but 'the Spirit of Jesus did not allow them' (Acts 16.7). And then Paul had his Macedonian vision. Prayer, discernment, listening, wise colleagues can all help us to examine our own motivations.

I would now like to consider the following themes: *missio Dei* and the role of the Holy Spirit, surprises, leadership and language. These are some of the themes that emerged from the five pioneers involved in church planting whom I interviewed for this paper, as well as others I have interacted with over the years. I have chosen the themes that were the most common across the interviews, and I have touched on some already.

Missio Dei

They all affirmed that God is already there – God is already at work in that place. They believed that their role was to discern what is already happening and to try to build on that. One couple, Miles and Chloe, interviewed on 3 November 2022 (all names are pseudonyms), are living on a new housing estate and avoid using the word 'church'. They said as soon as they use that word, people think of hiring a building and meeting at the same time every week. They said: 'We have been doing a lot of nothing. You know, the waiting and the discerning. It's actually quite difficult to sort of maintain, and to actually say, yeah we still trust God's going to work this out.'

They hope to develop a kind of community centre that can be used for lots of different purposes, one of which will be discussing faith. It is early days for them and they are struggling with diocesan expectations because they cannot yet describe in fine detail what they will do. They told me:

What does it look like now in the light of the next thing we've learnt or the next thing we've done? You know, it's not prescribed, we're not going there to do this, this and this, we're going there to find out and as a result of finding out, see what we do.

They explained to me that there is no diocesan plan to further fund the project when the original SDF funding runs out, so the pressure is on them to create something sustainable. For me, this raises questions about funding and how realistic some of the funding models are.

Miles and Chloe practised intentional listening, trying to discern what God was beginning to show them. In fact, they talk about 'building community, discovering church'. They say: 'God is at work out there, God is doing, it's almost like church exists. So there is God making the connections and relationships, and we just have to discover it or be an excuse to bring it together or discern it.' This is at the heart of the *missio Dei*. It is about watching, waiting, listening, discerning the Spirit of God already present and at work there. This may mean helping our imaginations to become unstuck so that we can see clearly. Our imaginations are more colonized than we think so our imaginings of what church might be are limited. The C of E is a social construct, as is the parish system. It may not be wrong or bad but there will be other ways of being and imagining church. Over the centuries and in other parts of the world, church has looked and is very different – under a tree, in a pub, online, in secret. Each generation and each context needs to translate or contextualize what it will look like for their context – and it is the locals who need to take the lead.

Surprises

All the folk I interviewed insisted that nothing went according to the plan they were either given or devised. Like Miles and Chloe, they all found the targets and expectations placed on them by the church to be unrealistic. Angela, interviewed on 28 October 2022, is ordained and working in an edge place – a tough, quite deprived area; she started slowly and quietly. She struggles with most of the church planting language and finds the models to be mainly evangelical and middle class. For example, she told me:

> I sometimes wonder whether the kind of original model is based on very prosperous middle-class folk who can move from church to church with ease and have access to private transport and wouldn't have a problem going to a different part of town. That really isn't the case with those whom I am working with at all.

During the first lockdown they distributed food parcels; from this came a kind of food cupboard, which had not been on the plan at all. She then had a regular breakfast meet-up and from there a small team gathered and from that a new worshipping community emerged where folk using the food cupboard gather regularly to discuss faith. This was a surprise for Angela and not what she had expected. All the folk I interviewed and many pioneer students I have spoken with over the years confirm this – it is one step at a time and hardly ever does it go according to human planning.

Angela says she sees genuine transformation happening:

> Whether that's from a faith perspective or not sometimes. So you know, people are clearing debts, people are becoming volunteers; they've become from the sort of people that felt the world owed them something to sort of genuinely giving back, and then growing in confidence, and their mental health has improved.

She told me that the targets she is expected to meet are 'bonkers'. She is required to report on the numbers of disciples. She wants to know how she is supposed to measure discipleship. She exclaimed in frustration:

> How do you measure it? What does it look like? Do they get to pray a prayer and then they're in? Is it baptisms? Is it how often they come along? ... Well one of my group bounces in and out of prison – are we going to mark him as not a disciple? ... It is just kind of like the commodification of it really; I've found it quite difficult.

Angela calls the group an ecclesial community that has emerged from the food cupboard, but it may not look anything like church as we know it. This is where the Spirit can surprise us and challenge our preconceptions. Taylor affirms that whatever the Spirit touches, the Spirit 'turns inside out'. We need more of this turning inside out, more imagination, more freedom to take risks and experiment without the weight of bureaucracy and unrealistic targets imposed on genuinely creative outcomes. We should not be surprised that the Spirit will astonish us – we just no longer expect it. Taylor reminds us of this on the first page of his book *The Go-Between God*, where he writes: 'The chief actor in the historic mission of the Christian church is the Holy Spirit.' He asserts that 'We have lost our nerve and our sense of direction and have turned the divine initiative into a human enterprise' (Taylor, 1972, p. 3). We are not to go it alone, and he reminds us that at the start of it all, Jesus told us to wait and not to deploy our own resources or strategy. He goes on to issue a warning:

> While we piously repeat the traditional assertion that without the Holy Spirit we can get nowhere in the Christian mission, we seem to press

on notwithstanding with our man-made programmes. I have not heard recently of committee business adjourned because those present were still awaiting the arrival of the Spirit of God. I have known projects abandoned for lack of funds, but not for lack of the gifts of the Spirit. Provided the human resources are adequate we take the spiritual for granted. In fact we have only the haziest idea of what we mean by resources other than human wealth, human skill and human character. (Taylor, 1972, p. 179)

Local leadership and language

Irene lived in her community for nearly ten years before something resembling church emerged. She was originally part of an organization that intentionally does not aim to plant a church. She, with some others, moved into the neighbourhood – a multicultural context – with the aim of loving God and neighbour. They all had jobs, they committed to a local church and they got to know their neighbours. Gradually people from the local neighbourhood dropped into their home on Thursday nights and this community grew. It was framed around welcome and hospitality; they shared a meal together and because it was a Christian community, they prayed at the end of the evening. We know that welcome and hospitality are key Christian practices, perhaps even disciplines. The Dutch Roman Catholic priest and writer on spiritualty Henri Nouwen has a lovely idea on hospitality as spaciousness: 'Hospitality ... means primarily the creation of a free space where the stranger can enter and become a friend instead of an enemy. Hospitality is not to change people, but to offer them space where change can take place' (Nouwen, 1976, pp. 68–9). And the North American Methodist scholar on hospitality Christine Pohl tells us: 'Churches that practise hospitality look a little bit messy' (Asbury Seminary, 2020).

Irene described the people who came as 'edge of church kind of people' as well as people from many other faith backgrounds. She said, in her interview in October 2022, that 'We never thought of this as church – it was just what we did.' But looking back on it, she thinks now that is was 'as much church as anything really'.

Then the original community broke up – people moved on, circumstances changed. So eventually the Thursday evening group became its own community within the local Anglican church, which Irene attended. She explained that this was a result of ten years of relational work of living in that community and making friends.

They recognized the need for local leadership and did try to hand over to local people. For example, they asked those coming if they could host the weekly meal in their homes, even on a rota basis. One woman did so for a few times, but it was too much for her and she could not manage it. Almost all those coming had unstable mental or physical health or difficult family circumstances, and so were unable to be committed. Additionally, as people with low levels of education, it was really hard for them to take a leadership role without constant support, for many reasons. In the current group, some changes have been made. They now use a simple Bible Study format, which can be led by anyone, and everyone is encouraged to have a go at leading. However, this is a slow process and will take a long time for confidence and competence to build. Time and patience are needed. Irene thinks that in lower-income and marginalized neighbourhoods, all this is a lot more complex and nuanced than just saying that local leadership is needed. Currently, this community is still operating under the auspices of the local Anglican church with oversight from the vicar.

Donovan reminds us that once the gospel is accepted, it belongs to the people and we need to trust that the Spirit will lead them towards a faithful expression of the faith. Bevans and Schroeder quote a Lutheran pastor who told them that 'unless we're willing to risk *losing* the gospel in the process of inculturation, we will never see the gospel become an integral part of a culture' (Bevans and Schroeder, 2011, p. 92; emphasis original). Only then can the locals be free to develop a faith community appropriate for their context.

I am intrigued by the idea of intentionally not planting a church. I realize that may not go down well! But let's play with this idea for a moment. One of the people interviewed on 7 December 2022, who lives in a medium-size city, asked me bluntly: 'What is the point? There is no shortage of churches … there are people of faith in all those churches to some degree … quietly living out lives of faith in real communities … They're on the rock face, trying to get alongside community … they are living real lives.' To put this in context, this person was reacting very strongly to a certain approach to church planting which, in his opinion, is imbued with a kind of 'finishing school' approach: a lot of resources, targets, and with little emphasis on looking after people. I know this is a particular approach, but his reaction to it was so strong, visceral almost, it made me wonder about the language and reputation of church planting.

What if we had a completely different approach? What if we used an entirely different vocabulary? How about this:

> We listen and learn first, to see what God is already doing in people's lives and communities. Then, where appropriate, through sensitive

evangelism and discipleship, we establish local Christian communities who will live as radical followers of Jesus.

Or:

We work with the poor to see their communities transformed. Because we live among them, we gain a deeper understanding of the local language and culture and can thus build deeper relationships. We recognize that the poor have resources to contribute to their own transformation. Sustainable transformation depends more on mobilizing those ideas, skills, energies and resources than on outside monetary contributions. Our gifts and external resources are offered to build the capacity of the poor community.

This is the language of the mission organization Servants.[2] Initially we may think it has a different focus – but does it? It is about transforming society and seeing local Christian communities established. That is what we are about and I think that this language picks up some of the themes we have considered: listening in the neighbourhood, discerning how God is already at work there, committing to living in the context to establish relationships, living and working on the edges, allowing the locals to engage in their own transformation and leadership.

Conclusion

To conclude, let me finish with a few questions:

- Where are the edges in your church planting?
- Where are you experiencing the Holy Spirit and how are you responding to the Spirit?
- What have been the surprises so far? Have you left any room for surprises?
- Who are the leaders? Do you have plans to hand over to the locals, and when?

We know that God is good. We know that God is love. We know that God brings the growth.

What then is Apollos? What is Paul? Servants through whom you came to believe, as the Lord assigned to each. I planted, Apollos watered, but

God gave the growth. So neither the one who plants nor the one who waters is anything, but only God who gives the growth. (1 Cor. 3.5–7)

Notes

1 https://freshexpressions.org.uk/oxford-diocese-launch-ambitious-church-planting-plan/ (accessed 29.08.2024).
2 Servants, https://servantsasia.org/who-we-are/strategies.

References

Allen, Roland, 1962, *Missionary Methods: St Paul's or Ours?*, Grand Rapids, MI: Eerdmans
Asbury Seminary, 2020, 'Dr. Christine Pohl: Making Room – Recovering Hospitality as a Christian Tradition' [podcast], *Thrive*, 29 September, https://thrive.asburyseminary.edu/dr-christine-pohl-making-room-recovering-hospitality-as-a-christian-tradition/ (accessed 2.08.2024).
Baker, Jonny and Cathy Ross, 2020, *Imagining Mission with John V. Taylor*, London: SCM Press.
Bevans, Stephen and Roger Schroeder, 2011, chapter 'Letting Go and Speaking Out, Prophetic Dialogue and the Spirituality of Inculturation', in *Prophetic Dialogue: Reflections on Christian Mission Today*, Maryknoll, NY: Orbis Books.
Dadswell, David and Cathy Ross, 2013, *Church Growth Research Project: Church Planting*, https://www.churchofengland.org/sites/default/files/2019-06/cgrp_church_planting_from_cgrd_website.pdf (accessed 29.08.2024).
Donovan, Vincent J., 2019, *Christianity Rediscovered: An Epistle from the Masai*, London: SCM Press.
Gutiérrez, Gustavo, 2013, 'Saying and Showing to the Poor: "God Loves You"', in Michael Griffin and Jennie Weiss Block (eds), *In the Company of the Poor: Conversations with Dr Paul Farmer and Fr. Gustavo Gutierrez*, Maryknoll, NY: Orbis Books.
Jennings, Willie James, 2020, *After Whiteness: An Education in Belonging*, Grand Rapids, MI: Eerdmans .
Johnston, Mark, 2018, 'Listening in the Neighbourhood', Dunedin, New Zealand: Knox College for Ministry and Leadership.
Lings, George, 2016, *The Day of Small Things: An Analysis of Fresh Expressions of Church in 21 Dioceses of the Church of England*, London: Church Army's Research Unit, https://churcharmy.org/wp-content/uploads/2021/04/the-day-of-small-things.pdf?x44099 (accessed 12.08.2024).
Nouwen, Henri, 1976, *Reaching Out: The Three Movements of the Spiritual Life*, Glasgow: William Collins.
Taylor, John V., 1964, *CMS Newsletter*, January, No. 267.
Taylor, John, V., 1965, *CMS Newsletter*, September, No. 285.
Taylor, John V., 1972, *The Go-Between God: The Holy Spirit and the Christian Mission*, London: SCM Press.
Taylor, John V., 1974, *CMS Newsletter*, June, No. 382.

17

Just What is it That You Want to Plant? A Dissenting Missional Ecclesiology

SIMON HALL AND ROY SEARLE

Introduction

This chapter is offered as a voice from the margins. Its authors come from one of the oldest dissenting traditions, and within that tradition they find themselves to be beloved and sometimes celebrated but, nonetheless, outsiders. While both have led in large and growing churches, they intentionally chose a different path many years ago. Roy co-founded the Northumbria Community, the first neomonastic community, and Simon co-founded Revive, what would now be called the first fresh expression of church[1] in the Baptist family. They recognize that their ecclesial ancestors did all this and more many centuries ago. The early Anabaptists in Europe formed communities around a rule of life and the first Baptists in Simon's home county of Yorkshire met in pubs as no one else would have them. They make no claim to novelty; rather, they write from their rich heritage as a movement that dissents from two spirits that haunt these times: autocracy and individualism.

The contention of this chapter can be stated quite simply. While a person reading these words might have a detailed and nuanced ecclesiology, if one were to ask the person on the Clapham omnibus what they understand by the word 'church', whether they are taking that bus to church or not, they are very, very likely to think of a building, of a service in that building, and of a person wearing a dog collar who is presiding over that service. The central problem with church planting is that it is 'church' planting, limited by this narrow and therefore unbiblical vision. If we have already decided what must grow, might we neglect or even dig up what God has planted in a community because it doesn't meet our expectations?

As a way to address the issues around church planting, we want to begin with Stefan Paas's metaphor (Paas, 2016, p. 1), in which he argues that the soil of Western Europe has been exhausted by both overfarming and a monocultural ecclesial agriculture. In this infertile soil, church planting in the future will have to be either multimillion pound 'biomes' like the UK's Eden Project or very small, hyper-local approaches to what we might call ecclesial rewilding, in which the soil is slowly nurtured back to health by gardeners who understand the land and local flora.

The challenge of the high-cost, high-intensity model, in which both plants and fertilizer are imported from other parts of the world, is that it actively prevents the growth of local plants, which will probably struggle in the foreign environment created. Only plants that are suited to the new, artificial environment can prosper there. When one visits the Eden Project in Cornwall, one drives past hundreds of private gardens, lovingly tended with the minimum of fuss and expense. This reflects a very human bias towards the spectacular, but when it came to agriculture, it was mustard that Jesus pointed us towards, a tiny seed that grows into a medium-sized bush.

A parallel metaphor that Simon has used is the end of the Cretaceous period, a time when the largest dinosaurs dominated life on earth. If we had been asked to bet on where future highly evolved life forms would emerge, it would have been reasonable to assume the large sauropods would be the safest option. It must have seemed unlikely that future dominance lay in the tiny furry mammals just trying to survive. However, the larger the creature, the harder it is to adapt to a rapidly changing environment. We are suggesting that the current cultural changes in the West amount to the emergence of a new post-Christendom epoch, for which past models of church are very likely to be unsuited. What we have traditionally called local church, with a sanctuary, full-time minister or priest, and manse or rectory, will soon be unsustainable in a majority of communities. This is a sociological and economic projection, not a theological assertion. If we believe in local church, we will have to work towards something that doesn't look like local church as we have known it. Perhaps we won't live to see these changes, but by the end of this century Christians in Western Europe will know whether our hypothesis was correct or not.

The temptation for all Christians who are concerned about the future is to look for the spectacular and follow the trend towards specialized megachurches, whether they be cathedrals, ethnic diaspora churches or charismatic warehouses. Such a move will inevitably accelerate the decline of local church and exacerbate what we might call ecclesial inequality: that the church and the gospel are becoming more easily available to particular socio-economic groups. Let us be absolutely clear: church as we know it is retreating most rapidly from the communities that already feel left behind in social, political and economic dimensions. And communities like those in Jaywick, Hartlepool, Girvan and rural Northumberland and Cornwall are abandoned. It would appear that our ecclesiastical authorities are still working on a spiritual version of 'trickle-down economics', which by now has been largely discredited (Merrick and Waugh, 2023).

An exclusive focus on large churches has other problems. Churches that attract commuters from a wide catchment area will inevitably find it difficult to respond to change when the majority of congregants have chosen the church precisely because it is what they prefer *as it is*. This is an example of the church's capture by market theory (Paas, 2016, pp. 126ff.), resulting in multiple planting in areas that already have many healthy churches. When such churches then plant copies of themselves, they are duplicating the consumer choices of a very limited segment of the religious marketplace: I like these songs; I like to meet at this time; this is what I want for my children and so on. As Dan White of the V3 church planting movement notes, one task of the missional church planter is to detoxify their planting team (and other Christians joining in the early days) of the idea that church is primarily there to meet their felt needs (White, 2015).

If the current changes in society are as seismic as we suspect, then we the Christian community should at the very least be spreading our bets between the big beasts and the tiny critters. (It remains to be seen whether the T-rexes can live in peace with the mammals without killing them.) We believe that the new, emerging future of the people of God is more likely to found in the small, the unstable and the insignificant. We can't show you what that future will be like – that is partly our point – but we can help to create an environment in which small things can prosper, however fleetingly. Of course, we are not the first to suggest that small can be beautiful, nor that the day of small things should not be despised (Zech. 4.10), although the implication is that the small will one day become large.

Our stories

At Portrack, an urban estate on Teesside, Roy's starting place was not a church but the gospel. It was about dwelling and discerning what the Spirit of God was doing in the neighbourhood. And in the process, the community began to discover signs of the kingdom of God on the streets. As a leader, Roy and his wife Shirley learnt to be guests, not hosts. They were called, along with others, to dwell and be in the neighbourhood (John 1.14). It was incarnational ministry.

Not confined or consumed by running church programmes and projects, Roy and the small church community found themselves engaged in issues of justice and community relations, working with the local Catholic church on 'common good' projects such as a job creation scheme, securing a butcher's van delivery service and operating a drug (prescription!) run. Consequently, as a church without walls, Portrack Baptist Church grew phenomenally, with many people coming to faith. Gospel transformation came to both individuals and the estate. The church continues to look and feel very different from many other church plants.

With the Northumbria Community, there was little initial intention to form a community and certainly no intention to set up a church. Roy and the other founders felt freed from any need to plant according to Western modernity's approach to challenges and opportunities with an obsession for design, control and strategy. The Northumbria Community began not with any vision, nor was there any clearly defined, formulaic strategy or programme. The community's beginnings were rooted in questions, explorations and a great deal of uncertainty.

The founders drew inspiration from the monastic, missional spirituality of the Celtic saints and embraced their contemplative and the apostolic ethos. Embracing the monastic 'one thing necessary',[2] seeking God, spiritual formation and discipleship, a community emerged that was connecting with lots of spiritual but not necessarily religious people. It felt very missional without being intentionally so. Seeking God and asking what it meant to live out the gospel in a changing world, the community's modus operandi was the very opposite of 1980s church growth strategy, with a steadfast resistance to taking control, being directive, reaching out, recruiting or marketing. The early years were programme- and project-light but people- and place-heavy. Prayer was central, followed by the geography and history of Northumbria. Buildings, services, congregating people together were either non-existent, irrelevant or minimal. Nonetheless the community has seen God bringing 'home' so many people, now thousands across the world, for whom it has become their primary place and family – their church.

Because the starting point was not church as the founders had known it, the community has ended up as something that is very different from what is often construed as a church plant. The Northumbria Community is part of the holy, catholic church, made up of people from very diverse backgrounds, traditions and experiences of life. This Roy believes to be a remarkably enriching thing and a beautiful life-giving fruit of planting the gospel without too much expectation.

In the same way, Crossing Places, the missional community Roy formed in rural North Northumberland, together with the many similar initiatives that he is privileged to see in his role as a Baptist Union Pioneer Ambassador, are not starting with planting a church but rather planting the gospel and seeing and serving what emerges. Crossing Places no longer exists today but the fruit of its ministry lives on and is flourishing; people are coming to faith, there is a re-imagining of church, particularly within the United Reformed Church, who now have a pioneer minister. The open-handed and inclusive approach to faith and spirituality has resulted in a greater sense of shalom and well-being throughout the neighbourhood, and that is seen in greater harmony and cohesion among the different groups and 'tribes'. The economy is growing in an area that has known considerable poverty and rural deprivation: signs of the kingdom that have come as the gospel has taken root within the area.

The team at Crossing Places learnt to be less determining and controlling and more cooperating with what the Spirit of God is doing, which cannot be confined by any ecclesiology. Roy has witnessed in so many pioneering initiatives the emergence of missional communities that happen to not look like congregations. Beyond city centres, market towns and affluent suburbs, it may be time to ask if the days of congregation are over and that we might get back to the roots that formed the DNA of the Baptist family, namely informal communities shaped by the gospel.

Simon's experience of planting was similarly led by observation of what *Abba* was already doing (John 5.19) in groups of people beyond the church. After experimenting with Christian community and running a dance worship club night, Simon was involved in founding Joy in Oxford, one of the first youth congregations in the UK, in 1991. Joy emerged from the remarkable evangelistic endeavours of Oxford Youth Works, which resulted in a significant community of non-church young people seeking discipleship. It was clear from the beginning that these young people were not going to be integrated into even the 'coolest' youth fellowship.

Later, Simon helped to found the Revive community in Leeds in 1997 as a church in youth culture, with an exciting – and draining – multimedia worship event in a city-centre gig venue. Similarly to Joy, everyone involved in Revive tended to identify church with a Sunday service, which was indeed progress from seeing it as a building. Yet this is a misconception that hampers both mission and discipleship, sucking life out of the world to continually rebuild a Temple that Jesus condemned. It is hard to argue that the Sunday service is the primary locus of either mission or discipleship, yet the proportion of both human and financial resources that go into facilitating it is astounding. Sam Wells (2015) draws out both the significance and limitations of collective worship, suggesting that when we gather, this is like the crowd hearing Jesus' call to discipleship. It is only the beginning of discipleship, and it is not mission, to attend a church service. Discipleship is how we respond to the call presented at collective worship; mission is how we participate in God's activity in the world. Yet institutional structures focus so much on the 'performance' of these services, and on attendance at them, that they tend to become an end in themselves, as if discipleship consists in attending them, and mission consists in inviting people to them.

Revive reached a point where the community realized that the imagined requirement to perform a high-quality multimedia worship event was not only exhausting the whole church, it was diverting attention away from the call to discipleship as presented in what Wells calls *A Nazareth Manifesto* (Wells, 2015). To fulfil that manifesto, the church stopped meeting on a Sunday altogether for some years, choosing instead to gather for four weekends every year. Today, despite being a community that includes artistic creatives and professional teachers, preachers and liturgists, the communities that make up Revive have made discipleship and mission their focus and have laid down the intense effort of a large weekly gathering. Instead, Revive is now a borderless network of small groups and projects. A light-touch entrepreneurial spirit means that some groups come and go, others change form regularly, and one or two become significant institutions in the city. There is no list of groups and projects that 'belong to' Revive: beyond basic safeguarding accountability, the empowering work of Revive means that folk can come to an arts centre, a women's employment project or an all-age discipleship group without hearing the name of Revive, even though the community's DNA is mixed in with the vision of the creators and the Spirit of the Creator. Simon's ministry moved from being that of the traditional shepherd-teacher to working in an apostolic mode: 'sending' others through training and mentoring, working at building relationships with others who had relevant skills and providing an overall vision of what God can do when we are allowed out of the building.

The times call for a dissenting ecclesiology

While hierarchical and centralized denominations might make their ecclesiology more explicit, it seems self-evident that nearly all denominations (and movements that claim not be denominations) make the a priori association of church with Sunday congregation. Within the Baptist denomination this traditional 'Christendom' model of church still predominates, despite the absence of canon law to enforce it. It is hard to think of presentations of Christian faith that don't centre on congregational worship,[3] thus reinforcing the cultural stereotype even among those with no religious affiliation. This is not to say that church is unimportant: far from it. We accept the criticism of Michael Frost and Alan Hirsch's famous maxim, Christology begets Missiology begets Ecclesiology (Frost and Hirsch, 2003), that it is too elite and individualistic, that most people meet Jesus in community, so that all three are in constant dialogue (see, for example, Fitch, 2009). Church is (almost) central to the gospel of God's reign. The issue is that those with power (and money) are defining church in such limited ways.

An alternative is to be found in the adventure of letting go of our controlling mechanisms, with their aims, objectives and desired ecclesiastical outcomes, to discover the Spirit of God at work in our neighbourhoods. Rewilding, pushing back some of the so-called progress of the Industrial Revolution's practices that, for example in agriculture, have contributed to damaging the natural environment, has some parallels in the approach to church that we believe is necessary. Among the contributions that Baptists can make to other denominations is our formal commitment to the simple teaching of Jesus: 'For where two or three are gathered in my name, I am there among them' (Matt. 18.20). To those not subject to canon law, we encourage you to celebrate your ability to rewild, to pioneer and plant without the institutional, prescribed strictures, and to make a distinct contribution to the ecclesial ecology of the UK. We can rewild the church, we can positively subvert hierarchical, top-down institutional expressions of church. We can use strategic thinking to flow out of discernment and innovation as opposed to controlling how things must be. We can challenge the way in which things are measured, including the prevailing and dominant emphasis on counting attenders and income. We can emphasize community over institution. We can celebrate the ministry of the whole body of Christ, dismantle the clergy/laity divide and challenge the drive towards the professionalization of ministry. Discerning, not from an established place but in the unfamiliar place we now find ourselves, what it means to be the people of God, learning to sing the Lord's song in a strange land. We are called to explore, pioneer and plant where the tide of Christendom in the Western world is receding, what some on both left and right are calling a new dark age (see Gail, 2016 and Dreher, 2017). We are certainly in a place where we have never been before.

At this moment in time, our concern is not only about the focus on the size or location of churches, it is not just that denominations have bought into a wonky ecclesiology focusing on the worship service, it is that this wonky theology has become institutionalized and reinforced by the powerbrokers and money-dealers: the standard Protestant definition of church is that it is where the word is correctly preached and the sacraments are correctly administered.

It is hard to think of an ecclesiology that could do more to centralize power, institutionalize priestly authority and focus attention narrowly on the administration of the worship service. It is hard to criticize the Commissioners of the Church of England and other denominations for measuring success according to attendance and income, because those things ensure the maintenance of the established church in its current form. But at what point do we find that Jesus is outside our temple, prophesying its necessary downfall?

When writing about universities, the philosopher John Dewey highlighted the ultimate paradox about institutions: that they are the enemy of best practice, as well as being the vehicle by which the idea of best practice is handed down to the next generation. This is as good an argument for institutional, established church as we can muster. However, the challenge we have today is that the best practice that is now being promoted concerns the survival of the institution, as if that on its own will make disciples. There is a danger that mission becomes a hollow pyramid or Ponzi scheme in which the actual fruit of the gospel – discipleship – is all but forgotten. Dewey suggested that we should not judge an institution by its conformity to some abstract principle (the problem with Frost and Hirsch above), but rather by its outcomes for specific groups of people. This pragmatic – Dewey called it 'experimentalist' – approach (Rondel, 2018) is nonetheless deeply theological, because the choice of people and the choice of outcomes must be chosen by our reading of the Scriptures and our understanding of the gospel.

In Matthew 28.16ff., Jesus instructs us to make disciples of every *ethne*, every people group. This simple instruction will take us into a whole variety of diverse places and with myriad groups of different people. What we are suggesting in the light of this commissioning by Jesus is that while there are essential core elements or values to any church, their expression has to be formed by the gospel and not some overarching, uniform model of church. Models cannot be easily replicated. What we should see in this renewed and much needed era of pioneering and church planting is gospel-shaped churches. In essence, to change the idiom, let the dog wag the tail! Let the gospel wag the church! We recognize that this call is far from new. The call for contextual mission and churches goes back a long way, reaching an apotheosis in David Bosch's *Transforming Mission* (1991) and a moment of popular acclaim with the report *Mission-shaped Church* (Archbishops' Council, 2004). But since then the forces of industrialization and marketization seem to be brushing over the tracks made by these pioneering works and the many pioneers that they represent around the world. Perhaps the fact that the turn to missiology came from the global South is one reason why 'the West' has failed to hear its lessons. Whatever the reason, we feel the need to reiterate these lessons once more.

Our question is quite simple: What might be the essential elements of an ecclesiology that centres on discipleship and mission instead of word and sacrament?

Jesus describes discipleship very simply: that people would learn to obey his teaching. His teaching was about character and behaviour, so we should be looking to see whether the fruit of the Spirit is emerging in our communities. We should expect transformation at the individual, community and civic levels. A gospel that focuses on privatized belief and experience does not represent the teaching of Jesus. More research is needed, but we believe that the kind of slow, contemplative and relational work that forms Christlike disciples may not be in harmony with what the institution needs to survive. It's over 100 years since Chesterton claimed that 'The Christian ideal has not been tried and found wanting. It has been found difficult; and left untried' (Chesterton, 1994, p. 38). Simon confesses that he had always assumed that this quote was about why people don't become Christians, but perhaps it's about why people who identify as Christians don't become disciples.

Dewey's question about outcomes is legitimate. A church can just as easily institutionalize abuse, apathy, nominalism, tribalism, prejudice or bad theology as love, joy, peace, patience, kindness, goodness, faithfulness and self-control. If our local churches are not displaying Christlike transformation, then what are they for? Jesus speaks disdainfully of converts (Matt. 23.15); a disciple is something else.

'Mission' is a highly contested word, and the notion of *missio Dei* even more so. To be sure, it is not a biblical phrase, although going and sending are everywhere. The famous verse in Matthew 28.19 begins with a present continuous, so that a better translation might be 'While you are going ...' or 'Wherever you go ...'. The going is taken for granted: God is eternally sending Godself and inviting us to participate. If we are to have any hope that we might follow this wind that blows where it will (John 3.8), then we need tabernacles rather than temples – at least for a while. And it's in the very nature of going that it is centrifugal, as the Pentecostal Spirit sends us out into the world, resisting the centripetal force of the institution.

We are not suggesting that the Eden Project needs to be closed, or that the T-rexes need to be slaughtered, just that in these times of societal upheaval we pay attention to the person growing fruit and veg on their window ledge, to the tiny furry creature just trying to get by. Those little critters can go places that dinosaurs can't.

The definition of church as word and sacrament is an institutional definition, which works to maintain the ecclesiology of the status quo. It requires a central authority to determine what right teaching and right worship are. If church is mission and discipleship, what we need is a community of the Spirit gathering in the name of Jesus; structural authority, buildings and priests may well be needed, but are matters of debate.

Such an assertion is, of course, the essence of dissent. As members of a dissenting denomination, this should not overly trouble us, but it places us outside mainstream Protestantism. Yet even in the car park of the Eden Project the weeds keep growing! Wherever we travel we meet people who love Jesus, or who are fascinated by him, but who struggle to connect the person of Jesus and his teachings with the very particular religious practices that have come to define the movement called Christianity. We do not have the time or energy to try to 'bring down the institution'. We ask only that the institution let the weeds grow and cherish them too. Perhaps in the cracks in the pavement we will discover a new grass or a flower that is more beautiful and resilient than its predecessors. The future may look dark to the institutions, but darkness is as light to God (Ps. 139.12). We have both been blessed by the fresh expressions movement and those who dissent even from that! We look with hope to the Myriad Project[4] within the Church of England, but also with mixed feelings as the inevitable survival instinct of the institution kicks in.

As we navigate the uncertainty and unfamiliarity of these changing times there is a chance that we might be able to go wherever the Spirit is going in the next millennium and in the process, walking humbly before God and one another, become true partners, established and emerging, institutional and dissident, equal partners in the work of the glorious gospel to the ends of the earth.

As a brief excursus, the internet is bringing about the birth of an entirely new genus of church, which may make all our talk redundant. Covid has accelerated people's detachment from physical engagement with place, whether that be workplace, play place, community place or worship place. In 2019 Simon was involved in setting up Edifi, Northern Baptist College's online training programme, and at the time all involved balked at the idea of getting a group of church leaders to engage with a new technology called Zoom. We imagined that we would need an in-person gathering to teach over-50s how to use social media such as WhatsApp. Now? Not so much. Perhaps circumstances will overtake us all and we will have to develop an ecclesiology that is as fluid as the internet. Nonetheless, the questions will remain the same: Is this thing that we are doing helping people grow into Christlikeness? Are people gathering together with God for the purposes of the gospel?

Notes

1 Over the years, Revive has also been called a youth congregation, an alt-worship community, an emerging church and a network of missional communities. The fluidity of the language indicates both the rapid change that popular and ecclesial cultures are experiencing and the nascency of the movement.

2 The word 'monk' comes from the Greek *monos*, meaning something like 'one alone'.

3 The film *Tyrannosaur* (2011) is a notable exception, displaying life in the home and Bible study group of a conservative evangelical couple. But be warned: what we see is a genuine horror.

4 https://ccx.org.uk/myriad/. Also see McGinley, 2023.

References

Archbishops' Council, 2004, *Mission-shaped Church: Church Planting and Fresh Expressions of Church in a Changing Context*, London: Church House Publishing.

Bosch, D., 1991, *Transforming Mission: Paradigm Shifts in the Theology of Mission*, Maryknoll, NY: Orbis Books.

Chesterton, G. K., 1994 (1910), *What's Wrong with the World*, Fort Collins, CO: Ignatius Press.

Dreher, R., 2017, *The Benedict Option*, New York: Sentinel.

Fitch, D., 2009, *Missiology Precedes Ecclesiology: The Epistemological Question*, https://www.missioalliance.org/missiology-precedes-ecclesiology-the-epistemological-problem/ (accessed 3.11.2023).

Frost, M. and A. Hirsch, 2003, *The Shaping of Things to Come: Innovation and Mission for the 21st Century*, Peabody, MA: Hendrickson.

Gail, W. B., 2016, 'A New Dark Age Looms', *New York Times*, 19 April, https://www.nytimes.com/2016/04/19/opinion/a-new-dark-age-looms.html (accessed 3.11.2023).

McGinley, J., 2023, *The Church of Tomorrow: Being a Christ-Centred People in a Changing World*, London: SPCK.

Merrick, J. and P. Waugh, 2023, 'Blair, Major and Brown Say Failure of "Trickle Down" Economics and Regional Inequality Contributed to Brexit', *The I*, https://inews.co.uk/news/politics/ex-pms-admit-regional-inequality-brexit-2704593 (accessed 26.10.2023).

Northumbria Community (no date), *A New Monasticism*, https://www.northumbriacommunity.org/who-we-are/introducing-the-community/a-new-monasticism/ (accessed 26.10.2023).

Paas, S., 2016, *Church Planting in the Secular West: Learning from the European Experience*, Grand Rapids, MI: Eerdmans.

Rondel, D., 2017, *Pragmatist Egalitarianism*, ch. 6, 'Institutions as Instruments: John Dewey's Democratic Egalitarianism', Oxford: Oxford University Press, pp. 89–112.

Wells, S., 2015, *A Nazareth Manifesto: Being with God*, Norwich: Canterbury Press.

White, D., 2015, 'Ecology of a Worship Gathering', https://danwhitejr.blogspot.com/2015/01/ecology-of-worship-gathering.html (accessed 31.10.2023).

18

Giving the Church Away: Fresh Theology for Church Planting?

MICHAEL MOYNAGH

Introduction

This chapter arises from a book in preparation (Moynagh, 2024). Drawing on the extensive literature on gifts, the book asks whether there might be a further model of the church, alongside Avery Dulles's six (1974), centred on giving the church to others. From this perspective, it reinterprets some of the classic themes in ecclesiology: the nature of the church, the four marks, the invisible/visible church and inclusion/exclusion. Its second part addresses the ethics of the church's self-donation, proposes an ethical framework for giving the church, and reinterprets liberation, proclamation and eucharistic models of the church in the light of this framework. The book's final chapter suggests ways giving the church away can encourage a less abusive and healthier church. Here, I introduce some of these themes by focusing on the generosity of God and asking how divine generosity is worked out in the church's mission.

The church is a gift

It is conventional today, of course, to root mission in in the *missio Dei*. But what is God's mission all about? As John Flett reminds us (2010, pp. 198–201), the *missio Dei* literally means the sending of God. However, sending is a rather thin concept. It can be understood in different ways. So what does it look like? As Flett points out, once you begin to answer that question, you are driven back to the idea of generosity. God is a missional God because God is fundamentally generous. From all eternity, the three persons of the Trinity have been giving themselves to one another in love. And as Kathryn Tanner puts it, this self-giving within God bubbles over like an overflowing fountain and becomes the mission of God (2005, p. 83).

So when we encounter God in the Bible, from the beginning to the end our encounter is with divine generosity. We meet a God who showers the world with gifts – of life, of redeemed life and of life recreated in the kingdom. In particular, divine generosity is revealed supremely in the gift of God's self in Jesus, whose life was defined by self-giving first in his ministry and then his death. Jesus is the epitome of generosity, which means that generosity must also be the epitome of the church. If self-giving is central to the head of the church, it must be central to the body. Through the Spirit, the church must give itself away *as a priority*, just as Jesus made self-giving his priority. And just as Jesus is revealed to the world primarily in a movement of self-donation, so the church is to show itself in a corresponding movement. The church is called to give itself to others. That is the essence of the church's mission.

Anthropologists emphasize that it is in the nature of gifts to be passed on. In this way they build relationships, which is one of their main social functions. A gift only remains a gift if the person intends to pass it on. Otherwise it becomes a possession. Now, passing on – or sharing – a gift can take a variety of forms. Recipients may literally share the gift, as when someone drinks the present of a bottle of wine with her friends. Or recipients may pass the gift on by using it to serve other people; the gift of a guitar is used to entertain others. Or recipients may share a gift by putting it on display so that others enjoy it, whether wearing some new scent or showing works of art. Or recipients may talk about their gifts: 'The holiday we were given was fantastic. We did so and so.' Or, again, recipients may transform a gift to pass it on, such as using a monetary gift to treat a friend to a meal. If gifts in general are shared, then presumably the church as a gift should also be shared. Were that not so, the church would cease to be a gift and become a possession.

In the case of the church, however, sharing the gift is an even greater imperative. The church should be shared not just because it is in the general character of gifts to be shared, but because it is in the originating nature of the church to be a gift – a gift not just to believers, but to people outside the church. All four Gospels describe how Jesus sent out the disciples, who became founders of the church. The disciples were sent to share the church with others. From the very beginning they passed the church on, and this transmission has continued ever since. Giving the church away is in the people of God's DNA.

This means that the church is not a gift in the sense that a box of chocolates might be a gift. You don't have to share the chocolates. You could consume them all on your own. Instead, the church is a gift more like a traditional board game. Traditionally it is in the nature of a board game to be played with others. You cannot enjoy the game without sharing it.

So it is with the church. The church is not a gift that you might or might not share with someone else. ('Actually, I'm going to eat all these chocolates myself.') Theologically, it is in the church's fundamental nature to be 'played' with others. Recipients of the church, therefore, must share the church with people outside not just because this is typical of gifts. Sharing the church is the manner in which God intends the church to be enjoyed.

Passing on communion in Christ

There are many ways for the church to be shared – or 'played' – with other people. The church can share its resources by using them to serve others or by joining with other organizations to campaign for social and environmental justice. The church can put itself on display through the quality of its life, so that being shared takes the form of being a beacon of what God is like. Members can describe their experience of church, of sharing life with Jesus, just as they might describe – and so pass on – their holiday experiences. When the church acts in these ways it behaves appropriately, like many other organizations. They too become gifts by sharing their resources, putting themselves on display and describing their experiences.

But there is one gift that no other organization can offer, and that is the gift of communal life in Jesus. No one else can offer this particular gift; only the church, through the Spirit. When recipients of the church share *this* gift – the gift of communal life in Christ – they offer to others the very essence of the church. That is because, as Rowan Williams so often said when he was archbishop, church happens when you encounter Jesus and when you encounter other people who have encountered Jesus. Church is a communal event, centred on Christ.

Now, when recipients of the church share the church in the form of communion in Jesus, they offer a gift that is especially precious. It is one thing to share the gift of a theatre trip with a friend, quite another to share your life. Likewise, it is one thing for the church to share its resources, for example, but it is a very different matter to share the heart of its life: communion in Jesus. Indeed, when the church offers the centre of its life to other people, it follows the example of Jesus, who gave his whole life for others. And this says something important about the church, because to offer the heart of your life is a precious gift in the extreme, and the gift of something precious is a sign of how much you love the other person. Precious gifts are reserved for precious people. So to give away communal life in Christ is to make a vivid statement about the extent of the church's love for the world. Thus it is not enough to campaign for justice or lovingly serve other people, hugely important though these are. The church is called to go further: like Jesus, it is to offer others its life, the heart of its existence, which is communion in Christ.

Giving in the form of new Christian communities

The church is called to give its very *self* away. But what does this involve? In some cases, the gift will be offered in the form of an invitation to join an existing congregation. But for many people such an invitation will be inappropriate. The existing congregation may be out of reach because of when, where and how it meets. This is something that people often forget: every congregation is exclusive by nature. Once you have decided to meet at a particular time, in a particular place, with a certain agenda and a certain style, you will attract some people but you are bound to exclude many others. You are bound to exclude all those who cannot come at that time (because they are on shift work or have family commitments, perhaps), all those who cannot travel to that place, all those who do not share your agenda (they are not interested in Jesus, maybe) and all those who find the style off-putting (who have a different taste in music possibly, or for whom sermons spell hierarchy and belong to a world that has passed). Every congregation is inevitably selective.

And this is typical of gifts. A gift is given to some people but not others. I give a present to the birthday boy but not to his sister. Gifts are exclusive by nature. And so if the church is a gift, a gift from God to the world, when the gift is passed on Christians will offer it in the first instance to some people but not others. This is a big problem for the church because we worship an inclusive God, who died on the cross with his arms outstretched in a welcome to everyone. So how do we square the circle? How can we offer a gift that is exclusive by nature to everyone? I would suggest that the answer is to start new congregations that meet at a time and place, with an agenda and style that *do* connect with people for whom the church is currently out of reach. In the Church of England, that is one of the ways to serve the *whole* parish. The more the church is passed on, the more it is passed from one group of people to the next, and then the next, and the next again, the more the church will come alive in the entirety of the parish.

In fact, I would suggest that there is no missional agenda of the church that potentially cannot be served by giving away these new communities. If it is discipleship in the workplace, we have examples of new Christian communities serving an office, a school and patients of a medical practice.

If the priority is a specific group – homeless people, abused women, asylum seekers, gay people, teenagers on a run-down estate or people with learning difficulties – a small team can listen to them, love and serve them, build community with them, introduce those interested to Jesus and encourage a Christian community to emerge. If the focus is the environment, social justice or global poverty, Christians can listen to people outside the church who share their concern, find ways of working together, form community as they do so and explore how Christian spirituality can make a contribution. New Christian communities can input into these and other missional agendas not by taking them over, but by offering communal life in Jesus in support of them. Thus offering these communities need not be one missional agenda among others. I would submit (bravely!) that they can be part of *every* missional agenda. There is potentially no missional challenge to which these communities cannot make a contribution.

For the benefit of the world

Indeed, multiplying Christian communities will probably proliferate other gifts that the Spirit offers through the church. The more new Christian communities are given away, the more the church's gifts of pastoral care, support for social and environmental justice, contributions to the creative arts through music and buildings for example, reconciliation and so on will be amplified. The church will accumulate more resources to share with others – more volunteers, funds and so forth. Giving the church to others will be for the benefit not of the church, but the world.

And this fits with certain types of giving. When blood is donated, for instance, there is the giver (the one who donates blood), the recipient (the hospital that receives and stores the blood) and the beneficiary (the patient who receives a blood transfusion). Likewise in charitable giving, there is the giver (the person who makes a donation), the recipient (the charity that receives the donation) and the beneficiary (those who benefit from the charity's work). The same should be true of the church's giving. When the church gives itself, communion in Christ, to others in the form of new Christian communities, there will be the giver (the parent congregation or church), the recipients (those who receive the new Christian community) and, not least in importance, the beneficiaries – those outside the church who benefit from the expansion of the church's capacity to give on many different fronts. This begins to answer the glaring objection: how can the church be a gift when it is so full of abuse and has so often misused its power? *Part* of the answer, which I say more about in my book, is that the church is best a gift when it is offered for the benefit of the world.

Receiving first

What might offering new Christian communities look like? After all, not all giving is healthy. Some can be manipulative and demeaning. Indeed, in some languages the words for gift and poison come from the same root. So what ethical boundaries might we place around the church's self-donation? A safe launch pad is for the church to be a *recipient* before it becomes a giver. After all, Jesus received before he gave. He received his humanity before he gave his life. As an infant, he received from his parents before intentionally giving back to them. In his public ministry, time and again he accepted hospitality from others before offering them his kingdom gifts.

Receiving before you give inverts the power dynamics involved in some forms of giving because, as I have said, giving can be a mixed blessing. Giving can be degrading if it leaves the recipient dependent on the giver. Not least, it can be a means of control when the gift comes with strings attached. But when the church receives before it gives, it upsets these power dynamics. Instead of making others dependent on the church, the church becomes dependent on them. Rather than giving with conditions, the church allows others to give to the church with obligations perhaps implicitly attached.

Receiving before giving puts generosity into the context of a mutual, two-way relationship. It provides a counter-blast, if you like, to paternalism. So often in the church, we want to do things for other people. We think that loving people means doing things *for* them. Yet one of the greatest acts of love is to allow people to do things for us, because when people give to us they are enabled to flourish. Someone who gives me a meal can express their cooking abilities. Someone else who takes me to a rugby match can share their love of rugby with me. Someone who drives me to the hospital can express tangibly their concern. Indeed, any act of giving (almost by definition) is an opportunity to show love. And when people show love, they reveal themselves at their best. That is why one of the greatest gifts we can offer is to allow others to be generous to us. For in the act of giving, the person puts their better side on display. So just as Jesus received before he gave, the church is wise when it does the same.

Giving appropriately

Having accepted gifts from others, the church is better placed to offer itself, communion in Jesus, as a gift. But this gift must be offered in a form that is appropriate to the potential recipients because it is in the nature of giving that we seek out gifts that are the right fit for the other person. If my friend were teetotal I would not give them a bottle of wine. So when the church offers the gift of becoming community in Jesus, it will ask what appropriate form that gift should take. Its generosity will not be marred by offering a gift that is unsuitable – that recipients have difficulty in receiving. Rather, the church's generosity will be expressed in the appropriateness of the gift – in the thought that has been put into it by standing in the recipients' shoes. And this of course speaks of contextualizing the gift.

At the same time, the gift must also be appropriate to the giver. A few years ago, my wife and I took two of our grandchildren to an exhibition of presents given to the royal family. What was striking was how many gifts made a statement about the giver. For example, there was a beautiful gift of three gold palm trees and a camel. Where was it from? Saudi Arabia. Gifts say something about those who give, in particular about what the giver thinks of the other person and the relationship between them. Something of the giver, if you like, accompanies the gift. So when a group of Christians offer others communion in Christ, they are entitled to ask: Does the gift reflect the sort of people we are? And a church or denomination is entitled to ask the same question. Which of course is when the debate begins! How far should the gift reflect the giver's traditions? How far should it be appropriate to the recipients? And if the expectations of the two are different, where should the balance lie?

In her discussion of giving, Lee Fennell describes the negotiation that occurs inside the giver's head. The giver enters imaginatively into the life of the other and asks: 'What would be an appropriate gift for me to offer? What would work for the recipient? What would work for me? And what would fit the nature of our relationship?' Fennell calls this internal conversation 'empathetic dialogue' (2002, pp. 85–101). I would suggest that something similar happens when new Christian communities are offered to others. In conversation with the potential recipients, the team involved asks: 'What would be a suitable form in which to offer communion in Christ? What would best work for the recipients? What would be suitable for us to offer? And what would fit this stage of the relationship between us?' Team members engage in 'empathetic dialogue' as they prayerfully seek to understand at depth the potential recipients, and imagine how best the church can be offered, taking into account their own identities, the identities of the recipients and the giver–receiver relationship. Hopefully, the result will be that receivers welcome the emerging Christian community, appreciating the thought behind it.

Letting go

Once communion in Christ has been offered, the gift must be released. This is because it is in the nature of giving that the giver lets the gift go. The other is allowed to receive the gift in their own way. If I give a toy car to my grandson but then all afternoon hold his hand showing him how to play with it, the present ceases to be a gift to the boy. It becomes in effect a gift to me, enabling me to relive my childhood! I have to let the gift go. But having released the gift, I may be surprised by how my grandchild plays with it. It may become a rocket, or a boat, or a tank. Likewise, the gift of communal life in Jesus only becomes a gift when it is released, when recipients are allowed to be community with him in their own way. Of course they will be guided by the Spirit; they will be given the resources of Scripture and the Christian tradition; and as with some gifts, they will need a certain amount of instruction in how to use these resources. But fundamentally, they will be learning how to receive the gift in a manner that works for them. And this may cause us some surprise. Let me give an example of what releasing the gift means. In Britain's East Midlands, 11 Alive emerged among families who did not connect with the existing church. They met café-style late Sunday mornings, with bacon butties, games for the kids, newspapers for adults and so on. At the end there was a short act of worship. Every eight weeks the community stayed for lunch, and after lunch broke into four teams. Each team prepared two acts of worship, which meant all the worship was organized for the next eight weeks. Each team was led by a church member, but *anyone* in the community could join the team, help prepare the worship and even help deliver it. An agnostic or atheist, for example, might introduce a song, read a poem or contribute to a short talk.

Tim, the minister, told me: 'This greatly accelerates people's journeys to faith.' I asked: 'How many atheists and agnostics do you have in your community?' The reply: 'At present, not many. That's because most have come to faith.' Releasing the gift of communion in Jesus is spiritual dynamite. Yet it's not always easy. Tim said that he loved preaching and leading worship. But in the past three years he had been up front in 11 Alive just once. This was not easy for him. A sacrifice was involved. And that's often the case with generosity: it hurts. So when we release the new Christian community and hand it over, we must not be surprised if the process feels painful.

Accepting the gift and giving back

When recipients accept the gift of communion in Christ they are drawn into community with others. Many gifts have this character. They draw you into a community of people who enjoy the same gift, even though this often goes unnoticed. For instance, a gift of swimming lessons connects the child to others who are enjoying the same experience. The gift of a pair of fashionable shoes connects the recipient to others who appreciate that style of footwear. True, these others will not all know each other. So they are not a community in a visible sense. But they are an implicit community. In a similar way, the gift of communal life in Jesus draws the recipients into a wider community, the community of the universal church. As in my shoes example, congregations within the whole church do not all know each other and often are not even aware of one another. Nevertheless, they are part of a real community, which comprises all those who have received communion in Christ. As part of this wider body, recipients contribute to the whole church and receive from it the blessings of the Christian tradition.

Finally, having accepted communion in Jesus, recipients will offer their own gifts back to the church. These will go beyond time, talents and money to include fresh insights into the meaning and application of the gospel. Not least as, ideally, recipients grow in their appreciation of the tradition, they will want to express their gratitude for it. Yet they will have no practical means of directly thanking those in earlier centuries who have contributed to the tradition. They will have no direct way of thanking Martin Luther, Cranmer, the Wesleys and many others who have made lasting inputs into the heritage of the church. They will be a bit like a pupil who as an adult comes to appreciate a particular teacher but has no means of directly thanking the person. Instead, the adult may express her gratitude by diligently passing on her own skill or knowledge to others. 'What you did for me,' she thinks, 'I'll do for other people.' Recipients of the church may act in a similar way. They may thank contributors to their Christian inheritance by passing on their own experience of the tradition, the essence of which is gathering around Jesus: 'Just as you passed on to us the gift of being a community with Christ, we too will pass on the gift to others.'[1]

Now, when the church is given away like this, Christians behave in a eucharistic manner. A piece of the congregation is broken off as the nucleus of a new Christian community. It is offered as the body of Christ to people outside the church. As people gather round they receive the gift, consume it and are transformed. Then, we pray, they repeat the process. Thus Holy Communion-like, in a 'liturgy after the liturgy', the body is passed on from one generation to the next and from one context to another. Which suggests that offering new Christian communities should not be a fringe part of the church's mission. It should be the core of the church's vocation – Catherine wheels that spin off multiple sparks of Godly love which benefit the world around.

A gift-based methodology

In conclusion, I believe the Spirit has gifted the church with a methodology to match this gift-based theology. In fresh expressions circles, we often talk about the missional journey that new Christian communities frequently travel: Prayerfully listen to the context. Find a simple way to love and serve people. Build community with them in the process. Create opportunities for people to explore Jesus if they want. Encourage an expression of church to emerge around those coming to faith. And then repeat the process, but in a way appropriate to the new context (Figure 1).

Figure 1: *A missional journey, underpinned by prayer and connection to the wider church*

Of course, real life is messier than a diagram, and so in practice the circles often overlap or pile on top of each other. Sometimes they are taken in a different order. But time and again, founders of new Christian communities travel this journey. Often they are not aware of it. They act intuitively. Only later do they realize that the path they travelled has been generalized into the journey just described. Our observation is that more and more church planters, of varying hues, are adopting this approach (see Paas and Schaeffer, 2021).

What is striking is the gift-and-response dynamic that underpins the journey. Each circle is an expression of generosity, which elicits further generosity in reply. And that response then becomes the basis of the next gift. So, for example, 'listening' is a gift that may call forth a generous response of information, ideas and a willingness to help, which then form the basis of the circle, 'love'. Generous 'love' elicits the gifts of engagement, of relationship and trust that form the basis of 'community'. The generous offer of 'community' elicits the gifts of enjoyment, gratitude, increased trust and deepening relationships. These create an openness to Jesus and lay down a foundation for 'sharing Jesus'. The latter, we pray, leads to the gifts of joy and fresh insights from those who accept the kingdom, which become building blocks for an expression of 'church' to take shape. This in turn elicits a response of enthusiasm and gratitude that encourages the journey to be repeated, but in a different way, to fit the new context. So the dynamic of generosity bringing forth further generosity is passed on from one setting to another.

Conclusion

The church, I would submit, is called to this life of self-donation. Might this be a theological frame for church planting? Whether tiny plants or large ones, whether actually called church planting or not, might generosity be what church planting is about? The church is to be drawn into God's mission of self-giving, gratefully joining the Spirit in giving the church to others for the benefit of the world. The church should do this by receiving first, giving appropriately and releasing the gift, and by welcoming recipients into the universal church as they accept the gift and in their turn pass it on to others with thanks. By giving away its self, communion in Christ, the church can become like Jesus – generous through and through.

Notes

1 Space prevents discussion of the transformation that results from giving the church, a theme picked up in Moynagh, 2024.

References

Dulles, Avery, 1974, *Models of the Church*, New York: Doubleday.
Fennell, Lee Anne, 2002, 'Unpacking the Gift: Illiquid Goods and Empathetic Dialogue', in Mark Osteen (ed.), *The Question of the Gift: Essays Across Disciplines*, Abingdon: Routledge, pp. 85–101.
Flett, John, 2010, *The Witness of God: The Trinity, Missio Dei, Karl Barth, and the Nature of Christian Community*, Grand Rapids, MI: Eerdmans.
Moynagh, Michael, 2024, *Giving the Church: The Christian Community Through the Looking Glass of Generosity*, London: SCM Press.
Paas, Stefan and Hans Schaeffer, 2021, 'Reconciled Community: On Finding a Soteriology for Fresh Expressions', *Ecclesiology* 17.3, pp. 325–47.
Tanner, Kathryn, 2005, *Economy of Grace*, Minneapolis, MN: Fortress Press.

19

Movement, Diversity and Leadership in the Early Roman Churches: Explorations of Church Planting Hints in Romans 16

JOHN VALENTINE

Introduction

What does a church plant look like? Is there a template, a model, a good and right way of doing it? Should church plants look like each other? These questions lurk around the edges of church planting theory and practice. If we delve a little deeper, there are all kinds of issues to think about in relation to culture, to leadership, to structures. Sometimes church planting is criticized for being based on a single model, which works in one culture but not in others, and is accused of being oblivious to context. What might the New Testament have to say to such matters?

May we look at a particular text, something straight from the life of the church plants in Rome? I think we will find things that startle and illuminate us, a freedom and an inspiration for our own church planting practice. I don't want to overstate the case; there is an air of exegetical archaeology about this, and we are joining up dots rather than seeing clearly delineated pictures. Nonetheless, it seems to me that, at the least, there is much that is suggestive and full of potential in these verses.

Romans 16.1–16 is the section of the letter where Paul greets various people. He commends Phoebe to the churches of Rome, before greeting a further 25 people, 23 of whom are named:

> I commend to you our sister Phoebe, a deacon of the church at Cenchreae, so that you may welcome her in the Lord as is fitting for the saints, and help her in whatever she may require from you, for she has been a benefactor of many and of myself as well.
>
> Greet Prisca and Aquila, who work with me in Christ Jesus, and who risked their necks for my life, to whom not only I give thanks,

but also all the churches of the Gentiles. Greet also the church in their house. Greet my beloved Epaenetus, who was the first convert in Asia for Christ. Greet Mary, who has worked very hard among you. Greet Andronicus and Junia, my relatives who were in prison with me; they are prominent among the apostles, and they were in Christ before I was. Greet Ampliatus, my beloved in the Lord. Greet Urbanus, our co-worker in Christ, and my beloved Stachys. Greet Apelles, who is approved in Christ. Greet those who belong to the family of Aristobulus. Greet my relative Herodion. Greet those in the Lord who belong to the family of Narcissus. Greet those workers in the Lord, Tryphaena and Tryphosa. Greet the beloved Persis, who has worked hard in the Lord. Greet Rufus, chosen in the Lord; and greet his mother – a mother to me also. Greet Asyncritus, Phlegon, Hermes, Patrobas, Hermas, and the brothers and sisters who are with them. Greet Philologus, Julia, Nereus and his sister, and Olympas, and all the saints who are with them. Greet one another with a holy kiss. All the churches of Christ greet you.

I think we can discern five distinct churches being greeted by Paul in this section, although Robert Jewett thinks there could be eight to ten (2007, p. 62).

- In verse 5, we read of 'the church in [the] house' of Prisca and Aquila.
- In verse 10, there is the 'family of Aristobulus'.
- In the next verse, 'the family of Narcissus'.
- Next, in verse 14, there is the suggestive list of five slave names 'and the brothers and sisters who are with them'.
- In the next verse, a further five individuals, four of whom are named, 'and all the saints who are with them'.
- We note too, by contrast, Paul's reference to 'all the churches of the Gentiles' in verse 4; 'All the churches of Christ' in verse 16; and to 'the whole church' in verse 23.

Interspersed with these churches, Paul refers to all kinds of individuals. He addresses them in different ways. He has significant history with some and appears to be working hard for connection with others. We can surmise something of what we might call the pre-Pauline or pre-Romans history of the first churches in Rome from the hints and gaps in these greetings.

The churches

May we look at each of these five churches, and describe and analyse what we can from them, before concluding with some possible implications for contemporary church planting?

First, the church that meets in the house of Prisca and Aquila (verse 5). From what we know from elsewhere, Prisca may well have been a freeborn woman from a noble Roman family. Her name usually precedes her husband's in the New Testament, which may well indicate that she is of higher social status. By contrast, Aquila was a Jew from Pontus (Acts 18.2), and was probably a freed slave. Whether through Prisca's money or their success in the tent-making trade (Acts 18.3), they had the money to travel and to have what must have been sizeable houses, large enough to accommodate a church. Archaeological evidence suggests that such houses would have been able to accommodate church gatherings of 35 to 50 people (Jewett, 2007, pp. 958–9). Prisca and Aquila may well have lived in the prestigious Aventine section of the city of ancient Rome.

Paul, of course, had long and close history with them. They met in Corinth (Acts 18.2). Luke tells us that they had had to leave Rome under the edict of the emperor Claudius in AD 49, when Jews and Jewish Christians were expelled. They travelled with Paul to Ephesus, where they had a 'church in their house' (1 Cor. 16.19). Romans 16 tells us of how they 'risked their necks' for Paul when he was in mortal danger (verse 4). And here they are again with another church meeting in their house (verse 5).

What might that church have been like?

In all likelihood, the leadership would have lain with Prisca and Aquila, who would have been patrons of the church – they would have provided the shared food for the meals, for instance. Leadership patterns would have closely mirrored those of secular Roman society, albeit transformed and softened by the impact of the gospel.

We note from elsewhere Prisca and Aquila's ability with people – they may well have been those who led Epaenetus to Christ (verse 5), and we know that they invested in the capable but inexperienced Apollos (Acts 18.26). Their church would have been marked by evangelistic focus and leadership development, with an awareness of what God was doing more widely than in Rome.

The leaders

A quick intermission from the churches: What of the leaders that Paul takes special care to greet? There is, for example, Mary (in verse 6), Andronicus and Julia (in verse 7) and Rufus and his mother (in verse 13). 'Mary' is a Latinized form of 'Miriam', so Mary was almost certainly Jewish. Paul's terminology that she 'has worked very hard among you' is practically technical language for her having been involved in mission and church planting in Rome. She would have been expelled from Rome by virtue of Claudius's edict of AD 49, and Paul may well have met her in the years immediately following. That puts her pioneering church planting work in Rome earlier than 49.

Andronicus and Junia date even earlier. Paul says that they were 'in Christ before I was' (verse 8), which puts their conversion pre-AD 34. He describes them as 'apostles': does this mean that they were among the 'five hundred brothers and sisters' to whom the risen Jesus appeared, 'most of whom are still alive', referred to by Paul in 1 Corinthians 15.6? Were they among the 'visitors from Rome' (Acts 2.10) in Jerusalem for the Day of Pentecost? Were they involved in the initial disputes over the organization of the fledgling church described in Acts 6.1–6? At any rate, they would have been highly esteemed by the early churches of Rome, and it may well have been Miriam, Andronicus and Junia who took the lion's share in the planting of the very first churches there.

The churches (again)

Back to the church plants themselves.

We next meet two categories of churches, what I will call the 'family' and the *insulae* churches. We read of 'those who belong to the family of Aristobulus' in verse 10, and 'those in the Lord who belong to the family of Narcissus' in verse 11. 'Family' is really 'household', the wider grouping of those who lived and worked and enjoyed a patron–client relationship with Aristobulus and Narcissus. These two men were probably dead, which is why Paul does not greet them, and they were probably not Christian, even though churches met in their houses. This means that the church members were slaves of these households. There is an intriguing possibility that both Aristobulus and Narcissus were intimately involved with the Roman administration, and it is possible that Narcissus fell out with Claudius, leading to his execution. We can only imagine the delicate and potentially perilous position that the slave churches were in that continued to meet in their households after they both died. What we have is highly intelligent and competent imperial administrators, meeting under the protection of households that were nonetheless at great risk.

The *insulae* or 'tenement' churches were probably located on the other side of the city, in the poor harbour and haulage areas; 90% of Rome's resident population lived in these tenement blocks. They were four or five storeys high, frequently with shops and businesses at ground level, with tiny rooms, shared latrines and washing facilities, at risk from fire and plague. The churches in these blocks would have met in the shops on the ground floor after hours or perhaps in rooms that could be combined.

It seems that these *insulae* churches operated differently from the house or family churches. Both have five individuals greeted by Paul. Does this imply a flat (or at any rate shared) leadership? And is there significance in how Paul speaks of 'the brothers and sisters' (verse 14) for the first tenement church, and 'all the saints who are with them' (verse 15) for the second? Maybe the first was intentionally egalitarian, rejecting a hierarchical model of leadership. And could the second have had an explicit ethos of holiness, perhaps more closely linked with the Jewish roots of early Christianity? We cannot know, but it makes you wonder.

Some implications for contemporary church planting

To finish with, what implications from these suggestive hints from the life of some of the very earliest churches might there be for contemporary church planting?

First of all, we sense a great energy and mobility shared between these church plants. Some of these names as well as Paul's references to shared history (which must have been beyond Rome, as we know that Paul had not yet visited there, 1.13) show us a sensitive situation into which Phoebe was about to enter. We know that the first churches in Rome must have been from substantially Jewish backgrounds, led by Jews who had become Christians. After the expulsion of the Jews and Jewish Christians by Claudius, the leadership, cultures and make-up of these churches must have been taken up by Gentile Christians. How challenging, then, for leaders such as Miriam, Andronicus and Junia to return to Rome, maybe to the very churches that they themselves had planted, and find them under very different leadership. The expansion of the church, the growth in numbers, the networking around the Mediterranean (and to other places too) must have been exhilarating but challenging. Paul's adverting to 'all the churches of the Gentiles' (verse 4) and to 'the whole church' (verse 23) in the context of a chapter focused on smaller individual churches with majorly Jewish origins speaks of a conflicted and uneasy situation.

Our own situation may have parallels, when different church origins, cultures and traditions can run into collision with the dynamics of growth, expansion and a different type of leadership from that of recent history.

This can be compounded by the staggering diversity of these early churches. Think of the combinations of Gentile and Jew in the early church, perhaps nowhere more starkly seen than in the marriage of Prisca and Aquila. Paula Gooder (2018) draws this out beautifully in her fictionalized account of the early Roman churches. Add into this the dynamics of slavery, freedmen and women, and patronage. Robert Jewett cites Peter Lampe to the effect that 'two-thirds of the names [in Romans 16.3–16] indicate Greek rather than Latin background, and hence confirm immigrant status … [And] of the 13 persons about whom something definite can be said, at least 9 point with great certainty to slave origins' (Jewett, 2007, p. 63; referring to Lampe, 2003, pp. 182–3). Scot McKnight draws out a fascinating and significant implication: 'We can guess that the most common language of the house churches [in Rome] was Greek, the second-most common Aramaic or Hebrew, and the third-most common Latin' (McKnight, 2019, p. 12).

This diversity and socio-economic complexity is carried over into the variety we see in the structures and leadership dynamics of these churches. A church structured around the patronage models of Roman society would have felt very different from those with flat, non-hierarchical, egalitarian leadership structures.

Perhaps we see this hinted at in how Paul addresses and describes the people he greets. Is it stretching things too far to see four categories of people here?

1. There are what he calls 'the apostles'. This is Andronicus and Junia, and others mentioned in verse 7, and Paul himself.
2. There are those who 'work hard in the Lord'. These are Miriam in verse 6; Urbanus in verse 9; Tryphaena and Tryphosa in verse 12; and Persis in verse 12. This language of 'working hard' is almost a term of art for Paul; it means engaging in the task of Christian mission, especially the work of church planting. He uses the verb 23 times and the noun 18 times (Jewett, 2007, p. 961).
3. Then there are those Paul singles out for special affection, those he addresses as 'beloved': Epaenetus in verse 5, Ampliatus in verse 8, Stachys in verse 9 and Persis in verse 12.
4. And last there are those who are simply named but not described.

One would not want to over-press these distinctions, but the repetitive nature of Paul's vocabulary and rhetoric are suggestive that more is going on here than lies on the surface. Could we be seeing something of how Paul structured his church planting movement? The first two categories (of the apostles and those working hard in the Lord) go together; in various ways they are the pioneers, the ones establishing these new churches. The last category could be the leaders of these churches, the pastors and teachers of the churches that the apostles, prophets and evangelists had founded. So what of the 'beloved' third category? Could these people be those being trained and developed for church plant leadership? Are these the apprentices? And if so, how telling it is that the atmosphere Paul is most keen to establish for their development is love.

Conclusion

In conclusion, what Romans 16 shows us is a network of churches in different parts of the ancient city of Rome, part of a wider movement that goes back to the resurrection of Jesus, which has been battered by the vicissitudes of Roman imperial policy and is now poised to spread to the farthest reaches of Europe. The churches are dramatically different – socially, economically, religiously, culturally, in terms of power, race and background. The churches vary between themselves in how they are structured, where they meet, how they are led.

Diversity and freedom to be different are a striking feature of these five early church plants. A major implication for contemporary church planting is the freedom for churches to be different from each other, to let context, the social make-up of the churches, the economic and power environments in which Christians live, shape the way they share a common life in Christ. This presents particularly sharp challenges to historic churches that have a clear and seemingly non-negotiable way of structuring their life and leadership.

If diversity is a striking feature of the churches of Romans 16, so also is unity. This may well have been Paul's primary reason for writing. He is wanting to secure a united support for Phoebe as she broaches the Spanish mission to a conflicted confederation of churches. Hence the overwhelming emphasis from Paul in the multiple references to 'in Christ' or 'in the Lord'. These churches, these leaders, are 'in Christ'. The diversity of their origins, histories, cultures and structures are surface features of a far deeper reality – the life of Jesus in which they all share. This leads to a life of holiness and affection, the 'holy kiss' of verse 16, and situates them within 'the whole church' of verse 23 and among 'all the churches of Christ' of verse 16.

Romans 16.1–16 show us not a single monolithic church in ancient Rome, but multiple churches, enjoying a shared energy from the presence of Christ among them, but displaying an astonishing variety – in terms of their origins, their history, their socio-economic and religious background – that manifests itself in their structures of meeting and leadership. Paul nowhere seeks to make them the same, but he urges a unity, a unity grounded in experience of Christ, a common affection and a shared mission. May our contemporary church planting networks and movements enjoy similar life, blessing and freedom to innovate, and find similar unity and shared purpose.

References

Gooder, Paula, 2018, *Phoebe: A Story*, London: Hodder & Stoughton.
Jewett, Robert, 2007, *Romans: A Commentary*, Minneapolis, MN: Fortress Press.
Lampe, Peter, 2003, *From Paul to Valentinus: Christians at Rome in the First Two Centuries*, trans. M. Steinhauser, Minneapolis, MN: Fortress Press.
McKnight, Scot, 2019, *Reading Romans Backwards: A Gospel in Search of Peace in the Midst of the Empire*, London: SCM Press.

Reflections on Part Four

As the five chapters in the final part of this book show, the work of church planting forces us to grapple deeply with questions of ecclesiology; for as Will Foulger evocatively describes, 'starting new churches – since the Church is God's – is a theological endeavour all the way down. Every decision we make about churches, from structure and resourcing through to styles of worship and buildings, says something about who we think God is and what He is doing in His world' (2024, p. 8). While this is surely true of all churches, the particular ecclesiological challenge of starting new churches is that often decisions have to be made for the first time (Should we 'worship first' or 'serve first'? What is our liturgical form? How should our leadership structures be organized? etc.). In this sense, starting new churches means that the ecclesiological questions confront us with force, and sometimes urgency. In many ways, church planting forces us to do ecclesiology more intentionally. It is for this reason that J. D. Payne describes church planting as lying at the intersection of 'ecclesiology' and 'missiology' (2009, p. 7).

One of the primary challenges these five chapters on ecclesiology have wrestled with is aptly summarized by Clare Watkins as 'the ecclesiological challenge'; that is, the challenge of 'articulating the sense in which the church can be understood as both "human and divine", both institution and of the Spirit' (2020, p. 2).[1] This theological question rightly raises methodological questions. Ought we start our enquiry by thinking about the nature of the church in pages of Scripture (as Valentine does in Chapter 19)? Should we take some insight from the voice of the 'person on the Clapham omnibus' (as Hall and Searle provocatively describe), or should we give weight to God's revelation of Godself as 'gift', as we heard from Moynagh?

The 'perennial' (Watkins, 2020, p. 2) challenge of doing ecclesiology in the tension of human and divine authority is particularly striking in the context of church planting. As we saw in Part One, the question of how the action and work of God interact with the structures and strategies of human agents is a crucial theological fault line in the discussion of church planting. If the discussion of the ecclesiology of church planting is to develop, these methodological questions about how we do ecclesiology must be addressed.

As Watkins highlights, we can see this tension played out acutely in the debate between systematic and practical theologians on the 'proper' mode of doing ecclesiology. For instance, in his influential work *Church, World and the Christian Life*, Nicholas Healy writes that 'In general, ecclesiology in our period has become highly systematic and theoretical, focused more upon discerning the right things to think about the church rather than orientated to the living, rather messy, confused and confusing body that the church's actuality is' (2000, p. 3). Healy's accusation that theologians are more interested in 'blueprint ecclesiologies' (pp. 25ff.) than getting their hands dirty with the complexities of real life and real people has shaped the conversation around church planting significantly. As evidenced by some of the chapters in Part Four of this book, to do ecclesiology properly is to hear the voices from the edge (Hall and Searle) or to listen to the voices in the neighbourhood (Ross).

Healy's challenge precipitated a move to the ethnographic, shaping the conversation around ecclesiology more broadly, particularly in the conversation around church planting. Yet as Watkins goes on to highlight, more than a decade after the publication of *Church, World and the Christian Life*, Healy is concerned that the ethnographic turn has not been entirely positive for ecclesiology:

> The ethnographic view undermines the notion that ... [what is observed can] ... constitute the church as a 'community' or moral person in a sufficiently rich and consistent way to work as a principle for theological or ecclesiological method. There is simply too much, materially, that is not shared. Indeed, the worldwide church ... when considered with a focus on detail, particularity and the exceptional, is arguably little more than a congeries of diverse forms of life, languages and meanings of the word 'God'. We cannot, then, start with the church as it exists; everything slips through our fingers unless we cement and shape according to our agenda, our construal of Christianity and our formation within our particular world. (Healy, 2012, p. 189, quoted in Watkins, 2020, p. 6)

Instead of swinging between the empirical and the doctrinal, Watkins urges us to find 'a way of speaking of the actual Church, which holds that earthly–heavenly tension in faithful continuity with the longer tradition'. And this means that 'Neither practical theological approaches nor doctrinal approaches, on their own, seem, as yet, to have developed the necessary vision or methodologies' to live faithfully in this tension. Thus, we need to find ways of developing 'more integrated methodologies' that can give us 'whole-theology articulation of the work God's Spirit in the world as it is' (Watkins, 2020, p. 7).

This challenge towards integrating the empirical and the theological in providing a theology of new churches is important. There are some clear examples of how we might develop a whole-theology articulation of new churches (see Foulger, 2024; Morris, 2019; Watkins, 2020). But it is also important to see that the end goal may not necessarily be for individual scholars to exemplify all aspects of the debate. Taking seriously Thomas Aquinas' depiction of theology as the 'queen of the sciences', we might take a lead from the epistemology of science more generally conceived. Science is often thought of as a team endeavour, with multiple and diverse areas of specialism offering complementary and overlapping discoveries in the pursuit of knowledge (see Wagenknecht, 2016). If the ecclesiology of church planting is to evolve in a more integrated way, we hope this will involve a more integrated theological community; that it won't be uncommon to hear diverse methodological voices in dialogue and conversation, as we have seen in the chapters here (and indeed in the book as a whole). For the theology of church planting will surely not be served only by scholars who specialize in every area of theology (indeed, one notable voice missing from the conversation on church planting theology is that of the biblical scholar). We hope that a flourishing of church planting theology will not be precipitated – as in the ecclesiology of the early 2000s – by extreme swings between disparate silos of theology, nor that all theologians will become internally integrated, but instead that a more integrated *community* of scholars might emerge, united around a desire to serve the church and its flourishing.

Note

1 With thanks to Helen Miller for alerting us to this discussion in Watkins' work.

References

Foulger, Will, 2024, *New Things: A Theological Investigation into the Work of Starting New Churches across 11 Dioceses in the Church of England*, https://www.cranmerhall.com/wp-content/uploads/2024/03/New-Things-Final-1.pdf (accessed 22.03.2024).

Healy, Nicholas, 2000, *Church, World and the Christian Life: Practical Prophetic Ecclesiology*, Cambridge: Cambridge University Press.

———, 2012, 'Ecclesiology, Ethnography and God: An Interplay of Reality Descriptions', in Pete Ward (ed.), *Perspectives on Ecclesiology and Ethnography*, Grand Rapids, MI: Eerdmans, pp. 182–99.

Morris, Helen D., 2019, *Flexible Church: Being the Church in the Contemporary World*. London: SCM Press.

Payne, J. D., 2009, *Discovering Church Planting: An Introduction to the Whats, Whys, and Hows of Global Church Planting*, Downers Grove, IL: InterVarsity Press.

Wagenknecht, Susann, 2016, *A Social Epistemology of Research Groups*, London: Palgrave Macmillan.

Watkins, Clare, 2020, *Disclosing Church: An Ecclesiology Learned from Conversations in Practice*, Oxford: Routledge.

Index of Names and Subjects

Acts (Book of) 24, 36–7, 59n3, 69, 109, 167, 176, 226, 258–9
agency, agents 13–14, 26–7, 35, 38, 41–3, 49–50, 63–6, 73–5, 77, 80–4, 87, 89, 96–7, 178–9, 181–2, 264
Allen, Roland 225
Anglo-Catholic tradition 16, 27, 185–9, 193, 196–202, 203–4, 212
apostle, apostles 24–5, 109, 257, 259–62

Baptist Church 233, 236–9, 242
Barth, Karl 26, 32n2, 42
being with 11, 162, 166–7, 177–9, 203
Bishop's Mission Order (BMO) 30, 185, 189–91, 194n2, 198, 211
Bosch, David 13, 17–18n1, 210, 240
buildings 17, 27, 29, 30, 163, 185, 187, 198, 201, 220, 222, 233, 236–8, 242, 248, 264

Christendom 4, 122, 139, 161, 167, 211, 234, 238–9
Christology 23, 27, 41–2, 59n4, 224, 239
Church Army 29, 116–17, 120, 122–5, 223
Church Mission Society (CMS) 222–4
Church of England 8, 12, 15, 21–3, 27–30, 69, 93, 96, 116, 118–19, 121, 123–4, 139, 153–5, 160, 167, 172, 186–7, 189, 194, 199, 203–4, 210, 213–14, 227, 240, 242, 247
Church Revitalisation Trust (CRT) 12, 30–1, 32n3
communion (eucharist, mass) 31, 45, 78, 185, 188–9, 191–2, 193, 199, 204, 222, 244, 252
congregation 21–2, 35, 39, 45, 54, 66, 69, 79, 97, 109–11, 112n1, 135, 159–61, 165, 168–9n3, n5, n6, n8, n11, n16, 172, 185, 187, 190–2, 197–8, 200–1, 211–14, 222, 226, 237–8, 243n1, 247–8, 252
context (contextual, contextualization) 4–5, 8, 11–16, 25, 32, 34–6, 38, 44–5, 47–8, 50, 54–5, 57, 59n6, 68–9, 80, 83, 86–8, 90, 92–4, 112, 122, 132–3, 135–6, 138–40, 149–51, 153–4, 160–4, 166–7, 176–7, 180–3, 191, 199, 209–12, 215–18, 222–5, 227, 229–31, 240, 250, 253–4, 256, 260, 262, 264
Corinthians (First) 39–40, 65–6, 129, 183, 232, 258–9

Corinthians (Second) 49
Cottrell, Stephen 118–19, 160, 186
creativity 16–17, 35, 45, 90, 92–3, 128, 132, 135–40
Croft, Steven 119, 197, 203
culture, 11, 24–5, 31, 35, 44, 47, 89–90, 93, 95, 101–6, 111–12, 123, 132–4, 140, 146–8, 153–5, 165, 167, 173, 181, 183, 210–15, 230–1, 237, 256

decline 15, 29, 31, 36, 96, 153–5, 160, 164, 173, 212, 234
denomination, denominational 86–7, 94, 116, 120, 124, 128, 153, 160, 164, 167, 168n4, 210, 214–15, 217, 238–40, 242, 250
discipleship 17, 36–7, 47–50, 52–5, 57–8, 74, 81, 87–95, 110, 138, 146, 161, 165, 167, 182, 213–15, 228, 231, 236–8, 240–2, 247
diversity 13–17, 44–5, 88, 101–3, 112, 119, 137, 203–4, 218, 225, 236, 240, 261–2, 265–6
doctrine (doctrinal) 26, 63, 213, 225, 265
Donovan, Vincent 149–50, 225, 230

early Church 37, 69, 109, 169n8, 212, 259, 261–2
ecumenism 21–2, 25
emerging church 31, 243n1
Ephesians (Epistle) 119
evangelical tradition 27, 43, 72, 74–5, 77–80, 84, 125, 151, 185–7, 189, 191, 193–4, 196–8, 203–4, 212, 227
evangelism, 6, 17n1, 21–2, 69, 81, 83, 117, 124–5, 187, 189, 223, 231, 237, 258, 262,
Exodus 176

Father (God), 6, 17n1, 23–4, 32n1, 56, 62–4, 68, 81–2, 118, 224
Flett, John 26, 244
Foulger, Will 2, 154–5, 169n12, 190, 203–4, 211, 225, 264, 266
fresh expressions 12, 29–32, 35–6, 47, 73, 75, 116, 118, 123–4, 197, 212, 223, 233, 242, 253
funding (see also, SDF) 3, 91, 117, 120–2, 148, 154–5, 160, 168n3, 172, 193, 197, 211, 215, 225, 227, 229, 248

Galatians (Book of) 49, 104
generosity (gift, giving) 4, 17, 92, 113n6, 185, 193, 212, 216–17, 244–54
gospel message 2–3, 7–8, 22, 24–6, 28, 32, 35–6, 38, 40, 43, 45, 48, 64, 69, 111, 125, 138, 140, 144, 147, 149–50, 159, 163, 181, 186, 189, 192, 196, 201, 210–11, 213–14, 216, 218, 222–3, 225, 230, 234–7, 239–42, 252, 258
grafting *see* revitalization
growth 22, 27, 30–1, 35–7, 39–40, 42, 45, 49–50, 54, 58, 65–6, 71, 78, 84, 87, 92–4, 101–5, 107–14, 119, 123, 125, 128, 138, 140, 141n15, 144–5, 148, 150, 160, 164–6, 176–8, 180–1, 183, 185–6, 191, 193–4, 200–2, 209–11, 215–16, 218, 222, 224–5, 228, 231, 233, 234, 236–7, 260–1

INDEX OF NAMES AND SUBJECTS

Hebrews (Book of) 63
hierarchy 130, 238–9, 247, 260–1
Holy Spirit (pneumatology) 14, 16, 17n1, 23, 26, 31, 32n1, 32n2, 34–5, 41, 42, 44–5, 48–50, 53, 56, 60, 62–4, 66–9, 71–2, 73–4, 79–84, 104–5, 108, 118, 138, 144, 148–52, 161, 166–8, 176, 179, 183, 203, 220–1, 224–32, 235, 237–9, 241–2, 245–6, 248, 251, 253, 254, 264
holiness 43, 84, 123–4, 147, 192, 260
Holy Trinity Brompton (HTB) 12, 197, 202
homogeneity 36, 88
house churches 141n9, 261

incarnation, incarnational 25, 41, 53, 63, 72, 103, 136, 166–7, 199, 215, 235
inclusivity 95, 180, 237, 247
innovation 17, 96, 134, 136–8, 140, 164, 165, 177, 190, 239
institution, 4, 15, 17, 27, 37, 59n6, 90, 94, 96–7, 103, 121, 128, 139–40, 151, 153–4, 165, 167–8, 211, 238–42, 264

James (Epistle) 111, 151
jazz 48, 136–7
Jennings, Willie James 176, 180, 223
John (Gospel of) 49, 56, 68, 112, 200, 224, 235, 237, 241
justice (injustice) 6, 15, 17n1, 41, 75, 109, 144, 147, 215, 236, 246–8

kingdom of God (kingdom of heaven) 6, 27, 48, 56–7, 147, 181, 211, 225, 235, 237, 245, 249, 254
Kwiyani, Harvey 84n3, 101, 108, 148–50

lay ministry (lay leadership) 41, 186, 189, 193, 201, 226
leadership 12, 15–17, 31, 34–5, 37, 50, 54, 57, 59n3, 64–8, 73, 75, 80, 85, 87, 91, 93–5, 97, 109–11, 118, 122, 132, 137, 140, 141n9, 142n19, 144, 153–5, 159–61, 163, 168n4, 179, 183, 185, 187–91, 193, 199–202, 211, 218–19, 222, 226, 229–31, 242, 256–63, 264
Lings, George 29–30, 116, 119, 123, 169n18, 223
liturgy, liturgical 31, 43, 97, 192, 194n4, 212–14, 216, 238, 252, 264
Luke (Gospel of) 109

management (managerialism) 30, 35, 44, 117, 120, 200
Mark (Gospel of) 209
Matthew (Gospel of) 47, 57, 181, 200, 239–41
Messy Church 47, 50, 54, 57, 59n5, 122
method (methodology) 34–41, 43, 45, 73, 99, 125, 128–9, 133, 138–9, 141n7, 142n17, 144, 146, 148, 155, 167, 172, 179, 182, 210, 212, 215–16, 253, 264–5
Methodism 144, 229
Milbank, John 28, 43–4
Milbank, Alison 28, 30–2, 35–6, 96, 189–91, 193, 204
missio dei 13–14, 23, 26–7,

29–32, 73–5, 80–4, 97, 112, 214, 224–7, 241, 244
mission, missiology 4–7, 9, 12–14, 16–17, 17n1, 19, 22–32, 26–7, 32n2, 35–6, 40, 45, 63, 68–9, 73–85, 91, 96–7, 102, 112, 118, 124–5, 135, 147–52, 154, 160–4, 167, 171–2, 178, 181, 185–94, 196–202, 203–4, 209–12, 215–18, 220–4, 228, 231, 235–9, 240–5, 247–8, 253–4, 259, 261–4
missional communities 14–15, 74–84, 159–64, 166–8, 167n5, 203, 210–11, 236–7, 243n1
Mission-shaped Church 12, 22, 27–30, 73, 118, 124–5, 197, 204, 210, 240
missionary 5, 22, 25–8, 32n2, 35, 39, 44, 102, 149–50, 163, 221, 225, 232
mixed ecology (economy) 11–12, 29–30, 32, 45, 117–20, 160, 165, 168, 186, 204, 218
modernity 52, 164–7, 236
monasticism, new monasticism 182, 233, 236
Moynagh, Michael 11, 17, 18n2, 36, 47, 73–5, 125, 203, 244–55, 264
multicultural 22, 229
music, musicians 79, 106, 136–7, 188–9, 247–8

new worshipping community 87, 125, 144, 172, 182, 211, 214, 226, 228
Newbigin, Lesslie 25, 216

ordination (ordained) 29–31, 65, 103, 122, 172, 190–1, 196, 201, 210, 222, 226–7

Orthodox tradition 182
orthodoxy (orthopraxy) 41, 52

Paas, Stefan 4–7, 9, 66, 125, 151, 167, 204, 210, 233, 235, 254
parish 7, 16, 21, 27–32, 34, 36, 44, 118–19, 145, 153, 173, 182, 185–6, 188–91, 194, 197–200, 209, 211, 218, 221, 227, 247
Paul (Apostle) 9, 17, 35, 38–41, 43–5, 49, 53, 63, 65–7, 69, 110–11, 129, 183, 225–6, 231, 256–63
Pentecost (day of) 23–4, 52, 259
Pentecostal tradition 59n3, 102, 108, 151
Peter (Epistle) 104
Philippians (Epistle) 23
pioneering (pioneers, pioneer ministry) 1, 5, 7–12, 15–16, 31, 34, 86–7, 91, 94, 111, 116–18, 120–5, 132, 139, 149, 153, 169n14, 172–83, 187, 197–8, 203–4, 209–10, 220, 226, 228, 237, 239–40, 259
pioneer spectrum 12
praxis 2, 8, 10, 13–14, 26, 51, 97, 209–15
prayer 14, 26–7, 31, 36, 38, 42, 54, 63–4, 66, 68–70, 73–82, 86, 91–2, 108, 159–60, 162–3, 168, 176, 183, 187–90, 192, 200, 210–11, 216, 220–1, 225–6, 228–9, 236, 250, 252–4
Protestantism 28, 42, 45, 101, 168, 239, 242
Psalms 103, 242

Reformation 23, 28, 101, 168
revitalization (grafting) 4, 12,

16, 30–2, 44, 73, 128, 185–94, 203, 211
resource churches 12, 15, 30–2, 117–19, 121, 123, 125, 168n3, 185–6
Revelation (Book of) 103
Romans (Epistle) 17, 63, 256–3
Root, Andrew 31, 36, 96, 164–5, 169n10, 169n11

sacraments 12, 16, 26, 29, 31, 44, 63
safeguarding 30, 147, 238
Save the Parish 30–1, 186, 194n1
Smith, James K. A. 52, 213
Strategic Development Fund (SDF) 3, 121, 160, 168n3, 172–3, 211, 225, 227
secularization, secular 27, 55, 61, 98, 125, 164, 167, 169n15, 198, 205, 258
Selvaratnam, Christian 15, 44, 69, 73, 85, 128–40, 153–4
sin 35, 56, 110
social action 74–5, 77, 189
Son (God the) 7, 17n1, 23–4, 26, 32n1, 43, 68, 71, 81–2, 103, 112, 118, 224
spirituality, 14, 38, 70, 74–5, 78–84, 92, 96–7, 151, 236–7, 248

Timothy (Epistle) 110
Thessalonians (Epistle) 39
Titus (Epistle) 111
Torrance, James B. 62–6, 71
tradition 6, 9, 14, 16, 30–1, 36, 45, 54, 136, 153–4, 167–8, 182–3, 185–7, 189, 191, 193, 196–7, 203–4, 209–10, 212, 215, 217, 232–3, 236, 250–2, 265
training 15, 30, 32n3, 64, 69, 94, 110, 117, 124, 128–32, 136–40, 153–5, 201, 215, 219–20, 238, 242, 262
Trinity (triune, trinitarian) 26–7, 50, 53, 56, 58, 62–3, 65–6, 68–72, 82–3, 118, 244

values 37, 44, 89, 95, 104, 107, 119, 129, 133, 139, 163–4, 179, 240
Vatican II 32n2
vision 1–2, 16–17, 30, 35, 56, 68–9, 80, 97, 118–19, 138, 140, 147, 200, 202–3, 211, 214–15, 226, 233, 236, 238, 265

Watkins, Clare 47, 50, 54, 81, 264–6
Wells, Samuel 124, 169n7
Williams, Rowan 42, 73, 117, 217, 246
worship 6–7, 11–12, 15, 17n1, 24, 28–9, 31, 34, 37, 43, 45, 62–5, 77, 79, 94, 125, 149–50, 160–1, 168n5, 172, 180–2, 188–9, 191–3, 198–9, 201–2, 203, 212–14, 216, 223, 237–40, 242, 247, 251, 264
worshippers 182, 198–9
worshipping 7, 15, 24, 29, 87, 91, 125, 144, 172, 182, 197, 211–14, 226, 228
Wright, N. T. 51–2, 55, 59n4